THE ART OF CAUSE MARKETING

THE ART OF CAUSE MARKETING

How to Use Advertising to Change Personal Behavior and Public Policy

RICHARD EARLE

NTC Business Books

NTC/Contemporary Publishing Group

Library of Congress Cataloging-in-Publication Data
Earle, Richard, 1932–
    The art of cause marketing: how to use advertising to change personal behavior and public policy / Richard Earle.
        p.   cm.
    Includes bibliographical references and index.
    ISBN 0-658-00122-1
    1. Social marketing.   I. Title.
HF5414.E18   2000
658.5—dc21   99-45663

Interior design by Monica Baziuk
Page layout and typesetting by Precision Graphics

Published by NTC Business Books
A division of NTC/Contemporary Publishing Group, Inc.
4255 West Touhy Avenue, Lincolnwood (Chicago), Illinois 60712-1975 U.S.A.
Printed in the United States of America
International Standard Book Number: 0-658-00122-1
00 01 02 03 04 05 LB 20 19 18 17 16 15 14 13 12 11 10 9 8 7 6 5 4 3 2 1

CONTENTS

PART 2

CAUSE MARKETING AT WORK

ACKNOWLEDGMENTS

A couple of years ago I went to a reunion at Amherst College. I noticed two things about my classmates, most of whom were starting to retire or think about it.

First, I noticed that we'd all stopped trying to impress each other. We all sort of reverted to the friendly and low-key guys we'd been as undergraduates. We all relaxed. That was good.

Second, I was taken with how many of us had started to "give back." We weren't spending our time figuring out which retirement community was closest to the golf course. An amazing number had decided to teach, to go into some distant jungle to bring medical advice, to participate in inner-city mentoring, or to organize voter initiatives. And yes, to write. To pass on what we'd learned. Since I'd spent most of my last thirty-five years writing, I figured I would tackle the last category. Because I too wanted to give something back.

It occurred to me one day that I'd probably lived through the golden period in advertising, so there's a bit of "memoir" in this. I brushed up against some remarkable people during that time, in the halls or screening rooms of the various agencies in which I worked. I watched them closely and absorbed from them like a sponge. At times I felt a little like that character in Herman Wouk's histories of World War II, *The Winds of War* and *War and Remembrance*, Pug Henry. Pug was always having tea with Hitler, doing special missions for FDR, or dodging bombs at Pearl Harbor. Just happened to be there. Like Forest Gump, some years later.

And I just happened to be there in New York in the '60s, '70s, and '80s, making ads with a lot of amazing people.

I had some outstanding mentors at the six agencies at which I worked. They weren't always the well-known people there, although some were. But each helped me and shaped me in ways they may not even be aware of. So I'd like to thank a few of them in this acknowledgment:

The late Gordon Webber took a chance and hired me all those years ago, with no advertising experience, at Benton & Bowles. He told me he saw something unique in me, but the most important thing he gave me was his own personal example that one could be a sensitive writer and a decent man and still thrive in advertising. Ed Anderson and Roy Eaton (who is now "giving back" as a concert pianist) were very important to my getting my feet on the ground in those days. At Doyle Dane Bernbach, there were Bernbach and Gage, and I watched them mainly from afar, although working with Bob Gage on Crackerjack was a class in itself. But it was Paula Green and Bill Taubin who really showed me how it was done. I was a very junior producer then, but just working with them and observing Paula wrestle with a piece of copy, and win brilliantly, was worth several semesters at any marketing school. At Grey, Manning Rubin hired me as a producer and then urged me to become a writer, and I'll always be grateful. The late Al Sarasohn let me spread my wings, and Ed Holzer pushed me headfirst back into cause marketing and was a great companion along the way. Ray Gaulke enthusiastically thrust me into a big job at Marsteller and was always supportive. Gene Novak, a significant mentor at Rumrill Hoyt, was another talented and decent man. At Compton (later Saatchi), Milt Gossett was the strong pillar behind everything that happened at the place. But Creative Director Kurt Willinger was as good a boss as anyone ever had, and did more for me than I probably knew or acknowledged at the time, and I'm very grateful. Phil Voss was a great field general, tough but always fair.

As for those who helped with this book, first and foremost, it wouldn't have happened without Barbara Fagan, a former teammate at Grey who called out of the blue the day I was thinking about all of this. She said, simply, "You must do it!" And then she helped immeasurably to pull it all together. It was Barbara who brought me to Loretta Barrett, who placed it, and who has been loyal and supportive and everything an agent should be.

Danielle Egan-Miller, my editor, took my ramblings and made them crisp and well organized, and pulled me back from boring you with too many old war stories.

Then there were all those who so generously talked into my tape recorder: Maria Falconetti, still the best researcher I ever worked with; Sid Furst, another brilliant prober; Susan MacMurchy, a fine practitioner and a good friend; the always loyal friends Morty and Jean Dubin (who graciously put me up at "Chez Dubin" during all those research trips to New York); Jackie Silver, with her many insights and good humor; Kiley and Company's Tom Kiley; Arnold Advertising's consumately professional Lisa Unsworth and Anne Miller; media specialist Richard Weinstein, the late Tom Cummings, and Kathy Scanlan at the Massachusetts Council on Compulsive Gambling; Tim Egan at the Rendon Group; Ron Wayland at the New England Broadcaster's Association; Ajibola Osinubi at MIG; Donna Gittens at Cause Media; the amazing Greg Connolly at the Massachusetts Department of Public Health; the immensely helpful Stacey Hammond at the Ad Council; Steve Dnistrian, Barbara Paley, and Josie Feliz at the Partnership for a Drug-Free America; former Marsteller colleagues Joe Goldberg and Milt Sutton; and Harvard's Dr. Howard Shaffer, who opened my eyes wide at a crucial point in the book's development and helped me put it all in perspective. Since I have referenced a lot of the work that was done for the Massachusetts Tobacco Control Program, I do want to tip my hat to some outstanding creative talent at Houston-Effler (later Houston Herstek Favat, and recently merged into Arnold Communications) who were responsible for some groundbreaking work: Creative Directors Rich Herstek and Pete Favat, Creative Supervisors Stu Cooperider and Dave Gardner, with strong contributions from Marc Gallucci, Mark Nardi, Todd Riddle, Ken Lewis, Roger Baldacci, Khari Street, and DeMane Davis.

And of course, I must salute the inspiring Iron Eyes Cody.

This book is dedicated to my remarkable daughters, Melissa Earle and Carol Burnham, who have grown into wonderful and fascinating adults, and who now get to hear all of Daddy's stories over again. And finally and most of all to Pat, my partner and inspiration for thirty-eight years, who quietly and constantly told me she knew I could do it, who helped me shape it, was my best critic, and put up with my screams when the computer ate those three chapters!

To all of you, this is my give-back after a lot of years of doing one of the best jobs you can do. My hope is that you will turn around and use your skills to do some good for this fragile and troubled planet on which we all have to live!

THE ART OF CAUSE MARKETING

INTRODUCTION

I worked on my first public service campaign in 1962. I had just joined the Benton & Bowles agency, and it had the American Red Cross account, a pro bono assignment from the Advertising Council. The project was tossed to a group of us juniors, and we were thrilled to get it. Nobody up the corporate ladder paid much attention to it, having bigger and more profitable fish to fry. We did a modest radio campaign. It was fine, but not inspired. I was amazed at how quickly it was approved.

The creative team on the campaign was invited to the Advertising Council's annual spring luncheon at the Waldorf. While watching presentations of the various campaigns, I found myself suddenly exposed to a whole parallel world of advertising "contributed for the public good" as the Ad Council slogan proclaimed.

Some of it deeply touched and motivated me, and a bit of it was just ordinary. I realized then and there that it was possible to use the techniques of marketing in a way that could have an important and beneficial impact on the public—a result that had nothing to do with detergent or analgesic market share, the things that consumed most hours of my workday. And I got very excited about that. I also realized that to do it right took some special skills.

Thirty years later, after retiring from a creative director post at Saatchi & Saatchi, I went back to see the folks at the Ad Council about a campaign for a small foundation. There on the wall, directly behind the receptionist, was a huge blowup of a poster featuring Iron Eyes Cody, the "Crying Indian" for the Keep America Beautiful campaign.

I remembered standing beside director Mike Elliot as that famous scene was filmed. I had heard the camera whir as the sun cleared a cloud and illuminated that beautiful man's face, picking up highlights on the carefully placed teardrop.

This was clearly a campaign the Ad Council felt represented the best of its genre. Standing in the lobby face-to-face once again with Iron Eyes, I developed a tear of my own. I was reminded of that lunch thirty years earlier, and the idealistic aspirations of a young copywriter.

I hasten to add, I didn't *create* the "Crying Indian." But as a newly hired creative director at Marsteller Advertising, the agency that did, I resurrected him from the old campaign file where he had been put aside after one year's airing, and wrote a new series of commercials and ads for him. Through the years he has became a true public service icon, right up there with Smokey Bear and McGruff the Crime Dog. The "Crying Indian" campaign has been listed as one of the best commercials of the century by *Advertising Age* and selected as one of the fifty greatest commercials of all time by both *Entertainment Weekly* and *TV Guide*. After a long hiatus, it was revived again for the '90s. More of that story later.

DOING WELL BY DOING GOOD

The relegating of public service campaigns to "stepchild" status, handled by agency juniors, has long since passed. Today the best and the brightest creative teams fight to get those assignments, with visions of Gold Lions and Clios decorating their bookshelves. And I also believe that most of them sincerely hunger for the opportunity to serve the public good with their talents.

The working title of this book was *Pro Bono*, from the Latin phrase *pro bono publico*, which translates "for the public good," and the art of applying carefully strategized marketing to serve the public good is certainly what this book is about. However, pro bono is a description generally applied by the industry to work done by advertising practitioners gratis or at cost, as a donation to a just cause. Since there has recently been an explosion of cause marketing campaigns created by agencies for a normal fee and placed in media that is paid for rather than donated, the more inclusive title, *The Art of Cause Marketing*, seemed more appropriate.

WHAT IS CAUSE MARKETING?

Cause marketing consists of using the skills of advertising to effect social change, to benefit individuals or society at large. To restate the classic definition, it is advertising in the service of the public.

Cause marketing seeks to impact personal behavior in a number of ways, including persuading the target to:

- avoid or discontinue risky practices like smoking, drug abuse, or unprotected sex
- discontinue antisocial actions such as littering or being careless with campfires
- seek counseling for destructive behavior such as compulsive gambling or spousal abuse
- take preventative measures such as getting inoculated, reducing cholesterol intake, or fastening a safety belt
- seek out and use information about various diseases
- reexamine personal attitudes toward issues like race and sexual preference
- identify and take action against inhumane or discriminatory practices
- organize, join, or give financial support to groups that benefit society
- become involved in community activities such as mentoring and monitoring neighborhood crime

Cause marketing can also help create or change public policy. In short, when properly employed, cause marketing informs about and creates action on behalf of a cause. Advertising which does that is also widely classified as "social marketing." However the term seemed too general for a practical text on creating advertising for causes, which is what this book was meant to be. The theoretical side of social marketing has been dealt with in a number of texts. But Doctor Howard Shaffer, director of the Division of Addictions at Harvard Medical School told me, "We have enough learned tomes and intellectual papers from people like me. What we most need now is a how-to guide. What we need is a cookbook!" So a cookbook this shall be!

"Cause-*related* marketing" is a label that has been defined by Kotler and Andreasen in their book *Strategic Marketing for Non-Profit Organizations* as "any effort by a corporation to increase its own sales by contributing to the objectives of one or more nonprofit organizations." We will touch on that sub-segment in Chapter Eight.

This text is written primarily for advertising professionals and students of advertising and communication. Public agency and private foundation administrators should also find it helpful in their roles as clients of those professionals. It will be a guide for anyone charged with using the tools of marketing to impact public policy or private behavior.

Because it does not advocate a radical departure from many of the basic tenets of advertising, this can be a good fundamental text for any student of the craft. Advertising is advertising, and most of the fundamental principles of strategy, art direction, copywriting, and research apply to this category as well. However, what makes the difference in most public service advertising is the complex psychological makeup of the target "consumer" for these messages.

To change deeply held attitudes, one needs a thorough understanding of the belief systems and motivations of the targets of that effort. And this requires sophisticated research, plus some very finely honed strategic and creative skills.

For example, most good product selling lines or slogans are fairly simple and straightforward. They generally present factual evidence of a product's superiority in language one hopes is mind-opening and memorable. But product selling lines usually don't come with deep psychological underpinnings. Cause advertising almost always does. Often it targets people who are addicted to drugs, alcohol, tobacco, or gambling. These targets of cause campaigns are frequently in denial about their problems, and therefore, not interested in your message. When cause campaign themes or slogans fail, it is more than likely because they contain no psychological or emotional "hook." The goal of most commercial advertising is simply to change purchasing patterns; the cause marketing campaign seeks to change *strongly ingrained behavior or firmly held beliefs*.

Is It Art?

Is it a little pompous to call this pursuit an art? I don't think so. It goes to a core difference between this type of advertising and product or service messages. That difference is why I believe even experienced practitioners of advertising can benefit from the principles outlined in this book.

An experienced art director–writer team can routinely produce an effective packaged-goods campaign. If that team is good, the work may be artful, but rarely is it art.

True art is something that moves people in important emotional and personal ways, something that stays with them and possibly affects their lives. Every year, the advertising award shows select a few product or service campaigns or ads that are truly works of art, and they are appropriately enshrined. But because the consequences are so far-reaching and because the objective is *always* to move people and affect their lives, it is very important that *every* piece of cause marketing be crafted as carefully as a serious work of art!

In addition to strictly pro bono efforts, many for-fee cause campaigns are funded these days by increased taxes mandated by voter initiatives, or by settlement monies from groups such as the tobacco industry. The result has usually been more professionally produced work that runs in prime-time paid media, as opposed to the typical Public Service Announcement (PSA) that often gets stuck in between the infomercials at four A.M. This, as we will see later, is probably the wave of the future.

During a long career at various advertising agencies I have done some public service campaigns that were strictly pro bono and some that were handled like any commercial account, earning the agency an appropriate fee. While the scope and complexity of that work has varied according to the size of the budget, the principles behind it are exactly the same.

Throughout those thirty-five years in advertising, I always eagerly sought cause marketing assignments. Even when working on agency packaged-goods accounts, I sometimes found myself dealing with public issues on behalf of corporate clients, such as the daunting task of having to write "recovery" campaigns after the two Tylenol poisoning incidents.

Recently, I have devoted virtually all of my time to advising cause marketing efforts. During this period I started to organize the precepts that form the core of this book. I served as advertising consultant to the Massachusetts Department of Public Health for their $13 million tax-funded anti-smoking campaign, and also helped develop campaigns for the Massachusetts Council on Compulsive Gambling and the Massachusetts Department of Environmental Protection, among others.

Because of my immersion in the Massachusetts Tobacco Control campaign, and knowledge of all aspects of its planning and execution,

I have employed many examples and illustrations from that effort. However, I do believe that they have relevance to campaigns in support of many other kinds of causes. A detailed case study of that campaign is found in Chapter Ten.

"LET'S DO SOME ADS!"

The number of cause marketing campaigns is ever increasing. In fact, because of the dominant role of the media in all our lives, sooner or later, almost every public interest group will say: "Let's do some ads!"

Some of the resulting work is still produced quickly and cheaply by unsophisticated PR people or small creative services. But today these are generally the exception to well-funded campaigns like the Massachusetts Tobacco Control Program or the efforts of the Partnership for a Drug-Free America.

However, even for-fee efforts from major agencies can fail, often due to the fact that they are merely applying the principles that successfully sell packaged goods or consumer services. As a result, we are flooded with a daily glut of well-intentioned cause ads, many of which fall far short of their worthy but complex objectives. In fact, much of that work may actually be counterproductive, nourishing cynicism among the very populations it seeks to reach, and fortifying barriers against the next media effort by anyone who dares to suggest a modification of their behavior.

For example, certainly Nancy Reagan was sincere about her anti-drug efforts aimed at the young. But expanding the "Just say no!" campaign (originally targeted to preteens) to all potential drug users was so simplistic and unconcerned about the psychological forces that contribute to teenage drug experimentation that we must assume most of those older kids merely laughed at it. As a very hip young man commented on MTV one night, "It's a little like telling a manic depressive to 'cheer up!'"

Then, as if no one had learned anything in ten years, Bob Dole, while raising the issue of increased drug use among the young in his 1996 presidential campaign, proudly unveiled the slogan, "Just *Don't* Do It!" That simplistic line also committed the offense of clumsily mimicking a carefully crafted youth campaign for Nike athletic shoes ("Just Do It!").

Lest this seem an overly harsh judgment of my former colleagues at the large agencies, let me state that I have made many of the same mistakes myself. My first major national public service campaign, the well-funded antidrug-abuse campaign for the National Institute of Mental Health (NIMH), was a flawed effort.

I was at that time an experienced creative vice president at a top ten agency, and was very proud of what we did. We won more than twenty prestigious industry awards with that effort, including a Gold Lion at the Cannes festival. There is no question that this highly visible campaign had a positive effect on my career as an advertising executive, yet looking back at it today I shudder at some of the mistakes we made.

For example, we graphically depicted drug use in some grim inner-city billboards. They were strikingly shot and the headline, "Slavery 1969," was strong. But the image of a needle in the arm could have been a turn-on to a heroin user, and those posters should never have been produced.

We also preached against marijuana use with the same intensity, language, and theme lines with which we railed against heroin, thus appearing to lack any real knowledge of our subject. It was all "drugs" and all equally destructive. Yet, clearly the severity of the effects and the potential dangers of each are quite different. So when we took the same hard line on the effects of marijuana use as we did on heroin, we lost credibility with our youthful audience. I tried to have the anti-pot spots eliminated from our campaign, but was told that since it was an official government campaign, we couldn't avoid it.

When the U.S. State Department called me some years later and asked me to travel with National Institute of Drug Abuse Director Robert DuPont to participate in an international conference on using the media to combat drug abuse, I accepted only if I could air our mistakes. To my surprise, the State Department agreed, and I did an elaborate mea culpa in what was, I hope, a constructive presentation.

Among other things, I told them that if you have, say, $10 million to spend in the media on drug abuse, then perhaps you should reallocate $9 million to creating education, counseling, and treatment programs, and use the balance in the media to advertise the availability of those services. To try and significantly stem the spread of drug addiction in thirty seconds on TV or in a half-page ad is very difficult. Not impossible, but difficult.

Sadly, today, more than twenty years later, many of the same mistakes continue to be repeated by respected advertising professionals. And if a public service campaign loses credibility with its target, it may lose everything. Those of us who have learned these lessons the hard way must take the responsibility of disseminating that learning to avoid repeating those mistakes.

HOW TO DO IT RIGHT

The following pages summarize lessons learned from years of personal experience. During those years I estimate I have been involved in the creation of more than one thousand broadcast commercials and an equal number of print, outdoor, and promotional pieces. I sometimes think that whatever could possibly happen during the production of advertising has happened to me at one time or other. I hope a retelling of some of the things I learned while living through those crises can help you navigate similar ones. And more to the point, perhaps the lessons learned from the cause campaigns with which I have been involved can help you steer clear of the many pitfalls inherent in this very specialized kind of advertising.

This book analyzes many examples of effective advertising in the cause marketing category, plus some that have fallen short.

Part 1 lays out the steps required to land and then develop a successful cause campaign.

The first chapter deals with some crucial considerations that must be addressed before any work can be created, including standard procedures used by cause committees in selecting advertising agencies for this type of account, and what factors you should consider in creating a winning agency pitch.

Chapter Two covers the importance of campaign planning and strategy, starting with such intertwined elements as budget and media and moving on to the crucial step of assembling the building blocks of a strong, simple strategy, including the often-overlooked but crucial areas of tone and style.

To help you further understand the addicted target, probably your most difficult challenge, Chapter Three explores the psychology of that special population.

Chapter Four is an overview of the nuts and bolts of the creative process, including the client presentation, with special attention paid to those factors that separate cause campaigns and cause clients from their for-profit cousins. The significance of logos and campaign themes to cause campaigns is discussed. And the special place of campaign icons in cause marketing is also covered, as we pay homage to Smokey, McGruff, and Iron Eyes Cody.

Chapter Five discusses television production for a cause campaign, with some thoughts about such matters as casting, including when to resist the urge to hire a celebrity spokesperson, and how to achieve first-rate broadcast production on a small public service budget.

Chapter Six covers the special factors that go into making effective cause radio, print, and outdoor advertising, and how these differ from the creation of broadcast advertising.

Copy research is arguably more important to a cause effort than to any other type of marketing. It's much better to predict if your campaign will work in the concept stage than to find out it didn't after the fact. Chapter Seven contains information about qualitative research: concept testing, focus groups, and mall intercepts and summarizes two case studies from the realm of issue advertising that were entirely driven by some fairly innovative research. Copy evaluation plays an especially significant role in cause marketing because the simple tools of sales figures and market share, surefire indicators of the effectiveness of a commercial product campaign, are missing. Yet proof of effectiveness is crucial to the placement and funding of most cause campaigns. Chapter Seven also includes a discussion of quantitative research and tracking as it applies to a cause effort, and techniques for effectively reaching special populations such as minority communities.

Chapter Eight covers the importance of preparing an efficient media plan, including the pros and cons of going the PSA route versus buying a paid media schedule, and contains a look at the new opportunities in on-line media. This chapter also examines the role of the Advertising Council in implementing and helping to place PSAs, plus ways to get your message out when you have virtually no budget.

Part 2 is a critical review of some of the most visible cause marketing efforts, with an analysis of how attention to, or a disregard for, the principles explored in Part 1 may have contributed to successes or missteps in these campaigns.

Chapter Nine is an analysis of the extensive work of that "Cause Colossus," the Partnership for a Drug-Free America, America's best-funded and most visible cause campaign. And Chapter Ten offers a detailed case study of the Massachusetts Tobacco Control Program.

Chapter Eleven is my top ten list of effective cause advertising campaigns, and Chapter Twelve summarizes with some final thoughts.

The book touches briefly on the areas of PR and promotions, corporate sponsorship, cause-*related* marketing, direct mail, and fund-raising. While these are all potentially important to any cause effort, they usually require the expertise of specialists and are usually subcontracted to those specialists by cause agencies.

For the benefit of administrators of cause marketing and students and others outside the advertising profession, a bit of "Advertising 101" is included—what good clients need to know to judge the effectiveness of the plan and the brief, the strategy, and the finished work. Even if your cause organization has the funding to hire a large full-service agency, judging that work will be easier if those principles are understood.

FIRST, DO NO HARM

I believe it is crucial that everyone involved with cause marketing take these principles seriously and carefully examine every communication placed before the public. Failure to do so may result in something much worse than just falling short of your objective. Daily, we see well-financed and beautifully produced public service advertising from experienced full-service agencies that may actually be counterproductive.

A long-running cause commercial, produced by a mainstream agency for the Partnership for a Drug-Free America and titled "The Burbs," shows a nicely dressed white preteen skateboarding through a neat suburban cul de sac. "Statistics show that 46 percent of all kids who smoke marijuana are inner-city youth. Guess who the other 54 percent are?" says the voice-over. The kid winds up with another preteen, and they start passing around a joint and toking expertly on it (see figure 9.1). Of course, the strategy was to shock middle-class suburban parents into action. These could be *their* kids; they'd better wake up and talk to them about drugs. But what about the kids watching over their shoulder? The preteens in the spot look like sensible kids having a wonderful time. Marijuana use appears normal. Quite appealing. But since media buys cannot be targeted precisely enough to eliminate youthful viewers, it's likely that sending the unintended message to kids—one that essentially normalizes youthful pot smoking—outweighs the benefit of shocking parents.

It is amazing how often the "product" (that passed-around "joint," drug paraphernalia, lit cigarettes, gambling activities, etc.) is portrayed in ads directed to abusers or compulsive users. Old habits die hard, and one of the major things the producer of any *selling* ad designs is the product "beauty shot." But putting the addictive substance or activity in the face of the user is just about the last thing you should do. You are very likely to evoke the memory of the "rush" that accompanies that use, and trigger the one response you wish to avoid.

Dr. Shaffer told me he once discovered that a recovering cocaine user under his care was contemplating a return to the drug after seeing an anti-cocaine commercial showing a line of coke being inhaled through a straw. The powder had been laid out across a photograph of a happy family gathering. The strategy was obvious: cocaine use can destroy a family.

But the much stronger subliminal message received by the addict was: "If that guy was willing to jeopardize his beautiful family just to snort that stuff, then the high has got to be amazing." And then he began to remember how amazing it was for him. He was *turned on* by the visual, ignored the verbal anti-drug message, and was stimulated to go out to buy some coke! (Dr. Shaffer reports that a therapy session successfully quelled the interest.)

The physician's creed states: "First, do no harm." That's clearly not a bad credo for anyone preparing public service communications. If you follow the basic steps in this book you will stand a good chance of serving that principle. And that's important because some well-intentioned public service campaigns do *a lot* of harm. However, if you are careful (and I hope this book can guide you in avoiding many of the pitfalls) you will be able to take some solid steps toward doing some good.

And when you do it right, and you start to see your campaign working and making an important difference in the lives of the people around you, you will have one of the most exciting and rewarding experiences of your career.

PART 1

DEVELOPING A CAUSE ADVERTISING CAMPAIGN

I

THE PITCH

RFRs, RFPs, and When to "Spec"

For several years I served on the new business team of Saatchi & Saatchi New York, at that time, a branch of the largest agency network in the world. We pitched our hearts out several times a month, and thanks to a pretty good agency reel and some smartly articulated, innovative marketing philosophies, we won a surprisingly high percentage of the accounts we went after.

For the past few years, while consulting in the area of cause marketing, I have served on a number of ad agency review panels, all on behalf of state government agencies. Having worked both sides of the street, I feel I can pass along a fairly comprehensive overview of what works to land a cause account, and what doesn't.

While on the agency team, we always tried to find out as much about the client group as we could, and would often adjust our pitch accordingly. As a member of several public agency review committees, I have come to realize that there are some very clear differences in the modus operandi of cause committees versus corporate client committees.

If you are an advertising professional pitching a piece of cause business, I hope this chapter will help inform that pitch.

THE CORPORATE PITCH

As a point of reference, let's take a look at practices usually employed whenever a corporate client decides to look for a new advertising agency, a routine familiar to most advertising professionals. A large company typically forms a search group from among its marketing executives, headed by the director of marketing. It is usually an experienced and professional group.

A list of possible agencies is collected, based on the marketing director's knowledge of available agencies, or gleaned from the American Association of Advertising Agencies members' directory ("The Red Book"). An announcement of the search is placed in *Advertising Age, Ad Week,* and newspaper ad columns, which usually results in a flurry of inquiries.

A selection of fifteen to twenty agencies is made, based on factors such as size of the agency (from reported billings and staff makeup), geographic location, client list, and reputation. In the corporate world, all of the above are carefully considered, plus, undeniably, personal contacts. An advertising partnership is a tough relationship, with many storms to be weathered together. A marketing director with any experience is bound to have an extensive network of friends and former associates in key positions at dozens of agencies. "I feel comfortable about working with you again, Charlie (or Mary)" is a tiebreaker in an agency selection more often than not.

The search group then requests a preliminary (written) submission. From this submission, a short list of two to five agencies will be drawn up and its members will be invited to make both a written proposal and ultimately an oral presentation—the usual dog and pony show. For these presentations, an assignment is often given, requesting some planning, strategizing, and usually some rough advertising addressing a specific marketing problem.

More often than not, this "rough" advertising becomes anything but, with agencies doing expensive research and production in the hope of winning a big and profitable piece of business.

Recently, more and more client companies are relying on search consultants, usually former high-ranking agency people who will accomplish, for a fee, much of the selection process.

THE CAUSE COMMITTEE

When it comes to selecting an advertising agency for a cause campaign, the situation is somewhat different. First, it is unlikely that the cause organization will have a staff member as experienced as most corporate marketing executives. An exception may be when a nonprofit committee or foundation is able to convince one of the search consultants to work for a modest fee out of respect for the worthiness of the cause.

With a government agency, operating with public or tax-generated money, this will usually not be permitted. First of all, any whiff of the old boy-girl network must fall by the wayside. Any member of the selection committee with a personal connection to any of the agency finalists is likely to be excused. Under the Freedom of Information laws, the whole process must be an open book.

The first step is the circulation of a Request for Response (RFR), which is basically an "are you interested" letter that spells out the scope and requirements of the proposed campaign. In so doing, it may be a simple letter or it may come close to the final Request for Proposal (RFP) in spelling out the details of the proposed contract. It is usually sent to a list of all eligible advertising agencies within a geographic area. The response can usually be a short "we are interested" letter, and most agencies who regularly reply to RFRs have these filed on their hard drives for easy adaptation to the cause at hand.

Contents of an RFR can contain some or all of these sections:

- description or purpose of procurement—a statement of the campaign's goals, scope, and any preferred qualifications such as ability to secure bonus ad placements, be responsive to multicultural needs, etc.
- acquisition method—fee for service, license, outright purchase, lease, etc.
- single or multiple contractor requirements
- duration of contract
- value of procurement—basically, the budget for the campaign
- performance and business specifications—the scope of service, which may include a schedule, development of materials, research proposal, etc.
- evaluation criteria
- general information section

The general information section can include a communication policy; communication is generally forbidden with members of the procuring body except as outlined in the RFR. It can also describe reasonable accommodation for bidders with disabilities and hardships, and "best value selection and negotiation," which essentially allows negotiation of a change in the contract specifications that may result in a more cost-effective delivery. Some state agencies even require applicants to

declare the nature of any business association they may have with controversial countries such as Northern Ireland and Burma!

Agencies that respond in the affirmative to the RFR are then sent
a more elaborate RFP by the cause organization.

Normal contents of an RFP are:

- statement of purpose
- background on the cause
- applicant eligibility, available funding, and contract period
- timetable, with various deadline dates
- the process: what will "qualify" the proposal (its required
  contents)
- bidder's conference invitation
- review and evaluation criteria
- oral presentation schedules (if appropriate)
- award notification procedure
- contract negotiation guidelines (often if some details are still to
  be worked out, and an agreement cannot be reached with the first
  prioritized bidder, the contract may be offered to the next prioritized bidder)
- contracting and subcontracting policies
- technical specifications, including overall objectives, scope of services (what the bidder is expected to provide—number of advertising units, minimum deliverables, performance objectives,
  monitoring, evaluation, timetable, and proof of fiscal soundness)
- applicant instructions, often including proposal format such as
  maximum pages to be allocated to each section and maximum
  overall length, project abstract, agency experience (including previous work and references), scope of work, staffing, and budget
- evaluation process and criteria, often including a copy of the evaluation form, specifying percentages of weight applied to each section

The advertising agency's response to the RFP should be a much
more elaborate package. An open meeting called a "bidder's conference"
is usually scheduled, and a senior member of the ad agency team should
be present and ask very specific questions. Since you will be putting a
lot of time and money into preparing the proposal, it should be very
clearly understood what is expected.

TO SPEC OR NOT TO SPEC

One of the big variables in RFPs is whether they will or will not ask for speculative creative work, and what the scope of that work should be. In a perfect world, I would argue that spec work should be kept at a minimum. There is no question that nothing flatters members of a selection committee more, particularly one made up of people from professions or disciplines other than advertising, than to see their cause come to life for the first time on tape, even if it is of the "quick and rough" variety. It can be a strong new business tool. Some agencies, as we have said, regularly spend major dollars producing speculative work if they believe the rewards of getting the business are great enough.

But none of the usual client-agency give-and-take has occurred before or during the preparation of speculative advertising. A smart agency will do a lot of planning research in preparation for this work, but the chances are that the design of that research may be flawed.

To expect that any advertising prepared for a pitch will be used unchanged in the ultimate campaign is usually a naïve hope. There are too many opportunities to make a mistake. And if the style or tone of voice is at odds with the taste of key client decision-makers, some lovingly produced work could bomb in the meeting and be the kiss of death for the pitch. There is, therefore, a strong risk involved.

In the final analysis, if it has *not* been asked for, the decision to do speculative work must rest with the individual agency's assessment of the situation. Generally, I would rather have the selection committee judge the creative ability of an agency by looking at its sample reel, but if you do no spec work and your competition does, you may be at a serious disadvantage.

Incidentally, when you submit an agency sample reel, be sure everything you show was created by staff that's still with the agency. If one or more of its creators has left, point that out and specify the degree of his or her contribution. Advertising, as we all know, is a collaborative effort, and you may have some key decision-makers still on board despite the departure of one or more of the players. But make that very clear in the response to the RFP. While serving on a review committee for a neighboring state agency with a small advertising community, I saw exactly the same spot on two different agency reels. It was the duty of the review committee to find out who did what. And we did. It turned out that the writer of the spots had made a fairly typical career move; he had switched agencies. The agency where he had written and produced the spot kept it on its reel; the new agency displayed it as an example of the newly arrived writer's work. We only counted it for the latter agency because the writer was there at the time, but we chided the applicant for not making clear that the agency had not produced the spot. You should always be explicit about the credits on submitted work.

Also, having endorsed a "no speculative work" stance, I should admit that I once advised a small agency preparing a pitch for a cause campaign to take that position. Basically, its proposal said: "Judge us on our past work. Hire us and we'll work together and develop a strategy and *then* produce some advertising we can all be proud of." I was encouraged in recommending that position by the fact that there had been no specific request in the RFP for speculative copy.

The agency lost to another agency that had done some very flashy layouts of some really terrible copy. It was in fact far below the ability level of the company I had been advising. But the selection committee had no basis on which to judge the quality of the work, nothing to compare it against since it was the only speculative work they saw. They were wowed by the simple fact of seeing their cause jump out at them from slick color layouts. "A clear win!" one of the evaluators told me later.

I have advised some of my cause client groups to eliminate any request for speculative work when preparing the RFP, but failing that, to at least hold the request down to asking for a solution to a fairly limited objective—a campaign aimed at preteens, for example. There's no question that the response it creates can deliver a quick snapshot of the agency's ability to think and organize a campaign. It will also level the playing field and limit everyone's spec work to the same assignment.

In my view the best spec situation is when the issuer of the RFP strictly enjoins the submitting agencies from including speculative work in the *written* proposal, but gives the finalists a creative brief and limited time frame in which to prepare a rough speculative campaign for the "oral." Therefore, ability to work to a tight deadline is measured along with creative ability.

The Massachusetts Tobacco Control RFP asked for some creative as part of the written RFP. Most of what was received in the written proposals was off the mark, but understandably so, due to the above-mentioned lack of any client-agency relationship. I helped the program director draft the letter inviting the finalists to the oral presentation, and as part of it, pointing out some strategic problems with the work. We summarized some of the specific criticisms. We also asked some fundamental client questions. There was a minimum of nit-picking; these were mainly Big Picture issues. The finalists were then invited to either completely rethink their work, modify it, or bring it back the way it was and defend it.

All but one staunchly, and somewhat haughtily, defended the unchanged work. One agency, Houston-Effler (later merged into Arnold Communications), brought back *some* of the original ads, well-defended, but also did some new work in response to the letter. In all, they very professionally addressed every point we had raised. (P.S.: they got the account!)

My experience in New York on a new business committee was always very stimulating. And despite the image of the New York ad scene as a tough, competitive world, when we lost a pitch, we generally graciously called the winner and congratulated them. We would then call the clients and ask them to critique our pitch (some were very candid in a postmortem, and we always learned from them). After that we picked ourselves up and went on to the next one. And that was the modus operandi for most of the agencies we went up against.

I have no idea whether it's generally true of advertising communities outside New York, or whether it's just a New England thing, but the animosity that was generated after our selection of an agency for the Massachusetts Tobacco Control campaign was astonishing to me.

One rejected agency group, which presented some good copy but seemed very disorganized in the pitch and projected a thinly disguised arrogance, started a lawsuit to protest the decision. The arrogance perception was proved soon after the lawsuit was thrown out. The agency loudly announced to the press that since their work was clearly superior, they would go ahead and produce their commercials at their own expense and offer them to any other state who wanted them. As far as I know, nobody took them up on it. They then told a reporter for a local paper that it was perfectly obvious that no one on the selection committee knew *anything* about advertising! As a member of that committee, did I take umbrage? A little!

If you are presenting to a government agency, be sure all your ducks are in a row. Even the most enlightened will still possess a somewhat bureaucratic mind-set. I watched an advertising agency in another state nearly win an anti-smoking account by the sheer weight of its buttoned-up presentation. Media, account management, PR, all were thoughtfully organized. Unfortunately, there was not a single moment in any of the creative work, either on the agency reel or in the spec ads, that came close to the degree of professionalism we felt the account demanded.

As was pointed out in what I think was the clinching argument during the decision discussion, no one watching TV and seeing the spots was going to have a clue about any of the smoothly organized infrastructure. All viewers would see was the commercial. And if it was inept and unpersuasive, the campaign funds would have been wasted. The agency came in a close second. However, had it presented even modestly better creative, it probably would have won the thing.

SOME PITCHING HINTS

To summarize, if you are pitching a cause campaign, the following hints can probably help:

- Structure your presentation logically. Spend a little extra time on your staff organization chart, clearly spelling out lines of responsibility.

- Do your research carefully, and make sure your creative is something you would be proud of. This sounds obvious, but there will be a temptation to try and dazzle these "bean counters" with some smoke and mirrors. Just remember, one of those bean counters might be me (or someone like me!).

- Consider videotaping your pre-creative focus groups. Cause groups may be unfamiliar with qualitative research, and the impact of seeing real people talk about their cause in a well-structured group can be very compelling.

- Try and have all your key players at the oral presentation. This is going to be a long collaborative effort, and the compatibility factor of the key players will be closely judged, even if it doesn't show up on any of the rating sheets. I have seen a pitch lost because *only* the CEO showed up, expecting to dazzle the group with his personality and status, only to leave them thirsting for a look at the "worker bees." I have also seen an account pitch lost because the quite prominent CEO was off pitching another (read by the committee as "*more important*") account.

- Pay a lot of attention to your budget. Again, try to think "bureaucrat" mentality here. Take a hard look at your fee. If the account has an ample budget and you stand to make decent profit on it, consider knocking a point or two off your fee, as a gesture to the worthiness of the cause. This could give you an edge if the vote is close.

For many years, the agency fee was a flat 15 to 18 percent of the media budget, but now that practice is rapidly changing, with less than 35 percent of agencies charging for services on that basis. Since it is an acknowledged fact that just about the same amount of work is required for a client with a $4 million budget as for an account with $10 or $15 million to spend, many agencies are working out other formulas, one being to guarantee a fee with a provision to take the greater of either the fee or a standard 15 percent media commission. This way, it lessens the suspicion that the agency is recommending more media than is necessary, just to inflate the fee.

Performance-related fees are also being put in place by some agencies and clients, the most significant being Procter and Gamble, although with the difficulties of evaluating performance in a cause account, this probably has little validity for the cause marketer.

So, let's assume you have mounted a well-structured, thoughtful but exciting pitch, and have been awarded the account. Congratulations! But let's *not* assume it's like any of the commercial accounts on your agency roster. It's not. And in the next few chapters we will review the normal steps of planning and making the ads, with a sharp look at the differences and possible pitfalls of a cause campaign.

2

PLANNING YOUR CAMPAIGN

Creating a Cause Advertising Strategy

Recently I got a call from a young program director at a nonprofit agency for which I occasionally consult. There was excitement in his voice. "We just got some funding from a state agency. They want us to produce a brochure. Will you help?"

"I'll be happy to," I said. "Who's your target?"

There was a long pause on the phone. The good news was that there was a sum of $50,000 available to that agency to create a piece of communication. The bad news was that he hadn't thought about *who* the agency was going to spend that money to reach. The most fundamental plank in the strategic foundation had not been considered.

Marshall McLuhan, the self-styled media guru of the '60s had a much-quoted thesis, first expressed in his eye-opening book, *Understanding Media*: "The medium is the message." Some of us thought at the time that we knew where he was going with that slogan, but it never made a lot of sense to any advertising professional.

McLuhan was obviously trying to shake up our conventional way of thinking about media. To upset our complacency, he theorized that the very carrier of the message was sufficiently "hot" or "cool" (his terms) to communicate, regardless of the content. Okay. He got our attention about how powerful each of the various media was. But none of this seemed in those days to have much relevance in the real world of selling.

If you are not using the medium to target a specific group, to aim a simple message of carefully chosen words at that target, to project a style or image or tone of voice that describes you and the attitudes you

hold, then for you, the medium *is* the message. You are doing marketing just to do marketing. And you are probably wasting your time.

The strategy or creative brief, as any beginning copywriter learns
early on, must be the firm foundation, the genesis of every piece of
advertising communication. And once the campaign is prepared, don't
put the strategy away in a file drawer, because it should be considered
during every evolutionary step.

Consider again the famous "Just say no!" campaign. Originally
conceived by an advertising agency for an Ad Council campaign on
behalf of the National Institute of Drug Abuse, it was a message aimed
at very young children, to arm them against the first time anyone tries
to initiate them into drug use. Nancy Reagan heard the phrase in an
NIDA film at a meeting in Oakland, and immediately adopted it as the
theme for a series of anti-drug presentations.

Unfortunately, Mrs. Reagan never understood the slogan was
intended for young children. According to Tom Adams of the conservative National Federation of Parents, she used the term with teenagers,
and even while visiting treatment centers. Quoted in *The Fix*, Michael
Massing's excellent book on the flawed "war" on drugs, Adams notes that
telling men and women in treatment to "just say no" was ridiculous.

By the time the campaign became the official government line on
drug prevention, the original very limited target—young kids—had
been largely forgotten. A campaign written for one very limited target
was being directed at another, with disastrous consequences. Because, as
we have said, it confirmed to the teen drug experimenters that the establishment, the government, was clueless.

STRATEGY: THE MOST IMPORTANT WORDS YOU WILL WRITE

A strategy must be the most carefully crafted set of words you write for
any marketing campaign. And the strategy for a cause marketing effort
is crucial to its success. Draft it, sniff it, refine it to its very essence.
Make it as simple and limited as you can. Then and only then should
the creative team start to work.

Good clients will keep the strategy in front of them at all times
during the copy approval process. Nine times out of ten, if the copy
doesn't feel right, it's because it's off strategy. Undisciplined writers will

sometimes become enamored of a turn of phrase or a joke or a dramatic situation that is so creative and unique that they just know it will guarantee them entry into the Advertising Hall of Fame. But if it's off strategy, it must be rejected, even if, as a piece of wordsmithing, it's pure poetry.

It's a good idea to begin any meeting in which advertising is being presented with a formal reading of the strategy. Sometimes the pursuit of an innovative idea has led the creative team to a piece of work that is ever-so-slightly off strategy. Reviewing the strategy just ahead of presenting the advertising should help expose that. If you are a creator of the campaign, I urge you to take the time before you present it to your client to do the same thing. Hold your work up against the strategic grid daily and make sure you are on solid ground. Because "slightly off strategy" belongs in the same category as "a little bit pregnant."

It is true that every so often good instincts may actually lead a creative team into an approach that *is* off strategy, but seems to be the right solution. Every so often, the strategy just may have been wrong to start with. If everyone agrees about that, then the presentation of advertising should stop until the strategy is redrawn. But this is a very rare occurrence.

A more frequent problem in the strategy phase arises when little attention is paid to the strategy as it is drafted and approved. Then some copy that was written strictly in accordance with the strategy is rejected. An analysis of that rejection may reveal that the problem is strategic rather than creative. This situation creates a waste of time and effort, and should be avoided at all costs.

As a consultant to a government agency, I once approved some charming copy in a preliminary meeting at the advertising agency. It was right on strategy, and I felt so good about it that I told them to just send it over to the program officials for what I was sure would be quick approval.

I got an angry call from the program head, saying "we would never say anything like that!" When I pointed out that it precisely and quite creatively expressed the principal strategic message, I was told again, rather firmly, that they would just never approve copy that said anything like that.

The truth of the matter was that the *strategy* should never have been approved because it raised an issue the sponsoring body wished to avoid. But no one had looked hard at it while it was being circulated.

A lot of talented people at the ad agency had wasted time and energy writing to an unacceptable strategy. Before they went back at the assignment, we made sure the strategy was rewritten.

The Narrower the Better

Incidentally, people often are surprised when I, as a former copywriter, insist that a rigid strategy is the writer's best friend. Creative teams may chafe a bit at first because it seems to restrict their creative exploration. But a narrowly crafted strategy will keep them from all those flights of foolish fancy that can so entrap and consume team members that they waste a lot of their (and ultimately everyone's) time. Ogilvy Creative Director Norman Berry, in the *Wall Street Journal*'s "Creative Leaders Series" said it best: "Vague strategies inhibit. Precise strategies *liberate*."

The relatively brief strategy document is never easy to come by. Just about everyone in the client organization will have an opinion about the best way to advance his or her cause, just as the president of nearly every company preparing an advertising campaign can hardly wait to list every single reason their product is the best.

The agency then has the tough task of determining which *one* of those reasons will make the strongest selling case versus the competitors. A healthy give-and-take between client and agency is crucial at this point.

This is where well-structured research comes in, and it can be an invaluable step in the strategy-writing process. Concept testing using competing benefit statements can save a lot of grief, if you're still not sure. It's certainly a lot cheaper to have a hand-lettered strategy card rejected by your target prospect than to have a fully produced commercial go down in flames in a focus group.

Marketing Strategy

The advent of "account planning," with its extensive pre-creative research regimen, may actually have helped nurture some of the most brilliantly creative and outrageously innovative advertising. That's because when it's done right, it eliminates much of the guesswork, and gives the creative group a detailed road map on how to get to the objective.

Planning a marketing strategy starts with a careful market analysis. In the case of a cause marketing effort, it will be a detailed analysis of the depths and causes of the problem the effort is designed to fix. It will include some preliminary focus groups to try out some aspects of the strategy, and a detailed psychological analysis of who the targets are and how they may be best reached.

If yours is a large television market, and your ideal target includes several demographic groups, you may decide to target only one of them, depending upon the size of your budget.

THE IMPACT OF THE BUDGET

Although establishing an available budget is just part of the puzzle, it is the crucial first piece. For many cause marketing campaigns, that budget may be quite small.

On several occasions a relatively inexperienced client has asked me how much a television spot costs. That's a little bit like asking, "How much is a car?"

You can get some decent wheels for under $10,000. You can also pay more than $500,000 for a custom Rolls. By the same token, you could spend $1.5 million on a TV spot, as many corporate clients do on a Super Bowl commercial. But if you have a very small budget, you must stay away from location shoots with a cast of thousands. It often surprises me how professionally a spot can be created employing some stock photos and music and a few hours in a good editing suite. Total cost? A few thousand.

In 1998, the average cost of an anti-smoking spot for the Massachusetts Department of Public Health was $150,000. The agency, in its pitch for the business had suggested a production budget of about half that per spot, assuming, I surmise, that the public health administrators would balk at spending production dollars at anything above that level. One of my first acts as consultant to the department was to urge them to double the amount.

Try if possible to stay away from low-budget production companies that will come to you professing a commitment to your cause and promising the moon. A quick look at their reel will give you a good idea of their professionalism. Usually the cracks will show.

Average TV viewers are quite intuitive when it comes to low-budget production. They may not be able to identify the flaws, but something about the spot may seem cheap, shoddy, amateurish. And the subliminal image of an amateur effort, can undercut the loftiest of goals. When Massachusetts mounted its anti-smoking effort, we were going up against some of the most slickly executed advertising ever produced, the multimillion dollar campaigns of the tobacco giants. It was important that the viewer perceive us as playing in the same league. Hence my strong plea for a higher production budget. (More on the details of production budgeting in Chapter Five.)

The key budget-related element to be considered at the strategy stage is how much media (if any) you can afford to buy. Some cause marketing campaigns are done strictly pro bono, and placed as PSAs to be run at the whim of the networks or local stations. Sadly, what this probably means is that your spot will rarely be seen by anyone other than insomniacs.

Or you may only have the money to buy a very limited schedule, with a very low frequency per viewer. In either of these cases, you may wish to consider a more startling execution. I guarantee that the posthumous Yul Brynner "Now that I'm gone, I'll tell you, don't smoke. . . . just don't smoke" anti-smoking spot was instantly impressed on the mind of any viewer on a single airing (see figure 11.1).

The notorious "Daisy" spot for the Lyndon Johnson presidential campaign that dissolved from a little girl plucking and counting daisy petals into the "ten . . . nine . . . eight" nuclear countdown ran only once before it was pulled following a public outcry. Still it remains solidly embedded in the collective national consciousness and is probably the most famous political ad ever made.

Obviously, a startling spot is also a risky spot. Do some well-focused research with your target. Let it and some heavy soul-searching convince you that you won't do your cause more harm than good as you put out something so strong it's instantly memorable.

CONTROVERSIAL ADS AND PRE-CLEARANCE

The experience of the Friends of Animals (FoA) may be instructive. This is a sincere group that has espoused some controversial positions. It opposes any use of natural fur, medical animal testing, and all animal hunting, and it proselytizes vegetarianism.

While taking no position on these issues, it is obvious to me that some are positions not held by a number of Americans. Although FoA strongly opposes violent protests, such as spraying paint or throwing buckets of blood on fur wearers, it may still be viewed with suspicion by many who lump FoA with the spray painters.

So, unlike a group that is opposed to something most people would oppose, such as littering or riding without a safety belt, FoA members take on a more difficult task of changing widely held attitudes about their causes, and possibly themselves.

The issues lend themselves to very intrusive campaigns. However, what good is the most edgy and effective commercial if it is never used, and therefore never seen?

FoA convinced filmmaker Tony Kaye to have one of his partner directors, Robert Espinoza, shoot a spot called "Evolve," created by a small (and wonderfully named) New York agency, Mad Dogs and Englishmen. The spot, although recognized by British Design & Art Direction and the Clio Awards, has never aired as a PSA and has run only once or twice as a paid commercial on cable.

"Evolve's" message is reasonably uncontroversial and offers a fairly intellectual appeal to reason. The payoff line is "Fur is a thing of the past." However, the visual is a shocker. The camera pans seductively up a shapely model wrapped in a floor-length fur coat. As we reach her head, we note that she has, thanks to special-effects artist Tim Considine, strikingly Neanderthal features and is gnawing savagely on what appears to be a huge piece of raw meat.

Although the poster version has been displayed in Times Square and in some Sony theaters, the TV spot was initially turned down cold by networks, local stations, and cable systems alike.

I'm not entirely sure why. Perhaps it was because the way the camera panned along the model, enough skin was revealed to imply that she was nude under the coat. Could it have been that Johnny Carson's fictional prudish NBC censor "Priscilla Goodbody" was still at her post? The Neanderthal makeup was, in the words of its designer, "convincing but not too grotesque," and I agree. It was just enough to startle you, but nothing you'd lose your supper over. It may have been that the blood at the end, with a few choice bits of flesh floating in it, breached some "good taste" guidelines, but that could have easily been addressed with a simple re-edit to a bloodless end title. This might have upset the director, but would not have destroyed the integrity of the core idea.

Robin Daniels, president of Mad Dogs and Englishmen, believes the ad was rejected simply because broadcasters did not wish to offend their other advertisers who sell fur. Certainly that's a factor when magazines that depend on cigarette revenues reject anti-smoking ads. However, that's seldom given as a reason. Sandra Lewis, FoA's New York director, tells me her favorite rejection rationale was that the spot would scare children! It doesn't matter that, as Sandra points out, some very bloody films have been aired by the same network in family viewing hours. Commercial clearance has always been more stringent. However, if it is truly a matter of taste, clearance can be negotiated at the planning stage, and sometimes a simple change can achieve approval.

Soliciting approval from the continuity-clearance people at the media outlets is a mandatory step, and I have found that their decisions often seem arbitrary. In their defense, I should make the comment that it has to be a terrible job. The only time they can get into serious trouble is when they say yes. If there's a hue and cry from the public after a controversial ad airs, the first words out of the network president's mouth will probably be "Who approved that?" So saying yes carries some corporate risk. Bottom line is, it's an imprecise science, and horse trading is allowed and even expected.

What can the cause marketer learn from this? Do your clearance process at storyboard stage, before you've spent your precious production dollars. Apparently that was not done for the FoA spot. It's particularly important if you're hoping to get PSA placement. But even if you are planning on using paid media, remember, it's *their* license, and *their* station or network, and *they* get to call the shots.

However, ingenious negotiating can often carry the day. Maybe for the FoA spot it could have been a simple matter of scrubbing the blood. Maybe FoA could have found a person in the clearance hierarchy who was sympathetic to its cause and might have guided it through the process. Possibly submitting the ad to the Advertising Council for consideration as an "endorsed" or "bulletin" campaign (described in Chapter Eight) would have provided an evaluation of the work's consistency with "generally respected American values," which is how the Ad Council describes its criteria.

So consider being edgy and intrusive if you have limited media money, because you'll certainly be remembered. But put it through the clearance process at storyboard stage, or you may wind up with an expensive piece of production that is only shown at the cause's annual meeting. FoA's Sandra Lewis told me about a spot produced some years ago by British photographer David Bailey for Greenpeace showing a bleeding fur coat. It was turned down, but Greenpeace generated great publicity over the rejection, including a "60 Minutes" segment. The resultant publicity was more than Greenpeace could have paid for. However, Sandra advises against provoking a turndown (and the ultimate news coverage it might generate) by producing something outrageous. "In order to make the news, the item may have to pander to the lowest levels of taste," she says, "and the sensationalism will alienate your serious supporters."

It may be prudent to articulate an opposite point of view here. To be truly intrusive and startling, a commercial has to be carefully crafted. If you're not certain whether your approach will be off-putting to a

Evolve

*(Seductive saxophone music
throughout)*

FIGURE 2.1 *Friends of Animals.* "Evolve" is a controversial spot that was not precleared. Virtually all media outlets rejected it, both as a PSA and as a paid commercial. *Courtesy of Friends of Animals Inc., and Mad Dogs and Englishmen, New York.*

substantial portion of your target, it may be best to stick with a straight-forward, mainstream presentation of your cause and hope it will get across to its target through repeated airings over several years.

Or, after reviewing your budget, you may come to a decision that will seem like heresy for this book. You may decide not to advertise in conventional media at all! Some combination of PR, direct mail, and the Web may be a better use of your money than spending it on a commercial that may never be seen!

In any event, go over your budget carefully. Plot out exactly what units of advertising you can reasonably create for the dollars you have, and spell them out in the strategy document.

ENTER "ACCOUNT PLANNING"

Many agencies lately have adopted a British practice called "account planning." Basically, it elevates a senior agency executive to the role of a planner who is charged with leading this pre-creative stage, guiding the research and market analysis, addressing the media effort, and coming up with a version of the conventional advertising strategy called the "creative brief."

According to Jon Steel's *Truth, Lies, and Advertising*, modern account planning was first practiced at the offices of hot British agency Boase Massimi and Pollitt. The "account planning" label was coined by Stephen King (the brainy adman, not the scary novelist) at the London office of J. Walter Thompson in 1968. The agency's head of planning, Chris Cowpe, described planners as "architects and guardians of their clients' brands" and "detectives who uncovered long-hidden clues in the data, and gently coerced consumers into revealing their inner secrets." They possess analytical and intuitive skills to interpret that data in an interesting and innovative way, unlike traditional agency researchers, who tend to be more reactive and bound by the literal findings of their research. According to Cowpe, planners are "proactive and imaginative, injecting their research-divined ideas into every stage of the advertising-development process."

THE TRADITIONAL ADVERTISING STRATEGY

Since the creative brief and the advertising strategy cover essentially the same ground, let's examine the fundamentals of the traditional strategy.

These elements are very familiar to every practitioner of advertising. However, let's review them from the perspective of a cause assignment. I will also include a comparison of some sections of the planner's brief which may differ slightly.

What follows is essentially a generic strategy form I have compiled based on years of preparing or approving strategies. *Your* agency may have a slightly different format. That's fine, as long as each of these elements is addressed. After analyzing the basic sections, I provide three actual cause strategies as examples of their implementation.

Strategy Elements

A typical strategy will contain the following elements:

1. Marketing Objective

What is the basic objective of your marketing effort? This is the first broad statement of your goals, but it still should be somewhat limited. Putting down a limited marketing objective will start to focus your thinking.

This section, typically titled "Why are we advertising at all?" in the planner's brief, is probably more helpful for product or service advertising since it describes the current business situation, such as "the consumer is unaware of our line-extension brand," or "we must convince the consumer that we have benefits that put us in the same league as the market leader."

This may seem less important for cause marketing because by the time most cause groups decide to advertise, the human or public need is often urgent and well-recognized by the people—for example, the need for funding for cancer or AIDS research. However, there may be situations when the need to do a campaign has not been clearly delineated. The impetus to advertise may simply be the result of a sudden infusion of funds from a philanthropic source, or the desire to achieve public visibility without any more pressing objective. In that case, hard answers to this first section may actually point the organization in another direction in which to utilize those funds.

2. Advertising Objective

An even more limited statement, the advertising objective spells out the specific objective, within the broader marketing goals, of this particular advertising effort, be it a commercial, television campaign, billboard, or brochure.

3. Target

Who do you want to talk to? What group do you need to reach? What are its demographics? The answer constitutes a definition, the narrower the better. As Jon Steel points out in *Truth, Lies, and Advertising,* "'men aged 35 and over with large household incomes' includes Bill Clinton, Billy Graham, Michael Jackson, Michael Jordan . . . Donald Trump, Bob Dole, the San Francisco police chief, and a large number of successful drug dealers."

A subsection in the traditional planner's brief adds: "What do we know about them?" This is one of the creative brief sections that I believe to be a great improvement over the conventional creative strategy. It is a helpful tool to allow the creative team to get a clear image of exactly who in the "Clinton-to-drug-dealers" laundry list they are writing to.

In his book *Hey, Whipple, Squeeze This,* copywriter Luke Sullivan, suggests pretending you're writing a letter and *visualizing* the person you're writing to. "She's not a 'female, 18 to 34, household income of blah-blah.' She's a woman named Jill who's been thinking about getting a newer, smaller car. She's in an airport, bored, trying to get a Gummi Bear out of her back tooth, and reading *Time* magazine backward."

Former Doyle Dane Bernbach (and later Saatchi & Saatchi/ Compton) creative director Bob Levenson also recommends putting aside the "male 18 to 34" stats and creating your own very personal prospect. "Keep in mind," he adds, "your prospect (even of your own creation) is likely to be smarter than you are, and much warier. He is, after all, not in advertising. You are."

4. Competitive Climate

What other messages are out there competing for the time, attention, and commitment of your target? This is important information to hold in mind before the writing process starts. It's simply a case of "know thy enemy." It is not a crucial part of the strategy statement, but it's a helpful tool.

When doing product or service advertising, this will consist of a review of all competitive brands' advertising. When doing cause marketing against an advertised product, such as tobacco, the process is very similar. It's a matter of seeing what's currently being said to promote product usage. However, when advocating a practice such as, say, trash recycling or breast self-examination, for which there is no organized opposition or competitor, this section should contain an analysis of prevailing public attitudes or psychological barriers to your position.

5. Principal Idea (Consumer Benefit)

What's the single most important thing you want to tell your target? This is the most difficult strategic element to pin down. If the copy contains more than one (or at the most, two) principal ideas, the result will be a less-effective communication.

John Hegarty, Creative Director of the London agency Bartle Bogle Hegarty, liked to write the Principal Idea statement across the top of a piece of blank paper, sometimes over a picture of the product, and tack it up on the wall above his desk. "There's the first ad in the campaign," he says. "Now it's my job to create something better!" Making that statement the headline for the first ad can be a good test of its simplicity and succinctness as a statement of the central idea. This is as appropriate for a cause campaign as for a product ad.

6. Support

Support points are facts that can be considered an arsenal of proof points to back up the principal benefit. There can be quite a number of them, and usually they are listed in order of importance. They can be as diversified as medical facts, usage statistics, or legal or health implications of the target's actions. Not all support points need to or should be used in every communication. These are the arrows in the quiver of the writer taking aim at your target. But if they don't directly support your principle idea, even if they are completely true, they should not be in the strategy.

7. Desired Action

This is a test of the Principal Idea. Simply stated, it asks: "What do you want your target audience to do, once they've received your message?" Again, in planner's terminology: "What are we trying to achieve?"

Is your principal idea strong enough *to provoke significant action on the part of your targets, or has it just been registered or noted?* And if you move them to act, is that action the one you want them to take?

8. Tone and Style

What is your tone of voice? For example, is this a message that can only be presented in a serious manner, or might it be freshened by the use of humor? Is your tone real? Reassuring? Startling?

Although tone and style are usually included as an essential strategy section, they are often considered less seriously than the other elements. They may appear to be just an executional *guideline*. However, when working on a cause campaign, they are to be ignored at your peril. Often, a well-crafted strategy is damaged when the language of the execution strikes the wrong chord; that is, when the style and tone of the words are at odds with the objective of the piece.

Unsophisticated copywriters will sometimes resort to humor, puns, or irreverent writing to show off their creativity, while the tone of that writing may be directly opposed to the tone and style objective. If the tone statement, for example, mandates sincerity and credibility, an overtly clever approach may be just the wrong tack and may seriously undermine an otherwise well-strategized message. Omitting the tone and style objective from the cause-campaign strategy can be a dangerous error.

9. Executional Requirements

Are you creating an entire campaign, or simply preparing a ½-page print ad? Assignment specifics are spelled out here.

Strategy Examples

The following are some strategy statements for two actual campaigns under the Massachusetts Department of Public Health Tobacco Control Program, prepared by the excellent team at Arnold Advertising in Boston. I have also included a strategy written for the Massachusetts Council on Compulsive Gambling. The comments within parentheses are mine.

> STRATEGY EXAMPLE 1: **A campaign from the Massachusetts Tobacco Control Program designed to address easy youth access to cigarettes.**

Marketing Objective Generate public discussion, debate, and action over the issue of youth access to tobacco through vending machines.

(Generating public debate and action is a proper overall goal.)

Advertising Objective Create awareness of the fact that, in most cases, with vending machines there is nothing to prevent kids from illegally obtaining cigarettes.

(The commercial will dramatize specific areas of ease of youth access to fuel that debate.)

Competitive Climate Freedom-of-access issues raised by the tobacco industry, and economic hardship claims by businesses maintaining vending machine service.

(There have been newspaper ads and well-orchestrated appearances at town council and licensing board meetings protesting economic hardship of any restriction.)

Target Massachusetts adults age eighteen and older, socioeconomic range, mid- to upper-level

Opinion and community leaders

(A fairly specific demographic. A good deal of "what we know about them." This will impact both the writing and ultimately, the media placement. The commercial is more likely to run on "Meet the Press" than "Married with Children." It still might benefit from a bit more of the "What do we know about them" meat on its bones.)

Principal Idea Access is the key to prevention. If kids can't get cigarettes while they're young, they are less likely to start smoking.

(Single-minded, straightforward.)

Support
- The majority of smokers (75 percent) begin smoking before they are eighteen years old.
- While an alcohol retailer stands to lose his license if he violates the law by selling to minors, there is little enforcement of the age limit for tobacco retailers. Vending machines have no legal liability at all.
- Approximately one million kids start smoking every year.
- Despite the fact that smoking in adults has been declining and drug and alcohol use by kids has been declining, youth smoking is on the rise.
- The tobacco industry needs to replace the three thousand smokers who quit or die each year in Massachusetts.

(All good points. All support the principal idea. Not all need be used in the commercial, but are available if needed.)

Desired Action If we could make it harder for kids to buy cigarettes, especially from vending machines, we could help keep them from becoming smokers.

(Get involved in setting or changing regulations in your community.)

Tone and Style
- Serious
- Urgent
- Conveys the feeling that no one wants kids to smoke

 (Unambiguous. You couldn't write a humorous spot to this strategy.)

Executional Requirements
- One thirty-second TV spot
- B&W newspaper ad to run in dailies
- Create a version of the print ad that allows local advocacy groups to put their logo on it

 Figure 2.2 shows one of two commercials written and produced to this strategy.

> **STRATEGY EXAMPLE 2: A campaign within the Massachusetts Tobacco Control Program to educate kids about the addictive nature of cigarettes.**

Marketing Objective To reduce smoking rates among kids at highest risk to start smoking.

(A broad objective. It encompasses all youth prevention efforts.)

Advertising Objective To educate kids about addiction—that by starting to smoke they are sacrificing their ability to choose to stop smoking. In their minds they may want to quit but their bodies won't let them.

(Disseminate some very specific information about addiction, ideas which, according to research, may not have occurred to or been taken seriously by the target.)

Competitive Climate Cigarette advertising depicting "cool," in-control smokers. General misperception among peers: "There's no danger in smoking a cigarette now and then. Only weak people become addicted."

(Both advertising and word-of-mouth create this climate.)

SINGER: Now I have children
of my own.

they ask their mother what will I
be? Will I be handsome?

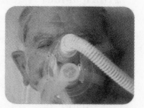

Will I be rich?

(I tell them) Que sera, sera,

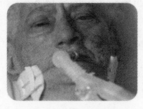

whatever will be will be,

One in three
children
who start smoking
will **die** from it.

the future's not ours to see,
(Title: One in three children who
start smoking will
die from it.)

It **doesn't** have to be.

Que sera
(Title: It doesn't have to be)

Urge your retailer to
support the law.

No tobacco sales to minors.

sera!
(Title: Urge your retailer to
support the law.)

FIGURE 2.2 *The Massachusetts Tobacco Control Program.* "Que Sera Sera" had its
original storyboard revised after the Sly and the Family Stone recording of the song
became available. Footage was recut to match song lyrics. *Courtesy of the Massachusetts
Department of Public Health.*

Target High-risk youth eleven to fourteen years old

Principal Idea The nicotine in cigarettes will control you. It slowly, but absolutely, will take away your body's physical ability to stop smoking.

(A strong and hopefully mind-opening idea.)

Support
- Once you start smoking, cigarettes will become an uncontrollable habit.
- Your body will need and crave nicotine every day . . . every hour.
- Can compare nicotine addiction to body's need for food, air, love, shelter.

(Clues to an appropriate execution are in this list.)

Desired Action I won't start smoking because I don't want to depend on cigarettes for the rest of my life. I never understood how strong addiction to cigarettes is.

(An action motivated by a revelation.)

Tone and Style
- Enlightening
- Heartfelt
- Honest
- Hit-ya-in-the-gut

(Some stylistic descriptions of the style. That's actually quite appropriate in this section, and can be very helpful to the writer.)

Executional Requirements
- Two thirty-second TV spots

Figure 2.3 shows one of two commercials produced to this strategy.

> **STRATEGY EXAMPLE 3: A campaign for the Massachusetts Council on Compulsive Gambling to educate families and loved ones about the nature of problem gambling and the availability of help.**

Marketing Objective Provide education and information on problem gambling as well as access to referral for treatment or self-help for problem gamblers and their families.

(Basically, the charter of the council.)

Advertising Objective Provide access to treatment for families or loved ones of problem gamblers.

(A much more limited objective.)

Competitive Climate

- Development efforts by neighboring casinos, racetracks, lottery.
- General perception among peers that gambling is a macho, social norm.
- Dopamine "rush" achieved by gambling. Desire to recapture it.

(This is a psychological manifestation that should be considered.)

"Breath"

(Sfx: Water splash)

(Whispering echo)
VO: Eventually you'll have to breathe.

It has nothing to do with willpower. *(Barely heard whisper)* Or choice. *(Whispering echo)* It's about need.

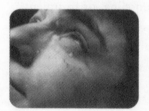

That's the way addiction feels.

(Underwater struggling sounds) Once you start smoking, you may not be able to stop.

(Normal talking voice) You'll need another cigarette . . . *(Inhale breath)* . . . like you'll need your next breath.

FIGURE 2.3 *The Massachusetts Tobacco Control Program.* "Breath" is a graphic analogy equating the need to take a breath underwater to the effects of nicotine addiction. *Courtesy of the Massachusetts Department of Public Health.*

Target Family and loved ones of compulsive gamblers.

(Due to the limited funding for the effort, this target was selected as most likely to be receptive to the message. The problem gambler may be denying there is a problem, and therefore may be harder to reach.)

Principal Message The compulsive gambling habit of your loved one can be destructive to them and their family. It is a hard addiction for them to break by themselves, but we can help.

(Actually two ideas, but they are closely linked.)

Support
- Compulsive gambling is a true addiction by the clinical definition.
- Compulsive gambling is a treatable disease.
- The dopamine rush makes the compulsive gambler return again and again to recapture the feeling.
- Some ways to determine if your loved one may have a gambling problem:
  - Seems constantly distracted regarding the family's welfare
  - Constant borrowing from family and friends
  - Lying about how they are spending their time and money
  - They have taken control of family's finances and money
  - Constant phone calls or mail from creditors

(A "laundry list" of symptoms of the problem.)

Desired Action Call the hotline for advice, counseling, or treatment options for your loved one.

(A very specific action.)

Tone and Style
- Sympathetic
- Credible
- Reassuring
- "Real"

(Important to reaching a reluctant target.)

Executional Requirements
- Two sixty-second radio spots
- Brochure

Radio Script

Client:	Massachusetts Council on Compulsive Gambling/ Massachusetts Department of Public Health
Title:	"Husband"
WOMAN:	At first, he's just gone every so often, and you think you can take it, 'cause you're not one of those possessive women, but then you realize he's gone quite a lot . . . and you think you can take it, 'cause that's just the way it goes, and then you find out he's gambling and you think you can take it, 'cause at least he's not with another woman . . . until you discover he's gambling . . . a lot. . . . and you think you can take it, because he won't listen when you tell him to stop, but when he gambles the grocery money, and you think you can take it, so, so what if he went a little crazy, just this once, until he tells you to clear your savings account . . . and he means *now* . . . or they'll break every bone in his body, and you're scared and shocked, but you think you can take it, 'cause he swore he won't gamble anymore, but you find out he stole money from his seven-year-old, and you think no . . . no, I don't think I can take it anymore!
ANNCR:	Call the Massachusetts Council on Compulsive Gambling at 1-800 GAM 1235. Compassion . . . understanding . . . solutions. For you and your family. Brought to you by the Massachusetts Department of Public Health.

FIGURE 2.4 *The Massachusetts Council on Compulsive Gambling.* "Husband" is a radio spot that offered a compassionate, real portrayal of a loved one's agony over a compulsive gambler. This commercial tripled the volume of hotline calls. *Courtesy of the Massachusetts Department of Public Health, Bureau of Substance Abuse Services in cooperation with the Massachusetts Council on Compulsive Gambling.*

Figure 2.4 shows one of two radio spots produced to this strategy.

Once the strategy has been researched, drafted, weighed, pondered, and made as rigid and limited as it can be, then you're ready to get going on what is always the most exciting aspect of your work: the execution.

SOME FINAL PLANNING CONSIDERATIONS

In case yours is an agency that has embraced the "planning" format or the creative brief, I want to reiterate a couple of points of difference before we leave this discussion.

Some creative briefs eliminate the support section containing the classic advertising "reasons why." I don't really understand why, and it's an element I strongly miss.

Also missing from many planning model creative briefs is a tone and style statement, something I consider crucial for the efficient execution of a cause campaign. Veteran researcher Maria Falconetti, with whom I worked at Compton, says that in her experience support and tone and style are rarely omitted from a creative brief. If they have become optional, I would strongly urge all cause marketers to consider them mandatory.

More and more, the creative brief, although based on client input, seems to be treated by planners as a purely internal document. Steel feels the client shouldn't need to see a written brief at all. However, if you replace the traditional creative strategy with a creative brief (as I understand the position of planning advocates to be), and a client, particularly a cause client, has not signed off on every word of it, you are asking for trouble. The client need not be present at the creative *briefing*, but they had better sign off on the brief.

As with any new advertising "magic bullet," particularly one which seems to be as effective a new business tool as planning, there are both ardent partisans and detractors. I can attest to its effectiveness in a pitch. The New York Saatchi office had not yet whole-heartedly embraced planning when we lost an account review for a large and long-held piece of business. The agency that won the business had, I'm told, dazzled the client with its decisive use of planning.

However, some of planning's detractors (most of them former senior agency researchers) have told me that a lot of agencies install a senior executive as a planner as an excuse to save the agency the money it used to spend on a large professional research staff. The highly placed planner (who, rather than being a strict researcher, may have come from an account management background) may then subcontract the research as needed, or perhaps even work with the client's researcher.

Planning's most ardent critics will tell you that it's only a slight reinvention of the wheel—standard pre-strategy research dressed up in fine British tweeds.

My own take on it lies somewhere in between. I believe planning is here to stay as an agency practice, especially in light of the fact that more and more clients are doing their own research or subcontracting it in the interest of getting what may be a more unbiased result. (Let's face it, many clients have long felt the agency research department is just a selling tool to "prove" the copy the agency wants to run is valid.) And if account planning results in more thoughtful and in-depth pre-strategy research, *and* gives more clout to those findings, how could I do anything but endorse it?

So if yours is a planning agency, fine, as long as you consider including those factors I feel should be specially applied to cause campaigns: support, and tone and style.

If yours is a traditional strategy company, don't feel inferior. Perfectly good advertising can be constructed to a standard creative strategy. Just be sure the good, careful probing of the target and objective that takes place prior to writing a creative brief is applied to writing your cause strategy. And some of the brief's innovations, such as "What do we know about the target?" can be very helpful if they are included in that strategy.

In the spirit of that important question, let's spend a little time examining some of what is known about the individual who is going to be your most difficult target—one who lives in an entirely different place from any target you have ever tried to reach with product or service advertising: the addicted target.

3

THE ADDICTED TARGET

The Toughest Challenge

The Massachusetts Council on Compulsive Gambling played a crucial role in my decision to write this book. I received a call from a staff member asking me to help devise an advertising strategy. I determined that I should first put together a fairly basic presentation on strategy construction, and spent a couple weeks researching the organization, its constituents, and its goals.

One day as I was poring over all this material, and some previous ad campaigns (most of which I didn't care for), I was asked if Tom Cummings (the council's founder) could take me to lunch.

I realized before the salads arrived that Tom was one of the most remarkable men I had ever met. He laid out his life story over that lunch, warts and all. I had the feeling he didn't mind revealing the personal difficulties that prompted him to found this organization, which is among the most influential in its field. In fact, I felt Tom believed it was important that I know all about them and understand them.

Tom's life and career as a revered Boston public school teacher had been nearly ruined by gambling. He went through all the steps of shame and anger and renewal that the problem gamblers his council reaches out to know so well. But he didn't just achieve recovery, a process he described as one of the most painful things he had ever done in his life; he made a decision to try to help others who were experiencing the same thing. Tom's dedication and determination allowed him to achieve funding, office space, and staff, and by sheer grit he moved the council into the respected national position it holds today.

Beyond that, Tom was a truly lovely man. After I made my strategy presentation, he sat back and shook his head. "I feel as if I just spent a semester in college," he said. That was the moment I decided that a book such as this was needed, for the Tom Cummingses of this world, and more important, for the marketing practitioners who set out to do advertising for them.

Tom passed away in 1998, shortly after we had both attended a meeting to plan a commercial based on the strategy we had devised together. Fortunately, he also had excellent basic executive instincts and had staffed the council well to run smoothly after he left it. Kathy Scanlon, his exceptional former right hand and now his successor as executive director, is carrying on beautifully.

But she also carries a touch of the sadness shared by the whole staff over not being able to drop into Tom's office to tell him some good news, or maybe some bad, and feel the warmth of his encouragement as he urged them to go back and attack the problem again with determination and enthusiasm.

Another extremely fortunate thing that came from my association with the council was an introduction to Dr. Howard Shaffer, director of the division on addictions at Harvard Medical School and an incisive and innovative thinker in the field. He is typical of the experts Tom's unique qualities attracted to the council. His conclusions on the nature of addiction, and his knowledge of the latest thinking in the field, have formed the basis for this chapter.

Why is a nationally respected scholar on the causes of addiction a key consultant to a council dealing with problem gambling? Because compulsive gambling is a classic addiction. And recognition of that fact (as opposed to considering compulsive gambling the result of weak will or lack of morality) is an important step toward obtaining help for the problem gambler.

Of all the target populations for cause marketing efforts, those who are addicted, be it to drugs, alcohol, gambling, or other destructive behavior, are unquestionably the most difficult to reach. If your cause is littering or recycling, then you may want to skip this discussion. But I also think you may find the subject as fascinating as I did.

ROOTS IN EDEN

The roots of man's tendency to become addicted to pleasure-granting activities go back, according to Dr. Shaffer, to a fundamental trait in the species. If you are a biblical scholar, you might even say they go right back to the Garden of Eden.

As Shaffer explains it, as long as we are "wired" to propagate the species, we will be at risk for addiction. The sexual act was designed to deliver a strong rush of pleasure, a "reward mechanism" if you will, for keeping the species going. The seeking and gaining of that pleasure is rarely a structured activity and is often spontaneous, without any rational thought or planning. Sex is not, as Dr. Shaffer puts it, "a negotiated activity." As Dr. Steven Hyman, director of NIMH, once said, "If we had to negotiate sex, we would have gone the way of the dinosaurs!"

If you equate this sexual search to people seeking the rewards of their addictive activity, which apparently delivers the same kind of rush, particularly in the anticipation phase, then you have taken a first step toward understanding the complexity of the condition with which your campaign messages must often deal. This is why Dr. Shaffer believes, that we will never totally do away with addiction.

AN EQUAL OPPORTUNITY PROBLEM

"Everyone is at risk for addiction. It's an equal opportunity problem," says Shaffer. More specifically, he points out that anyone with emotional problems, ranging from depression to anxiety to compulsive behavior is at higher risk. "Younger people are at higher risk," points out Howard, "because they are relatively vulnerable, and haven't matured a regulatory system for themselves." The elderly are also increasingly at risk because they often suffer from depression and are being medicated in ways that were not known a few years ago. Also at risk are children who are hyperactive or suffer from attention deficit disorder.

Dr. Shaffer cautions that these are rough cuts at various at-risk populations, and that membership in one of these groups is not necessarily a predictor of vulnerability to addiction. However, this list may help addiction-related causes establish targets for their messages. For example, in 1999 the Council on Compulsive Gambling mounted a radio campaign directed specifically at the families and loved ones of the elderly, many of whom are known to be gambling away their limited retirement funds.

BIOLOGY, PSYCHOLOGY, AND SOCIAL SETTING

What separates the addicted person from the experimenter, the alcoholic from the social drinker, the problem gambler from the casual poker player? Is there some genetic propensity, a genetic marker? For example, are children of alcoholics at greater risk? Dr. Shaffer says the "genetic marker" issue is too imprecise to draw any serious conclusions. There may be a tendency toward addiction in people who have the marker; however, many who grow up with it do not have the problem, and many who do not have it become addicted. Addiction may in fact be due to other factors. The child of an alcoholic has grown up in the same house with the drinker, for example, and therefore in the same social setting.

Addiction can usually be attributed to a confluence of biology, psychology ("mental health robustness"), and social setting. As an example of the latter, Dr. Shaffer cites the use of heroin by many soldiers during the Vietnam War who abandoned the practice after they were safely home. Meanwhile inner-city males, with little hope of changing their social setting, experience a very high rate of return to the habit even after extensive counseling. Clearly there was something about the social setting in Vietnam that contributed to use but not long-term addiction.

Dr. Shaffer also cites an interesting study called the "Rat Park Chronicle," published in 1980 in the *British Columbia Medical Journal*. Drs. B. K. Alexander, R. B. Coambs, and P. F. Hadaway crowded some rats into a teeming "rat city" but provided them access to some psychoactive medication, which they consumed avidly. Another group of rats was put in what was tantamount to an uncrowded park, and while they had similar access to the medications, they virtually ignored them.

We talked a lot about the neurological release that seemed central to the reward mechanism. There is some evidence that the neurotransmitter dopamine flows freely in anticipation of a reward, making us feel good. But dopamine is suppressed when the reward is achieved. Other neurotransmitters contribute to this process as well.

According to Dr. Shaffer, life seems to be in the chase and not the getting. This is why the "triggers" of that anticipation must be scrupulously avoided in your cause advertising. Depicting seductively exhaled smoke, roulette wheels spinning, or needles being readied can be very seductive to a person who is addicted, and trigger this anticipation "rush."

PROBLEM SOLVERS IN THE BRAIN

So how do we deal with this innate pleasure-seeking drive? When we were first "wired" to have reward systems as an incentive to procreate, theorizes Dr. Shaffer, the other parts of our brain responsible for rational thought were much more primitive.

Now, as we have evolved, we have a remarkable capacity for rational thought and problem-solving that, when employed, can interrupt the connection between impulse and behavior.

This gives some hope that education—planting knowledge about the risks and hazards of behavior—can be a deterrent. We still have the impulse, but now we have some facts to rationally apply to the situation, making it not nearly as rewarding.

A good example is in the use of condoms in the practice of safe sex. While some resisters still claim the condom gets in the way of the pleasure of the activity, the more logical individual will find a way to rationally integrate the practice into the activity in a way that does not diminish the reward.

Dr. Shaffer believes that public prevention campaigns should be designed "to promote integration of the thought into the process in such a way that the target is stimulated, not by an 'anti'-behavior message, but by a recognition of the behavior that is going on in that activity."

Once again, we should stay away from a "Just say no" (anti-behavior) campaign. Rather, design a message that says, "Of course you're going to want to try this, but have you thought about . . ." The message should be "Don't fight it . . . shape it!"

"Spots that meet people where they are, and then take them to where they may not want to be, are better than spots that tell them where they *should* be," Shaffer says. He admires the "Long Way Home" spot from the Partnership for a Drug-Free America (covered in more detail in Chapter Nine) because it does exactly this: it recognizes the situation as it exists and gives encouragement to build on positive aspects, rather than telling people how they *should* behave.

"Kids *will* seek pleasure. So many of the planners of these ads don't understand the universality of that need," Dr. Shaffer adds. "They don't grasp the complexity of the dark side of the human psyche. People are not rational all the time. As Albert Ellis said, 'We can't maintain mental health with consistency!'"

Incidentally, when I mentioned to Dr. Shaffer that Nancy Reagan reportedly told addicted individuals in recovery programs to "Just say no," he commented that they would all love to say no, but are unable to. That simplistic phrase would simply be frustrating for them, he theorized, and might even stimulate them to drug use because it would help convince them they were hopeless failures, unable to do what everybody else is doing.

CURRENT ADVERTISING, GOOD AND BAD

Dr. Shaffer and I also talked a bit about some of the current advertising in the drug and tobacco area. He believes spots that show social disdain, particularly for smokers, can be effective. He also likes the Massachusetts Department of Public Health "Pam Laffin" spot (covered in more detail in Chapter Ten) because the line, "I started to smoke because I thought it would make me look older," would hit kids exactly where they were. "That *is* the motivation for many of them," he says.

With one caveat, Dr. Shaffer felt that we should not stay away from describing the true dangers of tobacco and drugs, as long as we integrate them into *truthful* portrayals of the situations of the potential users. "When it comes to using tobacco and drugs, the more young people learn about the true dangers of these activities (if it's done in an honest and not disingenuous way) the less they'll do them." The exception, he says, are high-risk takers. "They'll do it more, exactly because it is so terrifying."

I also asked him about actor Carroll O'Connor's Partnership spot in which he discusses his son's drug-related suicide. I personally find this commercial very strong. We all love Carroll O'Connor. We know he lost his son to drugs. Our hearts go out to him. The end line of his spot is "Get between your kids and drugs *any way you can.*"

Dr. Shaffer told me he has spoken to many parents who will not talk to their kids about the subject just because of that spot. "That's a rough spot," said Howard. "The implication is for the parent to become a cop." It's punitive, he says, and may not be the best technique for maintaining the open dialogue that seems so beneficial. He notes that "if parents are too strong about abstention, what options do children have but to act out against that abstention? That's human nature. Parents who are police officers often raise kids who go out and break the law."

KIDS AT RISK

My conversation with Dr. Shaffer took place shortly after the horrendous school shootings in Colorado in 1999, and we couldn't help but reflect on that, as did most of the country during that awful time.

What struck us was the number of anomalies and the puzzlement of the nation's parents, who couldn't figure out how two intelligent kids in an affluent, safe neighborhood could commit such a senseless atrocity.

Shaffer noted that the rules for dealing with today's students, *and* for cause campaigns aimed at them, were put in place by a generation that probably had little understanding of the generation it was trying to reach. This is particularly true today, when social change is accelerating at such a pace.

Once again, we *must* recognize the complexity of this target of so much of cause advertising. Howard uses two slides to demonstrate this point when he lectures. They split up a quote from H. L. Mencken. Slide one says "For every complex problem, there's a simple solution . . .". Slide two continues ". . . that's wrong!"

No matter which way we pitch any of these programs as part of public policy, we are going to move some people away from dangerous substances. But at the same moment we move those people away, we're going to move some people *toward* them. The idea is to optimize the ratio: move more people away, and fewer people toward. "There are many of those spots that I hate," said Dr. Shaffer. "But they may do the job. After all, I'm not the target they're going after."

Dr. Shaffer draws an analogy to the "medication cocktail" approach to the treatment of AIDS. "When it comes to the youth population, there are no single 'magic bullets.' What we really need to do is layer our programs, to segment our approaches to the youth." My analysis of the Partnership for a Drug-Free America's progress indicates it is aggressively moving to do just that: to segment its efforts. I hope this means the group is moving away from warnings labeled simply "drugs," which, as we have discussed, can turn off a large number of youth targets, and instead is moving toward a segmented and truthful discussion of the risks of each *individual* drug.

Dr. Shaffer knows and admires General Barry McCaffrey, head of the government's Office of National Drug Control Policy, who is known to be an unusual proponent of interdiction, treatment, and education to reduce drug demand. Dr. Shaffer readily admits McCaffrey has a tough job, and that as the representative of the establishment, he *must* set a high moral tone. But he also feels the complexity of the target's psychology is such that mounting an effective campaign is a daunting task. Is this a discouraging conclusion? I don't think so. But it certainly mandates that everything done in this area be done slowly, cautiously, and thoughtfully.

Dr. Shaffer ended our last interview with a quote from John Kaplan:

"There's no situation so bad that you can't make it worse!"

During these conversations, Dr. Shaffer opened my mind to the many crucial psychological components of one of the targets we are trying to reach in our ads, and reinforced my view of the incredible difficulty of dealing with addictive substances in our advertising.

4

EXECUTION

Creation and Presentation

A s an advertising copywriter, I always considered the moment when the strategy was approved and we moved into execution mode to be the most exciting part of the whole process. There are no hard-and-fast rules about how to best make this time productive, since each advertising creative person works differently. In this chapter I describe some approaches that have worked for me and for some others I have known.

GETTING FROM "WHAT IF?" TO "THAT'S IT!"

Some of my best advertising memories have been of the days spent locked in a room with a good art director, free associating, playing "what if."

If you are an advertising creative person, this chapter offers some guidelines that certainly apply to any creative project, but are particularly applicable to cause marketing assignments. If you are on the account or client side, these insights into your creative team may be helpful as work comes to you for evaluation.

This is usually a time of exhilarating artistic freedom. But when it comes to cause marketing, that freedom must have significant limits. The strategy must be examined constantly during the process.

As I have said, one section of that strategy that is most applicable to cause marketing, and the one that is most often ignored, is tone and style.

"I've got a really crazy, silly idea . . ." says your partner, chuckling. You recheck the tone section. It says "Sympathetic. Credible. Reassuring." You must stop right there. Do it gently, so as not to kill your partner's spirit, or the excitement of the moment. But as we have said, a rigidly drawn and carefully researched strategy can be a tremendous time-saver. And unless you want to reopen the strategic discussion, that "crazy, silly" idea should be put in a file drawer for a different cause or product.

Or, perhaps you should both look *under* the silliness. There may be a germ of an idea that would survive a translation into a serious tone of voice.

It's OK to think cynical thoughts or joke around about your objectives as you work. A lot of great ideas start as jokes that, when explored, can be turned around to make a positive statement.

Tack everything up on the wall. Flip it onto the floor over in a corner of the office. Grab a pile of discarded magazines. Rip out related pictures and visuals, and tack them up. Scribble in a new headline or a line of dialogue.

Make a collage. Improvise a scene. Play all the parts. Yell, shout, pace. It will come. But here again, when your assignment is for a cause campaign, pay very close attention to the psychological considerations relating to your target (which should be listed in the target and competitive climate sections of the strategy).

For example, if your target is compulsive gamblers, consider that they are probably denying that addiction. In their minds, they are just having a little streak of bad luck and whatever they did to get the money for the next bet is just a temporary "loan" until they're even again. Sympathetically, you might lead them through the list of danger signs, and reassure them that what they have is a treatable condition, not a moral weakness. By no means put them down or treat them humorously.

SIGNING OFF

As you get close to an execution that is starting to sing, examine the strategy's executional requirements section. If it is for more than a single unit, ask yourself if you have just created a one-shot commercial that only works on TV, or whether you are truly designing a campaign. Does your end line just summarize the situation in that one spot, or could it be expanded and slightly generalized to be a true campaign theme? The best way to determine that is to use it in some quick layouts for a different medium.

I used to ask my creative teams, not entirely frivolously, "Is that a line you'd like to see in skywriting?"

Keeping Theme Lines Positive

When you're crafting a cause theme line, consider the impact of those words on people neutral to, or opposed to, your cause. Try to be positive. If you're pro something, be sure it is stated in a way most people would agree with. Or if you're against or out to stop something, make sure the thing you're "anti" is something that sounds hateful to most folks. Notice that the advocates of gun control never say they are for *gun control*. A lot of NRA types would start tearing down their posters. Advertising run by gun-control advocates says "Stop Handgun Violence!" Who could be against that? It *is* a negative, but it's opposing something everyone but a fanatic would oppose.

"Friends don't let friends drive drunk!" How much more positive that sounds than "Take away the keys!" Remember, we're talking about signing off here—the theme line. A headline could very well contain a shocking negative, but *end* on a hopeful note.

Both sides of our society's most divisive issue, abortion, adopt very positive labels. One group is not "against abortion," it's "pro life." And the other group is not "pro abortion" (something loudly linked with murder by its opponents), it's "pro choice."

Even the cause organization's name should resonate positively. It could have been the "Anti-Litter Council." Instead, it's "Keep America Beautiful." It could have been the "Anti-Drug Coalition." Instead, it's the "Partnership for a Drug-Free America."

In Massachusetts, the "Department of Public Health" (positive) signs all the anti-smoking spots, instead of the actual client, "Massachusetts Tobacco Control Program" (negative).

THE LOGO: HARD-WORKING ART THAT'S HARD WORK TO COME BY

If, in fact, it is decided that your entire campaign should have a theme line, then you may want to give serious consideration to commissioning a campaign logo. The advantages are many. Corporate logos such as the Nike "swoosh" or campaign logos like the "I Love New York" heart symbol, have, through synergistic placement on T-shirts, caps, buttons, uniforms, and of course, in all their ads, expanded the scope of the parent campaigns enormously.

Properly designed and placed, a good logo can have the effect of almost doubling your budget. Imagine the impact of seeing half the kids at a high school event sporting hats or T-shirts with your logo. And if it is wedded to a memorable TV execution (possibly computer-animated to grow out of the closing shots of the spot), then every kid on the street can remind you of the spot. That's a little like getting hundreds of mini-spots for free. The value of that extra exposure is inestimable!

There are a couple of cautions, however. Designing a logo is a very specialized business. In some cases, the cause group has already contracted to have a logo designed. But more and more, agencies are getting involved, particularly if the logo relates to a specific campaign. You may not actually create the thing, but you should direct the effort so it will be compatible and consistent with the advertising you are doing for the cause. By all means invite the art directors on your campaign to take a crack at it. But don't be surprised if they don't ring everyone's chimes with the results.

Better by far to convince your cause client to commission a firm that specializes in corporate identity programs. But be prepared—these services don't come cheap. And the process takes an amazing amount of time and energy. The more committees you present it to, the more different opinions you'll get. It's not like judging the impact of a commercial or a poster. The logo, in a simple graphic, must represent the entire effort. If you have a campaign theme line, the logo must be compatible with it. It should project everything the cause stands for, and do it directly as well as in subliminal ways. Research will help here, but don't expect definitive analysis. Focus groups may help you choose between several finalists, but they probably will not articulate very well the reasons for their choice.

Once you're close to selecting a logo, be sure to submit it to careful legal scrutiny. That ribbon graphic on every can of Coke seems simple, but be assured, its design was costly. And if your client's logo resembles it too closely, you can expect a call from some lawyers in Atlanta!

Once the logo is cleared and approved, you really have to *make it work*. You must carefully monitor its use, and make sure it is attached to everything you do. This is harder than it sounds. A new creative team on your campaign, fighting for every one of those valuable thirty seconds of screen time, will probably chafe at having to surrender precious seconds to something it didn't create and that may not exactly grow gracefully out of the story they are telling.

But if the logo is to work, it must be rigidly policed. The "Logo Czar," whether it is you or someone on your client's marketing committee, will be an unpopular but necessary guardian of a very valuable commodity.

It can take a couple of years before a logo embeds itself into the culture of a campaign. And every new hand through which it passes is likely to have a "not invented here" attitude that will manifest itself by trying to ignore it into logo oblivion.

But if your logo is good, if it connects with your target, then the value of its virtually free expansion of your reach is inestimable. You may make some enemies while guarding it rigidly, but you will certainly increase the value of your media effort many fold.

Just be sure that everyone loves it, because it's a very hard thing to erase once it's in place. A new head of NASA decided he hated the contemporary NASA all-type logo, which by that time was in place on everything from caps and T-shirts to interplanetary rockets. "Looks like a bunch of worms," he said, referring to the gently undulating letters, and for years NASA staffers moved ahead of his inspection visits, painting the offending logo out or shredding logo-imprinted stationery and brochures.

Nothing symbolizes the spirit of the organization more succinctly than its logo, but be very sure the top decision-makers love it because it's a very difficult task to obliterate it. And a change, after the public has gotten used to your logo, will be puzzling. People may ask if this is some new or competing organization.

The ancillary benefits of owning a good logo are incalculable. But the costs of changing it down the road are huge as well. Bottom line, in the words of the legendary American frontiersman Davy Crockett: "Be sure you're right, then go ahead."

CREATING AN ICON

Finding an ownable, memorable, and empathetic icon to represent your cause campaign is one of the hardest but most desirable things you can achieve. In recent cause marketing history, there have probably been four important ones: Smokey Bear, McGruff the Crime Dog, the Crash Test Dummies, and the Crying Indian.

Of the four, three are fantasy characters that can leap off the poster and TV screen and appear at your health fair or in your parade at any time. Because local actors can inhabit those furry suits, your icon can live forever.

Certainly, advertising icons have served many commercial products well. Most seem to have their origins in children's lore. Although they serve adult products, the Pillsbury Doughboy, Mr. Clean, Punchy the Hawaiian Punch brat, and Speedy Alka Seltzer are all basically children's fantasy figures. One of the best product icons is the child's toy, the Energizer Bunny, created by Chiat/Day. In fact, I doubt if the original spot was created to establish an icon; it was probably thought of as just a cute demo. But to extend this single spot and create an icon was true genius because the icon *is* a product demo, animating the single clear product benefit of longer life. And every time he is seen, whether in a point-of-purchase display or in some increasingly ludicrous but amusing TV commercial, the mind immediately reruns the product-specific theme line, "It keeps going and going and going. . . ."

FIGURE 4.1 *The Advertising Council.* "Smokey Bear." *Courtesy of the Advertising Council.*

And I believe the great public service icons all fall into the "children's character" category. McGruff, Smokey, the Crash Test Dummies, and the Crying Indian all support campaigns for which children can be the prime movers. Children can be among the most effective advocates for the desired consumer action, such as promoting outdoor fire safety, seat belt use, litter cleanup, etc.

Whether or not the two best-known tobacco icons, the Marlboro Man or Joe Camel are directed to children has been the subject of endless debate. In my opinion, they were probably not originally designed

FIGURE 4.2 *The Advertising Council.* "Crash Test Dummies." *Courtesy of the Advertising Council.*

FIGURE 4.3 *The Advertising Council.* "McGruff the Crime Dog." *Courtesy of the Advertising Council.*

to do that. But some subsequent research must have revealed to the corporations their strong resonance with kids.

An awareness of the effectiveness of these icons led us into an interesting "anti-icon" effort for the Massachusetts Department of Public Health campaign aimed at kids. We had a silly-looking live "talking" camel walk up to a microphone and say: "Cartoon images of me have been used to sell cigarettes. This is an outrage against me, my family . . . you'll never find a cigarette in my mouth. . . . They're bad."

In another (adult) spot, a look-alike of the Marlboro Man was filmed astride a horse in beautiful Lone Pine, California (the original Marlboro Country location), lighting up a cigarette. He then dropped

---

Camel

VO: Hello. Cartoon images of me have been used to sell cigarettes.

This is an outrage against me, my family, and my lovely wife Phyllis.

You'll never find a cigarette in my mouth...

a tasty desert rat, maybe, but never a cigarette. They're bad.

(*VO fades as camel walks off screen*)
A camel smoking, that's preposterous, outrageous.

I can't even light a match. I can't even get into a store to buy them . . .

FIGURE 4.4 *The Massachusetts Tobacco Control Program.* "Camel," a spot aimed at kids, denormalized an icon, Joe Camel, through satire. *Courtesy of the Massachusetts Department of Public Health.*

the lighted cigarette into his lap and nearly fell off his horse, screaming his head off as the steed galloped off into the sunset.

We felt these spots made good on the strategic objective to get people to laugh at these corporate icons rather than deify them. Research indicated we had succeeded, and we were able to buy placement in cinema theaters, where we knew we could reach our target with these "anti-icons."

An icon should be simple, it should be memorable, and the best should instantly recall the central idea of the campaign. The Crying Indian, Smokey, and the Crash Test Dummies do that. How many kids about to drop a candy wrapper see that Crying Indian in their minds and hesitate before littering? How many imagine they see Smokey staring at them from the edge of the clearing as they take extra care smothering a campfire? Do they hear Vince and Larry, the Crash Test Dummies, urging them to buckle up when they enter the family car?

Of all of them, the one that is a bit different is McGruff. He does have the ability to put a friendlier face on crime prevention. But "Take a bite out of crime" is pretty nonspecific. That may be the result of a much broader strategy objective.

But because of his recognition as a character and his ability to connect with kids and parents at school and community events, McGruff has become a durable icon. Subsequent commercials have cast him as a

---

Western

VO: There's a moment in every smoker's life when it becomes clear it's finally time to quit.

COWBOY: (*Drops lighted cigarette in lap*) Oww . . . owww!

COWBOY: I gotta quit!
SUPER: Massachusetts Department of Public Health

FIGURE 4.5 *The Massachusetts Tobacco Control Program.* "Western" denormalized the iconic Marlboro Man through satire. This commercial also ran in movie theaters. *Courtesy of the Massachusetts Department of Public Health.*

friendly and accepted "spokesdog" for recruiting teens in anti-crime activities, and neighbors into citizen-watch groups. And his nephew "Scruff" teaches kids how to protect themselves against violence in animated PSAs.

THE MOST FAMOUS ICON: THE CRYING INDIAN

As I mentioned in the introduction, I did not create the Crying Indian. This significant icon came from the fertile imagination of a team supervised by Milt Sutton, my predecessor as Marsteller Advertising creative director. The team included a writer named Hugh McGraw, who had left the agency by the time I came aboard, and an outstanding art director named Joe Goldberg, who was head art director at the Marsteller agency and with whom I had the privilege to work for two years.

Joe, who told me he fought hard during the creative process to keep the television ad simple and visual (a goal that led to the famous tear), actually took the classic poster photograph of Iron Eyes Cody that adorns the cover of this book. However, although I was not there at the birth of the campaign, I did write the second spot in the series, and as such had something to do with its revitalization and ultimate penetration into the national consciousness.

There's an old principal in advertising that's akin to the dreaded NIH (Not Invented Here). I call it NITY (Not Invented This Year). Long before the bulk of consumers are aware of your campaign, you probably will decide that it's tired. Undoubtedly you are factoring in all the meetings, creative agonies, shooting, editing, approval, revisions, and final airing. You were living with it for six months to a year before consumers even got their first look. That's where NITY comes in.

Consumers are only barely aware of it, but you're bored with it. Add to this the revolving personnel door at most advertising agencies, and you will probably have new people arriving on the account each year. They bring a bit of NIH to the NITY.

IN THE FIGHT AGAINST LITTER AND POLLUTION, WE STILL HAVE SO FAR TO GO

People start pollution. People can stop it.

FIGURE 4.6 *Keep America Beautiful.* A poster of Iron Eyes Cody from the "Crying Indian" campaign. *Courtesy of Keep America Beautiful.*

Anyone who is tempted to succumb to this kind of thinking should examine the campaigns of Procter and Gamble, arguably one of the most successful marketers in the world. When P&G created a Mrs. Olson or a Mr. Whipple or a Mr. Clean, it signed them up for the long run. Long after people in the advertising business were making "gagging" gestures every time one of them was mentioned, the marketing people at P&G were gently but firmly insisting on producing yet another adventure for these icons who had become comfortable friends to millions of consumers.

At Marsteller, the Crying Indian paddled down the river in a canoe, saw the pollution of the water as he landed, and wept that famous tear. Then he was given early retirement the next year, and a fairly forgettable commercial of kids cleaning up a vacant lot was produced and flew out under the radar.

I came to Marsteller as director of creative services the year after that and was presented the task of overseeing development of a new campaign for the Ad Council on behalf of the nonprofit organization, Keep America Beautiful. When I asked what had happened to the Crying Indian, I was told that was the "two years ago" campaign. I remember replying, "That's a little bit like shooting Smokey Bear!" Needless to say, we brought back the Indian, and the rest as they say, is a bit of advertising history.

Roger Powers, the dynamic director of Keep America Beautiful, strongly endorsed the return and was very supportive in every aspect of its revival. It was clear that he was keenly aware of the value of his icon, but had bowed to the wishes of his agency in approving the different campaign of the previous year.

Joe Goldberg and I were up in Toronto shooting a yogurt commercial, and he started sketching a storyboard showing the Indian on a horse. I began working on some words that delved a little more into the reverence Native Americans have for the land and nature. The execution came very quickly, but participating in its production was one of the great experiences in my career, most of which was due to the time I spent with the delightful Iron Eyes Cody.

When the "Crying Indian" concept was first approved, the casting call went out for a Native American actor, and Iron Eyes was near the top of any Hollywood casting director's "Indian" file. First of all, Iron Eyes was a "movie Indian." He had appeared in a number of Western films and was proudest of *A Man Called Horse*. And he would occasionally tell stories about hanging out on the Via Veneto with the cast of some spaghetti western he went over to work on. It was this side of the man that perhaps led to the scurrilous rumor that briefly circulated in the New Orleans press that Iron Eyes was actually an Italian actor masquerading as a Cherokee. It was a story roundly denied by Iron Eyes and the people around him. He was an actor second, a proud Cherokee first.

Because of this, there was a very serious side to Iron Eyes. He was very committed to Native American affairs and respectful of his heritage, which I have not the slightest doubt was authentic. He spoke very movingly between takes about his son, who had become something of a firebrand in his activism on behalf of Native American affairs, and about whom he was worried. He didn't want him to become like Russell Means, the oft-arrested Native American activist.

Iron Eyes was no less passionate than his son about his native heritage and the wrongs that needed righting. But he felt persuasion in the media was a much better route to those ends. When I asked him if he felt it was demeaning to the strong image of Native

Americans to show him crying, he said, "Oh, no. Indians cry—if they feel deeply about something."

A Chant to the Great Spirit

One day we were shooting in a glorious stand of tall pines, near a reservoir high in the Hollywood Hills. As the camera crew was rehearsing their moves, I heard a thrilling and mysterious sound echoing from the edge of the lake. It was Iron Eyes, standing at the edge of the water, chanting.

He was staring at the large rocks and tall trees reflected in the still waters in an almost trancelike state, and the strange words coming out of his mouth had no meaning to me. I waited respectfully until he had finished, and then asked him what that was.

"The Great Spirit Prayer," he replied. The prayer was part of his heritage. The words were in the Cherokee language, and I asked him to translate:

> *"Oh Great Spirit, whose voice in the wind I hear*
> *And whose breath gave life to all the world, hear me!*
> *Make me walk in beauty*
> *Make my heart respect all you have made*
> *Make me wise that I may know all you have taught my people*
> *The lessons you have hidden in every rock. . . . "*

I had been deeply worried about how to translate this famous icon into a radio campaign. We had committed to the Advertising Council to produce a full radio schedule in addition to the posters and television. The tear was exclusively visual. But the persona of Iron Eyes was not. I smiled a broad smile. "Iron Eyes . . . you've just given me the radio campaign. We'll score the television with a phrase underlining the moment of the tear, and then adapt that to a radio track. Will you speak it in Cherokee?" My thought was to have it simultaneously translated in an overlap over the music.

It was the first time that very reasonable and soft-spoken man said no.

"I chanted it once on the Carson show in Cherokee, and the audience laughed. It was so inappropriate and disrespectful. I don't want to risk that reaction again." And he was very firm about it, even though I felt that the original language would have been very moving. But of course, I respected his wishes, and the final track was just fine.

I called an old friend, Fred Karlin, who had done a number of commercial tracks for me in New York some years before. Fred had just pulled off the extraordinary feat of winning both an Academy Award (for the song "For All We Know" from *Lovers and Other Strangers*) and an Emmy (for the score to "The Autobiography of Miss Jane Pittman"). He wasn't doing television commercial work anymore, but when I mentioned Iron Eyes Cody and a spot in the "Crying Indian" series, he immediately cleared his calendar.

This is one of the great aspects of working in cause marketing. If the cause is important, hardly anyone will turn you down. For example, actor William Conrad had done the track on the first "Crying Indian" canoe spot. However, Conrad had just made the transition from his enormously successful show "Cannon" to a series called "Jake and the Fat Man" and was shooting around the clock to get ahead on a rigorous production schedule. His agent said he loved the cause, but simply couldn't get away to come to a studio. After several other entreaties, I finally persuaded him to record our copy on a tape deck while sitting in his trailer on the set late in the evening after shooting. His acting instincts were so good, there was no need for me to be present to direct the session. The one glitch was that the word count of the forty-five- and thirty-second versions was too long for Conrad's style of delivery, and his frustration with the shorter lengths was evident on the tape between takes. It's hard to predict the pacing of an actor when you're writing, and this was a little long for his impactful style. Had I been present, I would have made the cuts we ultimately used in constructing the final tracks.

Fred went into the studio with some wonderful film musicians, and Iron Eyes drove in from the valley for the session. He continued to stay interested and involved. It was obvious how impressed even these cynical studio players were to meet him. They'd worked with many stars, but Iron Eyes represented something different. He then recorded the prayer, and Fred did the most evocative things with the track. He layered some dissonanced tracking of voices, which he recorded using his own voice, and then conducted a most evocative downward passage on a solo cello to underscore the tear on film. It translated beautifully into radio as did the sonorous voice of Iron Eyes, and the very appropriate "Great Spirit Prayer."

Following that second spot, Iron Eyes started appearing in events such as the Rose Bowl Parade and traveling on behalf of Keep America Beautiful to civic events and "Green" conferences. As I recounted in the Introduction, a print of the poster hangs in the reception area at the Advertising Council, and both commercials were listed among the fifty greatest commercials of all time by *Entertainment Weekly.* The campaign was also voted one of the two best commercials of the century in an America On-Line millennium poll.

As I write this, I am looking at an obituary for Iron Eyes Cody, who died in 1999. It ran in the *New York Times, USA Today, Time,* and a number of other periodicals. He was given as much space as some heads of state. And I don't think the image has died with him. A revival of the campaign was produced by North Castle Partners for Earth Day 1998. It featured our original poster of Iron Eyes mounted on a bus shelter, with a special-effects animation of the tear falling as some kids thoughtlessly strew litter.

The bottom line is that the insertion into the national consciousness of the Crying Indian is so strong that he will live as an icon as long as anyone wants to put him up on the wall or rerun the spot.

Think long and hard about whether your cause could embrace an icon. Just like a memorable logo and theme line, it can extend the reach of your effort by rerunning your spot in the mind of everyone who sees it. Just like your logo, icons require a lot of care and feeding, a real commitment by everyone involved in the campaign to keep them a viable part of the effort. And this may mean mounting a strong defense against the forces of NIH and NITY.

But if you hit it just right, you may get the chance to tell your grandkids that you were there at the origin of a true bit of American folklore. I know I will!

THE CREATIVE PROCESS

There are so many roads to arriving at good creative work that I can't even try to describe them all. If you are a member of a creative team, you will have to establish those steps that work for you. As a copywriter I will simply suggest a few of mine.

At some point, after all the research and fact-finding and agony, an idea or execution is roughed out and the writing and sketching must begin. Although there are many different styles, mine happens to be that of a *re*writer.

Even if I am experiencing total writer's block, and that often happens, I will always write *something*. I usually hide it or file it on my hard drive under a coded label, so no one can see its inevitable ineptness. I then leave it alone for at least twelve hours. When I open it up and look at it again, I may hate 90 percent of it. But more often than not, there's a germ of an idea in the last 10 percent, usually the product of my subconscious. I often can't even remember writing *that*. But the instincts honed over a lot of years conspired to push it out of my subconscious. On one hand, I often can't believe how *bad* every other word on the page is. On the other, I can invariably find a small gem nestling there in the muck, and that will become the basis for the final execution.

Other writers I have known and respected do just the opposite. They let an idea germinate for days while pacing, jogging, taking in a movie, staring at the wall. Then they will put it down intact, and rarely change much from that point on. An excellent writer at an agency where I once worked became annoyed at the number of times his boss would walk by his open door, scowling as he noted that the guy was just sitting and staring out the window. He made up a small sign and tacked it to his doorframe. It said: "Even when I am not writing, I am writing!"

I had a delightful time reading through British Design & Art Direction's *Copy Book* in which thirty-two of the best American, British, Australian, and Asian copywriters told some of their secrets to approaching that blank piece of paper. Here are a few examples:

- Jim Durfee: "'Kill all your darlings.' If a single commandment could be burned into the mind of each beginning copywriter, it should be this one. Mark Twain wrote these words and lived by them. By shunning that darling of darlings—the pun headline— I'm left with no-nonsense straight talk."

- Adrian Holmes: "Any copywriter has to strike a deal with the reader. And as far as the reader is concerned, the deal is this: *I'll keep reading for as long as you keep me interested.*"
- Alfredo Marcantonio: "I write copy the way my grandmother made minestrone soup. I throw in every interesting ingredient I can find and slowly reduce them down."
- Luke Sullivan: "Your headline is introduction enough. In body copy, get right to it. Don't do a 'snappy last line' in the body copy. That's a tired old formula. End with the client's address and phone number."
- Paul Silverman: "Puns, these days, are risky business. But brilliant puns work. Anything brilliant can break any rule."
- Ed McCabe: "NEVER go ready, fire, aim. If you do, you'll always shoot yourself in the foot."

There's no hard-and-fast rule for arriving at brilliant copy. But however you get there, at the point when you think you've almost arrived, start pushing it through a number of evaluation grids.

Check It Out

First, there's the all-important strategic grid. Check off the following points:

- *Objective:* Does it fully accomplish the overall advertising objective?
- *Target:* Is it precisely written to your target audience? Does it speak their language? Does it push their unique buttons? Is it sensitive to the psychology of the person whose behavior you wish to change?
- *Principal Idea:* Does it have a clear, simple benefit?
- *Support:* Are the support points logical, and can they all be found in the strategy? Are there too many?
- *Desired Action:* Is the desired action clearly delineated?
- *Tone and Style:* Is everything about the language and imagery consistent with the tone and style statement?

Of course, copy that meets *all* the strategic guidelines may still fail to be a startling, persuasive execution. Here, then, are some executional evaluation criteria that may help:

- *Is it credible?* If it's broadcast, read it aloud. If it's to be underscored, pull out a CD and read it over the music. If it's dialogue, get some cohorts together and read it with them. If possible, record it and listen to it over and over. Do you *believe* the dialogue? Make sure it sounds real.

- *Is it rushed or cluttered?* Remember that in a thirty-second commercial there is only a limited amount of dialogue. My rule of thumb is not to exceed seventy-five to eighty words. Keep it simple!
- *Does it grab them right away?* Is it unique enough to cut through the clutter? Even if it is, but doesn't get their attention in the first seven seconds, it may still fall victim to the remote control.
- *Does it set up the problem or conflict early?* "Problem-Solution" is an old, but tried-and-true device, and it's particularly applicable to cause advertising. Set up the problem as dramatically as possible, and directly connect the solution to your cause organization.
- *Does your print pop?* If it's a print ad, do a fairly tight layout to size, and paste it in a magazine or newspaper. Turn the page and come upon it as if by accident. Does it "pop"? Does it grab you? Does it jump out at you? Does it demand to be read?

How much easier to make a piece of work bulletproof at this stage than to have to bring it back after the presentation and fix it later. It will also make it much easier to present and defend if you have checked it against every point in the strategy. It's also a good defense against a sudden idea by your client administrators. If it's not on the strategy, it can't be considered.

THE PRESENTATION

Of course, the best copy in the world will die on the page if it's not successfully presented to the client. And this is a crucial next step. With commercial clients, you are probably presenting to experienced ad managers or marketing directors. They will know what you're up to and where you're heading. With a cause organization, it is unlikely that there will be an experienced marketing pro in place. In fact, you may be presenting to a committee of public health officials, social workers, community activists, and so on. They may not be used to judging advertising in storyboard or layout form, and may need special care and handling. This is not meant as a put-down of some very smart, committed, sincere individuals. They have simply not lived through the steps of advertising preparation. They have hired you as their expert to bring it off, but now they are in the position of having to judge your work while it's still in an unformed state.

For several years, I taught presentation skills in the American Association of Advertising Agencies' post-graduate course for working advertising personnel in New York. What I told them was that when it comes to that crucial copy presentation, every successful team must find its own special techniques. All are valid if they sell copy. But the presentation step is crucial. If you fail to cross this hurdle, the campaign dies right there. I will list a few things I have learned and taught over the years.

First, rehearse the presentation extensively. Place all your materials and props carefully so they come easily to hand. Sometimes the most relaxed presentations are the most rehearsed. Nervousness and lack of preparation should have no impact on a good piece of copy, but they do, particularly with an unsophisticated client, as your cause client is likely to be. But don't let yourself slide into slickness either; that can be equally off-putting.

If you are a good natural actor, then you should by all means act out a broadcast spot at the meeting. If you do, take some time to set the stage. Be a storyteller. If you are not a performer, then you are much better off finding a bit of tape of a similar commercial, or more likely, a similar scene from a movie or a TV show. Let's take a page right out of the infamous Hollywood pitch:

> *Imagine* National Lampoon's Christmas Vacation, *only it's a bunch of teenagers instead of a family. The kid playing the Chevy Chase part is trying to be very cool, to impress the girls. He pulls out a pack of cigarettes while he's standing on a snowboard on top of a mountain. As he tries to put a cigarette in his mouth, the snowboard starts to slide. He does a total wipeout right in front of the girls.*

You see what I mean.

The "Rip-o-Matic"

Using actual scraps ripped from magazines, or clips from rented movie cassettes, can help this process a lot, especially with a client group that may be unfamiliar with the storyboard vernacular. At an agency where

I once worked, this technique became known as "Rip-o-Matics." The wipeout scene in *Christmas Vacation* is a classic and will get a big laugh in the meeting. This can help the sale enormously if you're a less-than-inspired presenter.

But there's also a caution here. A scene played by Chevy Chase in a $40 million feature may be hysterical, and if you present it as "something like this" you may have everyone in the approval process nodding along. But with your limited budget and talent pool, you'd better be sure you can deliver something near that level of quality, or there may be disappointment from that moment on. Similarly, a piece of print photography by, say, Richard Avedon or Francesco Scavullo may convey the mood perfectly. But if you don't have the budget to hire someone of that quality (and you probably won't), you may hurt your cause more than help it, because however carefully you produce the final ad, it will be a letdown.

At the very least, if you use some "rip-off" art or video, be sure you downplay the specifics and say something like "this is just to give you a general idea, or this is just for the mood of the scene."

Sometimes, it's better to use a piece of stock art, footage, or music in the pitch that you know you can deliver for the final execution. More and more these days excellent stock houses are delivering world-class music and affordable visuals. This may be a much better route for a limited-budget cause client than commissioning original work. When the Massachusetts Department of Public Health filmed that brutal parody of the Marlboro Man riding off into the sunset (and dropping the lit cigarette on his crotch), we lusted for the *Magnificent Seven* music we remembered from the original TV spots. Of course, we couldn't buy it. Then, to our surprise, the producer found an affordable piece of stock music from a British supplier that delivered a very similar dynamic.

There are, of course, two pitfalls with purchasing stock visuals and tracks. First, you can't own it exclusively. Our Marlboro Man parody commercial track showed up the same year behind a steakburger promotion for a local restaurant chain.

Second, you should check the provenance of any stock film footage very carefully. Many years ago, I produced a spot for Bufferin analgesic tablets depicting the end of a headache. We found some stock footage of happy imagery to intercut with footage of a relieved and happy actress striding down the street. We had a champagne cork popping, the audience cheering at a beauty pageant, and some grainy footage from the U.S.S.R. of a group of ballerinas lyrically executing elegant turns.

An angry client called within a week of the first network airing. A lawyer had filed a nuisance suit on behalf of Melissa Hayden, then a prima ballerina in George Ballanchine's New York City Ballet Company. I was told to please "deal with it."

At first, I was sure it had to be a misunderstanding because we had bought the rights to the footage from a stock service that assured me it was a performance at the Bolshoi Theater in Moscow. Since the U.S.S.R. had no copyright agreement with the United States at that time, the film should have been free and clear. But then I had a nervous hunch and insisted on going into the company's file to see the actual index card describing the scene. It *was* shot at the Bolshoi Theatre in Moscow. Then I spotted some small type at the bottom of the card: "Tour of New York City Ballet, 1975." My heart sank. The stock house covered its rear by pointing out that it only owned the rights to the film footage, not any of the talent on it.

We settled on behalf of the client for many thousands of dollars. The agency attorney told me later that Madame Hayden had a wonderful lawyer, a very theatrical gentleman who reached back to Shakespeare's *Tempest* when he insisted that with our crass analgesic commercial we had "turned this glorious Miranda into a Caliban!"

So by all means use stock, but buyer beware!

Painting a Picture

If you do have good presentation skills, then use *them* to paint an imaginary picture. Some of the most sophisticated art directors I ever worked with do storyboards that are just one step up from children's stick figures. That way, the final product will always be that much more magical. But with a less sophisticated client, this may be riskier than full renderings or stock photos.

There follow some other presentation techniques that may be particularly important when presenting to the less sophisticated cause client:

- *Read the strategy aloud first.* That way, the translation of the strategy into advertising will be obvious and will enhance the appreciation of the appropriateness of the work. Or, perchance, if it's off strategy, everyone will realize it right at the outset.

- *Present in ascending order of preference.* End with the one you really want to sell, and *never* present anything you wouldn't be happy to produce. Sometimes a client will gravitate to a particular execution for unexpected reasons and may be unwilling to be sold off it. Therefore, there should be no "straw men" in your presentation because you may wind up living with them.

- *Show the "safe" executions first.* A risky execution may represent a more distinctive and "mind-sticking" approach to the problem. But always make sure the client realizes the risk and shares the responsibility of taking it with you. Show a "safe" execution first, so the comfort level will be high from the outset. Then say something like "Now, if you really want to try something that will cut through the clutter. . . ." Presented in any other order, the risky one might well scare the client, who could spend the rest of the meeting wondering if the agency they selected has lost their minds!

- *Hold the comments, please!* Always politely ask the client to delay commenting until after *all* the advertising is presented. If clients truly hate any of the early executions, they are saved the unpleasant task of dumping on them and upsetting a creative team that may actually strike gold with an execution later in the meeting. Holding comments lets clients focus on the "brilliant" ones—and spares some ego bruising.

- *First the pictures, then the words.* When presenting copy from a storyboard, always take an unsophisticated client through the visuals first. Point to the first frame: "We see a young man nervously ringing the doorbell outside a nice suburban home. It is twilight. He is just putting out a cigarette, and is coughing." Frame 2: "A young woman, obviously his girlfriend, opens the door and greets him warmly." Frame 3: "We see him being introduced to the rest of the family. He is still coughing."

    And so on. Notice, you have not yet read any of the dialogue or any voice-over announcer copy. You clearly explain all the visuals, so they can be held in the imagination of the client group as you read the copy. If there's a surprise ending (as there was in the above-referenced board) you cover that frame and announce that there's going to be an unexpected twist at the end.

- *Describe everything.* Indicate facial expressions, reactions, camera angles, sound effects. Leave nothing to chance. After you have fully explained all the visuals and asked if there are any questions, you point to the frames and immediately read the copy in "real time." The pacing, timing, and impact of the spot is then approximated. Even the surprise ending comes with appropriate impact, and the client's reaction to the spot should approximate that of the home viewer. Then, almost immediately, it should be read to them, again in "real time."

  Many times I have seen excellent concepts go down in flames as a nervous writer gets all caught up in trying to insert descriptions of the action and technical effects between words of dialogue. ("'Hello,' she says, smiling. He is coughing a lot. 'I want you to meet my family.' We cut to interior of the house—it's a nice suburban home, you know, with flowers in vases and a little dog. The father, mother, grandfather, and little brother are all there. 'Mom, Dad, I'd like you to meet . . .' He's still coughing, the mother looks concerned. Tommy. . . .") And so on. The rhythm is shot. Too much time is taken to explain details that will be instantly understood in the final film. If these are all laid out and explained during the setup, they will be held in the memory and grasped in real time.

- *Hide the script.* Don't *ever* pass out a script or a board before you present a commercial. Remember when teacher passed out a test and told everybody in the class to put it facedown on the desk until told to start? How many kids peeked? Well, you'd be amazed at how many important corporate executives will peek at your copy even if you ask them not to. And I guarantee your cause clients will. Even if you tell them firmly to follow along, they *will* start reading ahead. It's all too interesting and exciting. And your presentation will very likely be a disaster.

- *Make the surprise surprising.* The other danger of too much disclosure is that surprise ending. You're going to hire a great director and wonderful actors to blow away the home viewer. But if half the room at your presentation has read ahead of you, the big punch will fizzle. You're going to be competing with your own words on paper. And why should you? It's your show. Cover it up, and reveal the surprise as you read the spot.

The Thrill of the Show

There's something else to keep in mind when presenting advertising executions to a committee from a public agency or nonprofit organization, the usual clients for a cause marketing effort. Most of their lives are spent with dry reports. You are bringing a bit of show business to them. They may be a pushover for some smoke and mirrors in the meeting. This is both a blessing and a curse.

Rational judgment by committee members may be compromised by that sizzle. They may be wowed by the wrong spot. Even worse, they may want to join in the fun you are apparently having and become players.

I'm told Joe Cronin, the legendary Red Sox manager, used to occasionally put himself into a game as a pinch hitter, but stopped when he no longer could hit home runs. One of the worst aspects of the built-in bureaucracy of government-agency clients is the tendency to *have* to get their hands on the work. Perhaps it comes from decades of collaborating on agency documents. Or years of applying group thinking to projects. I don't mean to be too harsh. For certain functions of any organization that may be exactly what's required. But it can be devastating to the creative process when it comes to constructing the specifics of advertising.

As David Ogilvy said: "Don't keep a dog and bark yourself. Any fool can write a bad advertisement, but it takes a genius to keep his hands off a good one."

Interference may be hard to avoid with cause clients, but be aware of the tendency, and as you build confidence with their representatives, try to gently head it off.

I once consulted on a brochure that had to be approved by a division of a large public agency. We had hired a good freelance writer to craft the words, and the first draft was sent over to the public agency for approval. When it came back, there were nearly seventy-five "corrections" written in the margins in various handwritings, with things crossed out and inserted, words and phrases changed and altered. And more often than not, the changes were not made to correct substance or facts; they were *stylistic* changes!

Over my objections, these changes were all inserted in the text and the draft was retyped and submitted to the head of the sponsoring agency. The reaction: "We paid a professional to write this mess?" And a mess it was.

I was told later that one mid-level manager had literally gone from cubicle to cubicle throughout the agency pointing to sentences and asking, "What do you think of this? What do you think of that?" The manager then wrote in almost every suggestion as a change.

My only solution was to urge that we sit together in a room with the writer and a *small* client committee to discuss the comments, letting the writer accept or make a case for rejecting them, or suggest revisions that were more consistent with his overall style. Slowly, the camel was turned back into a thoroughbred, and we finally got our brochure out. Late, but at least cogent.

Robert Townsend, former CEO of Avis and author of a wonderfully iconoclastic book about business called *Up the Organization,* told me once about the time he approved Bill Bernbach's recommended campaign for the rent-a-car company. "We're number two so we try harder" went the famous line, written by Paula Green.

Research had showed the approach to be risky. After all, didn't Americans like to go with winners? "We're Number One" foam fingers are wagged at football games every weekend. But Bernbach convinced Townsend that the very humanity of the theme line would cause his company to stand out, and the CEO bought it.

Bernbach bought him a nice lunch to thank him for being a uniquely helpful and sophisticated client. Feeling very good about himself, Townsend told me that along about dessert he asked Bernbach if there was anything else he could do to make the client-agency relationship any easier. Actually, Bernbach told him, there *was* something that needed fixing. Avis had a vice president for marketing who was charged with approving ads. Since the rent-a-car business was a fast-paced retail account, there were many ads a week that needed approval to meet the fast-changing market, and the marketing VP was often unavailable until the last minute, jeopardizing insertion dates.

"Okay," said Townsend. "I have twelve vice presidents. From this moment on, they're all authorized to approve ads!"

"There's one more thing," said Bernbach, according to Townsend. "If I have the art department make up a sign, will you see to it that it's hung in every vice president's office?"

"Sure," replied Townsend. "What will it say?"

"Approve or Disapprove. Don't Improve!"

Amen!

5

TELEVISION PRODUCTION

Rolling!

I started in advertising as a broadcast producer. I had recently moved to New York City from Boston where I had been a producer-director for WBZ-TV and had briefly produced shows for a summer theater. I knew about actors and I knew about television. In those days, most agencies knew very little about TV, so my somewhat specialized knowledge became a valuable resume asset.

Even several years later, after a savvy head of production at Grey Manning Rubin decided I really should be writing and moved me to the position of copy supervisor, I still felt most at home in a television or radio studio. Even though I have been on the set of more than one thousand commercials, I still get a kick out of it. I feel like that kid from a small town in Massachusetts who has sneaked onto a Hollywood set!

Walking onto a darkened soundstage can be both exciting and intimidating. And the dizzying cost of some aspects of it can be perplexing. One of those same clients who asked me how much a TV spot costs, declared, when I told him what he should expect to spend on his commercial, "That's crazy. That's over $8,000 a second. And six of those seconds are just a shot of my product!"

Everybody wants their advertising to run on TV. This will certainly be true of your cause clients. It is the most visible, glamorous forum for their message and can often be the most impactful way to dramatize a cause. It can also be perceived as a measure of the importance of the organization that it is a highly visible presence on television. This can have a positive secondary effect on such things as fund-raising and the ability to attract the attention and support of community leaders.

Also, as we will see in the chapter on media, television is the most effective way to reach the *most* people. However, it can be very expensive. A less-costly-to-produce medium, like radio, may not reach the highest numbers but may be the most efficient way to reach the *right* people.

Let's assume that all of the above have been considered early on in the planning stage. You have agreed for the right reasons that television should be part of your media mix, and have written a spot or a pool of commercials that has been enthusiastically approved. Let's take a moment to review the many steps normally required to get you on the air, with an eye to identifying areas of particular concern to the cause marketer. The broadcast producer, either an agency staffer or a freelance specialist, is taken through the storyboard and casts an experienced eye over it. Be very clear at that point what your budget is. The first words out of the mouth of the producer will probably be, "You can't shoot it for that!"

HOW TO SHOOT IT "FOR *THAT*"

If, in fact, yours is an elaborate production and you can't see any way to change it materially, the first thing to do is examine your overall budget for the campaign. Maybe there's a spot coming up that can be executed for less, so you can convince your client to rob from the Peter that's coming along to pay for the Paul at hand.

Or if you can group several commercials in a pool to be shot as part of the same job, your per-commercial cost will go way down. You still hire just one casting director, one stylist, one designer, and one production manager. A day on a set with a full crew costs just the same (in New York or Los Angeles it averages about $60,000) whether you shoot one thirty-second spot or parts of two or three of them! Put another way, if you can shoot four spots in two days, you get your basic production at a little more than half the cost. If you share logo artwork, music, even some common scenes, the savings compound.

THE DIRECTOR AS ARCHITECT

One place I urge you not to skimp is on the director, even though the really good ones command an astounding daily fee. In my opinion, they are worth every penny. The best analogy I can quote is one I've used often with clients who balk at the many thousands per day the big guys demand.

On a section of Park Avenue in New York I used to cross daily on my way to work, there stand two buildings on two adjacent blocks. The first is one of those anonymous "square wedding cakes" that line that magnificent boulevard. It used to house the home office of a large bank. I have no idea who the architect was, but he was obviously merely a pair of hands.

Just next door is the Seagram Building, celebrated as one of the finest examples of modern urban architecture. My heart always swells as I pass it. Now the interesting thing is that the girders and the glass for each building probably cost just about the same. What made the crucial difference in the Seagram Building was the consulting architect, breakthrough designer and Renaissance man Ludwig Mies van der Rohe. Now, I'm sure they paid top dollar to get the eminent Mies van der Rohe to come to New York and collaborate with Phillip Johnson on the design of a skyscraper. But as a percentage of the total cost, I'll bet it wasn't that much more than hiring the anonymous architect across the street. And what a difference! People passing those two blocks will notice it for years to come.

By the same token, the cost of lighting up a studio for a journeyman director is generally pretty much the same as it is for that small handful of brilliant artists who have not been wooed by the world of features, or even if they have, still embrace the challenge of doing our thirty-second movies.

They may insist on a first-tier group of key crew members, and may burn a bit more film to get it just right, so plan to spend something more for support. But overall, the basic studio and crew costs are pretty much the same. Spend the few extra thousands for the A-list director and you'll get an end result that will soar like the Seagram Building. Look at all the directors' sample reels you can, and pretty soon you'll know who's great and who's not.

And because you are involved in a cause marketing effort, it's not unlikely that with a little persuasion you can get A-list directors to work at something less than the fee they'd charge McDonald's or GM.

As the Massachusetts Department of Public Health campaign started making the rounds of the award shows, some world-class directors we might have considered untouchable started changing their schedules for us. One year, a difficult but brilliant man named Tony Kaye (who was that year's "hot" director and therefore virtually "unbookable") told us he had seen some of our work in festivals in Cannes and London and would gladly clear his busy schedule to shoot for us. That year, the agency received the national Clio for best public service commercial, thanks to Mr. Kaye.

Tony has moved on to feature films, as have many commercial directors, cinematographers, and composers. When I first went on the set years ago at Benton & Bowles, those who shot commercials were very separate from the feature filmmakers. Cinematographers on feature sets had a very distinct type of lighting. Most actresses' heads were flooded with a "halo light" so that, indeed, a heavenly halo seemed to frame their hair. Camera moves were via elaborate dollies and cranes. A zoom lens was a toy. And the worst thing you could do was let the sun flare out the lens during a shot.

The young people who made commercials had to find their own way, and because a lot of us at the agencies were constantly trying to push the envelope for a new look to our work, we urged the young commercial-makers to do the same.

Pretty soon, our spots with the snap zooms, handheld cameras, and lens flares were being examined by a Hollywood that discovered there was a youth market for its films for whom the vocabulary of commercials was the norm, and many of our commercial-trained cinematographers and directors "crossed over."

As a young advertising person, it was quite a kick to see the cinematography of Owen Roizman (*The French Connection*), Adam Hollender (*Midnight Cowboy*), Ernesto Capparos (*The Miracle Worker*), or Mike Nebbia (*Alice's Restaurant*), or the direction of Nicholas Roeg (*The Man Who Fell to Earth*) or Michael Cimino (*The Deerhunter* and *Heaven's Gate*—yes, he often went over budget on our spots, too!) on the big screen, and know that months before they had been shooting commercials you had written!

HOW TO KEEP THE MONEY IN-STATE

If your cause campaign is funded by state-controlled money, as many tobacco-control spots are, and that state is not New York or California, there may be a lot of political pressure to keep the production dollars in-state by hiring local film or tape production companies. This is fine, as long as they can deliver professionally and if they will accept an out-of-state director. If you have a hot or up-and-coming director in your city, you have no problems. But more than likely, the director you want is in one of the large production centers. In most cases, some kind of co-production deal can be worked out, or you can find a production manager who will ensure that crew and studio facilities are all local and the majority of the money will be spent in-state.

Sometimes, to get just the right location or director's touch, you may have to shoot in New York City or L.A., where most of the talented directors are based. In that case, let's hope you have established a strong liaison with your state's officials and can make the case that to spend the state's money on an unprofessional production would be to waste it. What this will require is the admission that the best local providers do not operate on the level of the companies in the major media production centers. Unfortunately, this is generally true.

So, once you've got a budget approved and an exciting director lined up you have to be sure the thing doesn't spin out of control. And as you well know, it can!

WHEN A CHANGE IS FREE, AND WHEN IT'S NOT

The most important thing to consider as you approach a production is to always keep in mind when changes are free and when they are costly.

The first set of free changes comes in the pre-production meeting. This is one of the most important moments in any production. If it is properly structured, it is the time to give all the people who will have a say on the final commercial a chance to air their preferences, and to be sure they understand exactly what the director's vision is.

It is surprising how often busy cause clients will pass on a pre-production meeting. "I trust you guys," they'll say magnanimously. Probably they assume it'll be a lot of technical mumbo jumbo they won't really understand. When the first cut is screened, if location and wardrobe and casting are all suddenly a problem, there's a very big price tag on every change. But accommodating the taste and desires of that client at the pre-pro meeting is free!

If clients or their fully authorized representatives will not come to the meeting, you have to make very sure that every detail that would be costly to change is discussed and placed under their noses—particularly casting. They shouldn't have to sit through the whole audition reel, but they'd better sign off on the selected actors. And, for that matter, all the important details of your approach to the board.

CASTING: THE KEY

Good casting can be responsible for 50 percent of the success of your spot. First, you've got to tap the best talent pool. Here again, as with proposing an out-of-state director, it may require all the political skills you can muster.

The Massachusetts Department of Public Health Tobacco Control Program is funded by additional cigarette taxes paid by Massachusetts citizens. So, in essence, the taxpayers have paid for it. The state legislators must vote to approve the budget every year. Now imagine the task of explaining to those legislators why you are casting for Massachusetts commercials in New York and Los Angeles. And the truth of the situation can be very unpalatable to an ardent state official. That truth is, as soon as actors get to be any good at their craft, they leave and go to either New York or L.A., where the hard-to-find acting jobs are.

"You mean, there aren't any decent actors left in Massachusetts?" Sadly, in most cases, no. But because it is a state campaign, they always run a complete casting call in the state and, occasionally, find someone great. But I would say in only about three out of ten cases is the talent up to the task. And this element is responsible for nearly 50 percent of the success of the commercial! It is an area you must never stint on.

There's another factor you must consider when casting out of state: the regional accent. Usually, middle-of-the-road, accentless English is okay. But if your spot is portraying a working stiff, don't cast a guy with a Brooklyn accent to play a Gloucester fisherman. Actually, working as much as I have lately in Massachusetts, I have become increasingly aware of how nearly impossible it is to affect a Boston accent if you weren't born and bred in the Bay State. "Pahk yuh cah" doesn't cut it, and will lose the Bay State audience in a flash. I once searched for a week for an actor with an authentic Arkansas twang for a spot to run in Little Rock. Since Bill Clinton was elected, they all think they can do it. But they can't. The actor we finally found was living in L.A., but he had grown up in Clinton's home state.

All this aside, the program administrators must be convinced to have the courage to approve the politically dangerous move to search out of state. The regional campaigns I've seen that have looked the most amateurish were usually condemned to that condition by homegrown talent. Obviously, we're talking about principal actors here. Smaller parts and extras should always come from your local talent pool.

The CDC Media Resource

Incidentally, with the cooperation of ASSIST (American Stop Smoking Intervention Study for Cancer Prevention), a partnership of the National Cancer Institute of Bethesda, Maryland, the American Cancer Society of Atlanta, and the Centers for Disease Control, the Massachusetts Tobacco Control talent contracts were written so the spots could be used in any other state, or nationally, without renegotiation. They are available from the CDC, together with commercials from Arizona and several other states, ready for re-tagging and local sponsorship. In some cases talent use for PSAs has been paid for; in others, a talent fee is required, but reduced if the spot is "in-cycle." Customized tagging costs approximately $950 for television and $1,200 for radio. Tape copies are $15 for VHS TV spots (other formats are also available) and $5 for radio. Print and outdoor spots are also available at comparably low prices. Information on the more than two hundred TV spots, one hundred radio spots, seventy-five print ads, and twenty-five outdoor ads available through the CDC can be obtained at the Resource Center at Cygnus Corporation, 5640 Nicholson Lane, Suite 300, Rockville, MD 20852. You can also call (301) 231-7537, fax (301) 984-8527, or visit the CDC website at http://www.cdc.gov/tobacco.

Just the Tape, Please!

There's another aspect of casting that I adopted early on and have never varied from: I make it a point never to meet the talent during the casting process. Let the casting director handle the audition and send you the tape. Actors can be very charming. If you're a theater and film buff, as I am, you will invariably meet people you have admired on the stage or screen. They love to talk shop. They will charm you. It's part of their job. But you are casting for a *role* in your very small film, not a personality showcase. The camera can turn these personable people into whole other creatures. It loves some of them; it doesn't treat others very well.

There are actors I have loved on the set and hated in the rushes. There are performers I have come to truly despise by the end of a shooting day that have projected such warmth and charm on film that I could swear they have been metamorphosed by some strange power. So just send the tape, please. Even under crude audition lighting, if they've got it, the camera will capture it.

"Insider" Talent

Another situation that arises more often than one might suspect and that must be avoided like the plague is "insider" talent. I dare say at least half the copywriters in the business believe they can read their words better than any actor alive. After all, who better to interpret the nuances of those words than their creator? And yet it's one of the worst things they can do because objectivity goes right out the window. Who's going to critique the reading? How much better to hire the best actors in the business and sit there in the booth and make sure everything you wanted is delivered. And, if you've cast really well, to be surprised and delighted by the fresh nuances they bring to the copy that are often beyond your wildest dreams.

Hal Riney is the only major agency creative person who reads his own copy regularly and gets away with it. He's as good as any voice-over talent out there. And yet I often wonder who reins him in when it isn't going well. He wrote the copy. He owns the agency. And he can carry it off because he's so good. But he's one of a kind. Another agency principal I know who does it all the time, and who shall remain unnamed here because I don't want to embarrass him, is almost the anti-Riney. His droning, gravel-voiced articulations of his copy are so dreary that half the value of his excellent words is lost. He is a world-class writer, but sadly, he continues to want to do it all. How skillful a seducer is the creative ego!

And the only thing worse than reading your own copy is letting yourself be persuaded to hire a member of the agency or client group, or one of their relatives, to appear in the spot. Who's going to criticize *that* performance?

The last time it happened to me, a staff member of the public agency I was consulting with approached me about doing the voice-over for a spot we were producing. Above all, there was the ethical question about what he would do with the residual money (nonunion talent must be paid the same as union talent—a clever clause inserted in the contract by union negotiators to avoid a rash of low-fee "scab" performances). Fortunately, an old story I told him ended that idea on the spot.

A young account executive at an agency I worked at had a wife who was a struggling actress. "Why don't you use my wife? She's terrific!" was his mantra each time we went into pre-production. Finally, we couldn't stand it and gave in, foolishly casting her as a lead in a regional spot.

The president of the client company, a rather crude self-made man who had had no involvement with the production process was ushered into the screening room to view the rough cut of his new campaign.

"Who cast that ugly broad?" he boomed in the darkness. When the lights came up, there was probably the longest silence in that agency staff's history.

The Celebrity Spokesperson

There's another aspect of casting that will inevitably arise in any cause marketing situation: the celebrity spokesperson. The thought of a Bill Cosby or a Mark McGuire speaking your message sends a shiver of excitement down the spine of any campaign manager. "That'll get us noticed; it'll make our cause famous."

It might. But I would urge a lot of caution when this idea arises, as it inevitably will. I will never forget sitting in the audience of a Bob Hope special one night in Burbank. While the crew was making last-minute lighting changes for the hour TV special, a series of cue cards was placed on an easel in front of the aging comedian. One at a time they were peeled off, as Bob, standing "in one," in front of a curtain, rattled off the copy; public service announcements for every possible disease and cause, bam-bam-bam. One take and done. Now this is not meant as a put-down of a revered entertainer who always gave generously of his time. But I would contend that by the nature of that one take in front of a curtain, the spots were minimally effective. There was *Bob Hope,* talking about your cause. But it's doubtful if the message had any more impact than just the mere association with a celebrity.

I really think that unless the celebrity has a unique association with the cause (Doug Flutie and his autistic son, Yul Brynner dying from lung cancer), it's a lazy answer to your problem. It's borrowed interest, and often the star power overwhelms all possible subtleties in your message.

Also, remember that this is the age of tabloid journalism. I can't really put down that category because I actually helped to grow it. A few years back I confess I did write a fairly notorious but incredibly successful line for a tabloid media campaign—"Enquiring minds want to know"—helped along by a brilliant videotape innovator named Alex Weill and a group of video artists at a company called Charlex. And I honestly think that if you treat that stuff as entertainment and don't take it too seriously, it deserves its place in our culture.

But what this means is that if you go the celebrity route, you'd better only cast one that's a certifiable saint. The last thing you want is your spokesman for sober driving splashed all over the supermarket checkout racks pleading to a DUI charge.

And if you think a music or film or sports hero is the way to convince our young people, think again. The very cynical generation of kids today believes generally that if you pay celebrities to say anything, they'll say it!

Musicians' Assistance

The Partnership for a Drug-Free America has taken that risk. Its Music/MAP (Musicians' Assistance Program) spots with rock stars like Kiss and Lauryn Hill are well produced, and I think a couple are very effective.

But others may be less effective with the kids they're meant to reach. Some of the spokespersons are obviously sincere about the drug-related mistakes they've made, and are clearly "damaged goods." Others seem fat and successful and appear to be giving lip service to the party line, which can be paraphrased as "Trust me, kids, I've been there. Don't use drugs!"

I can hear the kids now saying, "Oh, sure!"

We will analyze several of these spots in Chapter Nine. I think it may be instructive to see why some seem to work and the others, written obviously to the same strategy, may be less successful.

The Sports Connection

Sports celebrities are similarly tempting. Boston is one of the great sports towns, and the pressure to use our own star players and coaches on the state's anti-smoking effort could not be resisted. But we threw away a lot of tape over the years. Some who worked on the account said jokingly that if any athletes saw our crew coming they'd better duck into the clubhouse because we really were the professional sports version of Typhoid Mary!

Roger Clemens was spokesman for the Massachusetts Department of Public Health. He left the next year to play for Toronto. New England Patriot Marion Butts appeared in a charming spot titled "Butts vs. butts." He was traded by the end of the season. Bill Parcells agreed to let us edit some news footage of him into a spot on the new smoke-free environment at Foxboro. One season later he was hanging his coach's whistle on a hook in the New Jersey Meadowlands! And now all that expensive production sits on a shelf.

The Soccer Models

Probably the best use Massachusetts made of athletes was a spot co-funded by the CDC.

The members of the U.S. Women's Soccer Team were filmed posing like models in a Virginia Slims ad. A well-known photographer famous for his *Rolling Stone* covers was hired to direct. (Here again, he was happy to work with us because of the cause, clearing his busy schedule and keeping his fee down.)

These very attractive athletes say: "Cigarette advertising might lead you to believe that smoking is sophisticated, that cigarettes make you attractive . . . but we've done all those things without cigarettes, plus some things that cigarettes could never claim to do." Then there's an explosion of rough-and-tumble soccer action, and the announcer proclaims: "You don't get to be a champion by taking cigarette breaks."

In this case, we didn't play Typhoid Mary for the team. It went on to win the Gold Medal at the Atlanta Olympics and the 1999 World Cup. And Mia Hamm, one of the "models," has become a major media star. That didn't hurt the use of the spot and the accompanying poster either! That's somewhat equivalent to Lauryn Hill from the Partnership for a Drug-Free America spot winning so many Grammys in 1999. But let one of them be photographed with a cigarette, and for the kids, the backfire will be as loud as the Olympic cheers.

If you feel you must use a celebrity, try to cast for an association with your cause that is so strong it will overwhelm the mere celebrity of the spokesperson. The attractive young soccer players who seemed to have it all, and who would certainly have been slowed down by smoker's lungs, are a pretty good example of this. The accompanying PR, if you can be certain it will be positive, is a plus, and PR events built around that association will make the papers and the evening news. The pressure from your clients to use celebrities will be enormous. And you can be sure they'll show up at the shoot with their kids and grandkids in tow.

Models

(Music) GIRL 1: Cigarette advertising might lead you to believe that smoking is sophisticated.

GIRL 2: That cigarettes make you attractive. GIRL 3: That they make you popular.

GIRL 4: That somehow you can express yourself by smoking. GIRL 2: But we've done all those things

GIRL 1: without cigarettes, GIRL 2: along with some things GIRL 3: cigarettes could never claim to do.

(Sfx: Salsa music, cheering)

VO: You don't get to be a champion by taking cigarette breaks.

FIGURE 5.1 *The Massachusetts Tobacco Control Program/The Centers for Disease Control.* "Models" presented members of the World Champion U.S. Women's Soccer Team, first filmed a la Virginia Slims models, then taking the field and playing the way smokers never could. The spot featured Mia Hamm, Julie Foudy, and other positive role models. *Courtesy of the Massachusetts Department of Public Health.*

But (and this is just one man's opinion) mostly it's still a cop-out. It's mainly borrowed interest. You can do better!

Okay, you've cast your spot, and had a good meeting of minds in your pre-production meeting. If there's still a key decision-maker who can *not* be coaxed into the loop at this point, there are a couple of things you should consider that can save you a costly change later.

Double Casting—A Last Resort

While double casting (and therefore double shooting) is to be generally avoided, if it is not possible to check other key creative details with your ultimate approval source, there's always the famous "shoot it both ways" solution. This has a price tag and should only be done if there's real doubt. You're wasting time and film, and probably the director's patience. But it's considerably less costly than reshooting it after the set is struck.

EFFICIENCY ON THE SET

Even on the set, there are expensive changes and cheap ones. Urge your client to pay attention to all the early rehearsals. Once actors get a style of reading or a set of lines in their heads, they're going to blow many takes if they have to change later on. So sidle up to the director and make him or her aware of any concerns you have very early in the process.

Obviously, it's easy to watch a videotape shoot on a monitor in the booth. But most every film set today also has a video tap on the camera so the client can view the shot, something that was unheard of when I first started in the business. This is very sensible progress.

Make sure the monitor is fired up early in the day, and make sure it's placed as far away from the live set as possible. Roll tape on early rehearsals if you can. Then anybody who has a voice in final approval gets to observe and review it in private, raise doubts and concerns, and ultimately send them to the director. And there should only be one messenger, usually the agency producer.

Work out that line of communication early. And make it discreet. Try to have the conversation with the director out of earshot of the cast and crew. The most destructive thing on a set is hearing a buzz of comments from the client-agency group on the sidelines.

Long before use of the video monitor became common, there was a wonderful fable that circulated around the industry about a client's nephew who was invited to tag along on a shoot. He was about twelve but was already a student of film, and uncle had bought him a director's viewfinder to hang around his neck. He was about twenty feet to one side of the camera, viewing each take through his shiny black toy and making progressively louder comments. The actor on the set was craning his neck to hear them. After all, he was with the client.

"No good," shouted the exasperated director after a badly messed-up take. "Ready to go again right away!"

"Looked good to me!" said the nephew.

"Okay, then," snapped the director, "print yours!"

Isolating the talent is exceptionally important. Actors and actresses are often insecure about their performance. They will always be looking toward the client for approval or disapproval. That is why I always attempt to keep actors and clients as far apart as possible. And here you have to be very diplomatic because actors and actresses are charming and eager to please, and it's great fun for your clients to schmooze with them on the set. But when it comes to specifics of the performance, there should only be one father (or mother) figure on the set, and that must be the director.

This is particularly true when it comes to children. If possible, diplomatically move actual fathers and mothers as far away as you can.

I was once shooting a Life cereal commercial in a difficult location in a field in Puerto Rico (the only location we could find in January that resembled an Iowa farm in spring). As we made each take, we were knocked out by the natural quality of the little boy. He had a very serious faraway look as he spooned the cereal. It didn't bother us a bit when he told the prop man he hated the stuff. We let him spit it out between takes. But when we were rolling, he shoveled it down, was completely natural, and very, very good!

But the admission that he hated the cereal bothered his mother. She took him off to the side and hugged him a lot and whispered in his ear.

On the next take, he turned right to camera, rolled his eyes, patted his tummy, and uttered a big "Yum-yum!" The director almost had a fit. Needless to say, Mom was almost immediately treated to a shopping trip in San Juan, courtesy of the producer. And we finally did get a lovely spot.

Back to what's cheap and what's not. Try to get anyone who is a decision-maker to the set *early*. You can try as many different wardrobe and hair and makeup variations as you want. That's cheap. Since film is often shot out of sequence, it all must match. So if we've spent the morning making a master shot, and the client arrives for lunch and decides he hates the color of the actress's blouse, or even a curl in her hairdo, you've just wasted a morning because anything that doesn't match must be reshot. Expensive. Very expensive.

If you feel something is wrong, don't jump in after the first rehearsal, because the director and talent may be trying some different approaches. But don't wait too long, either. Go in while it's still cheap.

If the director has made a number of takes he or she considers acceptable and is just going for a protection take or two, it's very late in the game to raise your concerns. Directors will listen, but if the change is agreed upon, everything that went before is trashed. Also expensive.

The Value of Alternatives

Another thing that can save you money in the editorial phase is to have some alternatives up your sleeve. There's a caution here. Don't shoot so many variations that you fall behind and go into expensive overtime. But if you notice the director is right on or a little ahead of schedule, plot some variations that might give you some creative flexibility in the editorial suite. It's amazing how often they will turn good into great in the final cut.

Considering the cost of a day in the studio, it doesn't make any sense to wrap early. You get no refunds! The one exception to this is the talent. Wrapping the talent early can save money. So if you are planning any variations toward the end, try to do those employing talent first. Save the hand shots or inserts for last.

However, despite the value of inspiration and the delight you may feel in the new ideas that exist in the on-the-set variations, it's a good idea to always shoot the board, even if you only do a couple of takes on the original setup. A variation that seemed wonderful on the set may sour in the cold darkness of the screening room.

Now comes the moment of truth. You sit in a darkened room and look at the dailies. (In the East they're sometimes called "rushes," which means this is only a New York joke—Pharaoh: "Good heavens daughter . . . where on earth did you get that ugly kid?" Daughter: "That's funny, he looked great in the rushes!")

Let's hope you get what you went on the set for, plus some alternatives. Thanks to the new computerized editing programs, it's all done now in a cool and comfortable editing suite. Here again, there's cheap and expensive. In most cases, you're paying for all that humming equipment by the hour. So assembling a couple of alternative versions is easy and cheap. If you have any doubts about the most effective cut, do it two or three ways. And by all means, make sure your client sees it in this form. Fortunately, what is still called a "rough cut" (which used to be bunches of film with splicing tape and grease-pencil marks all over them) is now, thanks to computerized editing, pretty darn smooth.

Asking for the Order

You are always going to be frustrated by the short amount of screen time in a thirty-second commercial. Resist the temptation at the end to shortchange the logo and particularly the toll-free hotline number or an address. Many cause campaigns rely on a hotline, post office box, or website address as a way to connect their target viewers with counseling or help, or as a place for them to send contributions or requests for brochures or information. This is the cause version of that tried-and-true advertising principle: "Be sure to ask for the order!"

Wherever possible, seek the assignment of a box number, toll-free number, or website that is simple and memorable. To my way of thinking, an acronym number is worth its weight in gold. Viewers aren't sitting, poised in front of their TVs with pencil in hand, waiting to write down that all-important link to your organization.

"What was that number?" they'll ask, and four commercials later when they've found pencil and paper, it's gone from their mind. *Unless, you make it easy to remember.* Our hotline number for people trying to quit smoking in Massachusetts is 1-800-TRY TO STOP. Very easy to retain. Incidentally, you may have picked up, as several of our callers did, that "TRY TO STOP" is two digits longer than the standard seven-digit phone number. Not to worry. As long as there's no extension number involved, you can have an acronym number longer than seven digits.

The call goes through once you have completed the seven digits. Several more punched numbers don't affect a thing!

A Yellow Pages listing, while comparatively expensive, is another way to allow viewers to remember and react long after your ad has flickered off the screen. The Massachusetts Council on Compulsive Gambling adds the line "Or look in the Yellow Pages under gambling," and that source of information is easy to remember long after the actual number is forgotten. It's an important addition for that particular cause since the impetus for viewers to call to get help for a family member may well come later, once they realize their loved one may have the serious problem described in the commercial.

Lately, most organizations have established websites, and what a wonderful source of actionable information they can be! We'll talk a little later about the Internet, the one-to-one medium, but it's appropriate to note here that a carefully chosen Web address, one that is mind-sticking, is another excellent way to increase the efficiency of your ad. Once again, you want viewers to take that desired action step in your strategy, and if they can't remember how to find you, your advertising is wasted. Fortunately, a good Web search engine can deliver your site even if only a key word is remembered.

If you can't obtain an acronym number or a Yellow Pages listing, make sure your number or post office box is simple: "555-1000," "Box 1234," and so on. And be sure your title is on the screen long enough to be read aloud *three* times. We writers will always try to skimp on that in favor of our deathless prose. But you must resist shortchanging the titles at all cost. You may blow away the audience with your spot, but if viewers don't remember how to act on that emotion, if they don't know how to reach you, you've wasted a lot of time and money.

Rough to Smooth

Any change made in a rough cut at this off-line editorial stage is still pretty cheap. Once you go on-line and correct colors and insert final titles and special effects, the cost of a change is huge. So be sure everyone's on board at the rough-cut stage, including the top people. Of course, you should show them a final release tape as a fail-safe, but a change at *that* point has many dollar signs written across it.

THE FIRST IMPRESSION

There's another phenomenon I have observed that has turned me into a screening-room nut: *the client's first impression stays forever.* So if there's any way you can do it, especially in this era of a VCR in every office, try to get the chance to set the controls on the monitor carefully before the client enters the room.

Fiddling with the volume or color balance or sharpness during the thirty seconds of the first viewing is disastrous. At that moment, your agency head or organization president is just another viewer sitting at home. And that first reaction will always overshadow whatever they see thereafter, even if it all becomes greatly improved. Anything that distracts during that first impression may kill the big "Wow!" you're hoping to achieve.

If there's anything about that first cut that's still rough and could distract from the emotional impact of the moment, explain it ahead of time. Don't make a federal case out of it, as too lengthy a preamble will scare or annoy clients. But let nothing on the screen bother them or distract them during that first screening. The music should swell but not overpower, the dialogue should be clear, the color should look as good as you can make it, and the moment should be exciting.

Run it again immediately, once or twice. With luck any concerns they had during the first showing should go away after the second or third run. And if you've done your job, that excitement will be there for *everyone* in your target audience who sees your very artful, very expensive, very impactful thirty-second movie.

6

RADIO AND PRINT

Hot and Hotter!

Radio is the medium everyone expected would die as soon as we became sophisticated in the uses of television. But it's still going strong. And if a radio campaign is well-done, it may be the best answer to getting your message out to the people with good reach and frequency at a fraction of the cost of television. I particularly like doing radio. In some ways, it is a vastly more creative medium than TV. Marshall McLuhan was on to something, I think, when he called it the "hot medium" (as opposed to television, which he described as being "cool"). What he meant was simply that on TV, everything is laid out for you. You are taken by the hand, and told how to react, and what to feel. It is a couch potato's dream, not requiring much participation on the part of the viewer.

Radio, on the other hand, if properly done, forces the listener into becoming your collaborator. The listener's imagination is engaged. They must paint a face in their mind to go with the voice. The scenery created as they hear the swelling music is very personal and unique to each listener. Humor and surprise twists in the copy are easier because they're not telegraphed. You can't see them coming.

And as a participant in the process, a "co-creator" if you will, the listener is likely to *retain* more of your message. Hence, this medium, in McLuhan's theory, is hot! In his book *Understanding Media*, McLuhan suggests that the famous Nixon-Kennedy debate would have produced a different outcome had it been broadcast only on radio. Those who heard the broadcast on radio perceived Nixon as superior, while on television he appeared phony, McLuhan says, referring to the "used-car salesman" look we all started to associate with "Tricky Dick." Nixon became a cartoon on TV. But on radio, McLuhan apparently surmises, Nixon's intelligence might have won the day.

My wife Pat, at that time a young Kennedy staffer, remembers the day of that debate quite clearly. Nixon was nervous, she recalls, having spent many sleepless hours preparing for the debate. A frantic makeup person was fussing to try and hide his five-o'clock shadow. Kennedy on the other hand spent the day receiving steam and massage treatments. He arrived just before the debate, slightly tanned and very relaxed. He was clearly the first true television candidate, and many feel the images projected in that debate were largely responsible for his slim margin of victory in 1960.

McLuhan even poses the outrageous but certainly interesting theory that if TV had been available on a large scale during Hitler's reign he would have vanished quickly, or perhaps never come to power at all. Stripped of the loving godlike imagery in his Leni Riefenstahl-directed propaganda films, Hitler might have been reduced to a Charlie Chaplin clown in the cool medium of live TV. Radio captured only the intensity of his commanding voice.

Since those days radio has become very much a niche medium: talk radio in all flavors (conservative, liberal, female, jock); music for every taste from rock and heavy metal to country and classical; all news, all financial, all Christian. You get the picture. So if your targets are from a very narrow demographic, you can reach them efficiently (and quite cheaply) through radio. And because radio is fast and inexpensive to produce, it can be very topical, reflecting current trends or news stories. Topical commercials in an all-news format are particularly effective.

One of my clients, the Massachusetts Council on Compulsive Gambling, finds that the ability of radio to reach the avid sports fan or even the late-night listener (both groups heavily populated by the council's target) makes radio an excellent choice for its messages. Dramatic and empathetic case studies (see figure 2.4) were well served by radio, at a fraction of the cost of filming or taping them for TV.

Bob Mehrman, a Boston radio personality whose lungs were devastated by smoking-caused cancer, agreed to be the subject of a radio campaign judged "Best of Show" at the annual Boston advertising community's "Hatch" awards (the first time a radio campaign had been so honored). The audio juxtaposition of Mehrman's smooth, pre-cancer voice (edited from one of his earlier broadcasts) next to the product of an audiovox device (the only way he can now speak) made for one of the most compelling cause-radio campaigns I know of. In many ways it is as shocking as the Yul Brynnner TV spot. We are hearing the death of a voice, the only tool of this man's trade, due to smoking. (See figure 10.7.)

While these opportunities are rare, keeping the unique qualities of radio in mind can allow you to produce some very cost-efficient and effective cause commercials in this often ignored medium.

A FEW CAUTIONS FOR RADIO

I want to offer some cautions regarding creating radio. Again, most were learned the hard way! First, since the cost of a sixty-second ad in radio is only slightly more than that of a thirty-second ad, sixty seconds is the length of choice. Try to keep the copy down to about 160 words. However, listeners are used to the fast-paced dynamic of the thirty-second TV spot, so don't relax into the longer length so completely that you bore them.

Also, don't forget that you don't have any visuals to support the copy. You have to explain a little more. As with TV, this is particularly significant when there's a phone number or an address to be remembered. With no graphic on the screen, be sure to repeat a phone number at least twice, or ideally, three times. And here more than ever, an acronym phone number, a clever website address, or a post office box with a number in the thousands is crucial.

Music and sound effects are very important in radio. Some years ago comedian and sometime advertising man Stan Freberg produced a classic spot to promote the use of radio as an advertising medium. A delightful life-size fantasy mountain of whipped cream and pudding was created in an imaginary landscape. A fleet of planes droned over it, dropping cherries. It was all done with sound effects, and the mind painted the fabulous picture. "Now try to do that in TV," droned the dry Mr. Freberg at the end of the spot.

If you are using music, be sure you consider the environment in which the spot will run. A track that might be considered "elevator music" by youthful listeners of a heavy-metal rock station would set your cause back enormously. By the same token, the twanging of some Nashville guitar licks following on the heels of a Mozart overture on an all-classical station would certainly create a negative response.

In this age of electronic instrumentation and synthesizer sophistication, it is possible to find a composer-arranger who will create a very interesting track that is part music, part evocative sound effects for very little expense, particularly if there are no live players to hire and record.

SOME CASTING CONSIDERATIONS

I spoke earlier about the liabilities of celebrity spokespersons. But there always exists a positive opportunity in the use of unidentified "star" voices in radio (and as anonymous voice-overs on TV). It's particularly viable when your cause is something a celebrity strongly believes in.

Some "drop dead" star names, including some Academy Award–winning actors, have been quite willing to lend their considerable acting talents to unidentified TV-commercial voice-over tracks or radio spots, while they might strongly resist playing on-camera roles. Somehow, the anonymous voice-over maintains their "sell-out" virginity. They're just playing a role, not endorsing a product or cause. Yes, that *is* Donald Sutherland and Joe Pesce and Kelsey Grammar pitching those cars!

Voice anonymity in cause marketing avoids the liability of the celebrities overwhelming the message while still giving you the acting skills that made them stars. And most of them have not achieved star status by accident.

Just listen to the radio commercials done by your local furniture dealer or banker and you'll realize how difficult it is to be an effective commercial "voice." If you can't coax a famous voice to do your track, be sure to cast carefully because, when it comes to radio, casting is at least 75 percent of the success of the spot!

Another recent innovation that opens the door to the whole world of voice talent is the phone patch. They can sit comfortably in their favorite recording studio in Hollywood or New York or London, and you can direct them via a phone patch as if you were right there with them.

This is also an option today for TV voice-overs. It just requires that you send a tape of the spot to the studio. It does eliminate your ability to absorb the impact of a full playback to picture, but the plus of getting a great performance should make up for that slight inconvenience. Just be sure you have a stopwatch at the ready.

And when it comes to timing your copy, I find it's a good idea to come to the session with some carefully thought-out cuts. It's amazing to me how much variation there is in voice-over talent in terms of the ability to time copy. Some will read 150 words in sixty seconds and sound rushed. Others handle up to 185 words and seem to be drawling like Andy Griffith.

I generally tend to write a little on the long side but with clearly delineated cuts marked on the script, so there's no time wasted when the session clock starts ticking. These cuts, if they're substantive, should also probably be discussed with the client in advance. If that's not possible, tape both versions, one rushed, the other smoother. The reason for the cuts should be obvious to the approval group.

Voice recording has also benefited greatly from the computer age. In the pre-digital age, the razor blade on the tape block in the hands of a skilled editor used to get the job done, but the ability to mouse-click into a wave pattern visually displayed on the screen is light-years ahead. This means the great moment that sometimes occurs in an otherwise overlong or glitch-filled take can be lifted out and inserted in another take to make your track finally "sing."

The more recording you're involved with, the more you'll train your ear. Often I have accepted a technically perfect take, but urged the talent to go back and do one more "just for fun," and had the track go from competent to brilliant. There's always a moment in a recording session when I hear the copy as if for the first time. It may be take twenty-five, but it's the one to buy. You know the words by heart, but suddenly you're hearing them fresh, as if you were the first listener, sitting at home.

The opposite is often true with nonprofessional talent. You may want to construct a campaign based on the stories of real people. If you're working with "civilians," always roll tape the moment they enter the studio because, more often than not with nonprofessionals, the rehearsal is as good as it gets. It's spontaneous, it's real, and the more you try to direct them, the more you try to turn them into actors, the more unreal it all becomes. But if you can capture the sincerity of a real person, deeply affected by your cause, it can be magical.

Radio is alive and well, years after its predicted demise, and it may very well be the primary medium for the limited-budget cause campaign.

And, as McLuhan said, it's hot!

PRINT—EVEN HOTTER

Radio is hot, but under McLuhan's definition print is even hotter. Since I started in the advertising business as a television producer, I came to learn the techniques of print advertising somewhat late in my career. I had been assigned as copy supervisor on a television-heavy account during the days when we still did mainly sixty-second commercials and thirty-second spots were merely cut-down adaptations of the originals. The client decided one day that he also wanted to do some print. We worked up some layouts in both full-page and half-page formats.

When I got back to the agency, I reported to my boss that the client "liked the full-page ad a lot, but had a few problems with the :30!" He laughed until tears came to his eyes. "Okay, TV guy," he said. "We'd better get you some training in print. And don't think it's going to be easy. It's definitely the hardest kind of advertising to sell." When I asked why, he replied, "Because it doesn't present a moving target!"

And how right he was. A TV spot is a much easier sell. As you present it, usually from a crudely sketched storyboard, you're challenging the client's imagination: "Picture a sunrise over the ocean. The music swells, and we see an elderly couple, walking along the beach in slow motion. Got it?" They usually do get it because their imagination has been engaged. And in rough-cut form, it's even easier because it flashes by in thirty seconds, with a whole array of executional devices to play on the client's emotions: music, adroitly timed dialogue, animated graphics, etc. But the print ad just sits there, seeming to say, "Criticize me!"

Some Print Fundamentals

Let's examine some fundamentals of print. Media placement will dictate a lot of the decisions you make about format. Print is a very selective environment. The readers have picked up that publication because they're interested in its content. They are probably paying a lot more attention than TV viewers who may just be letting it all wash over them.

If your environment is a glossy magazine, you may wish to let a startling visual carry your message. A witty or intriguing headline may be all you need. Certainly your copy should be brief and to the point.

If, however, you are on the op-ed page of a serious newspaper, then a thoughtful long-copy approach may be completely appropriate.

Writing thoughtful, reader-friendly long-copy ads is a dying skill, but there is still a need for that talent.

When the chairman of Johnson and Johnson finally agreed we should break our silence and speak to the public after the tragic Tylenol poisonings, we bought full-page newspaper ads full of copy, with a very straightforward headline: "A Message from the Makers of Tylenol."

Everyone in the country was aware of the product-tampering deaths (a network news director told us it received more coverage than anything since the Vietnam War), so everyone knew what the ad was about. That simple headline was as dramatic as anything "creative" we might have crafted. And the news value of the tragic incidents forced widespread readership of the long-copy message from the corporation. They had been waiting to hear from us.

One caution in writing long print copy: make every word count. Don't let meaningless phrases take over your ad. Give them facts!

In most print ads, the illustration is the most important element. And photography is consistently more memorable than artwork. If it's appropriate, caption the illustration. Captions always get more readership than body copy. If the illustration is the major attention-grabber, the headline ranks not far behind. Readers of most newspapers and magazines are basically skimming. Something about your visual and headline must grab them by their sleeve and say "Read me!" Sometimes, the graphic is so striking it does the job for you, and sometimes it can do it without any copy other than a signature line. But in most cases, it's a combination of headline and visual that clinches it.

Because a headline must work so hard, there is probably a greater tendency in print to reach for the pun or the cute twist. When this works, in the hands of a skillful writer, it's magical. "It's small and ugly but it gets you there," read the headline for Volkswagen over a visual of the moon-landing lunar module. "In one American state, the penalty for exposing yourself is death," read the headline in a British ad for Timberland Out-erwear over visuals of bleak Mount Washington terrain in winter and the company's Gore-tex coat. In the cause area, a well-known ad for People for the Ethical Treatment of Animals (PETA) showed a screaming monkey strapped inside a diabolical-looking lab device. The headline read, "Imagine having your body left to science while you're still in it."

But these are the rare exceptions. The fastest way to spot a novice or inexperienced writer is when you see a pun or double entendre in the headline that ignores the core of the message. These writers assume the sheer artfulness of the twist will grab the reader, while ignoring the fact that the whole ad must present the image of the sponsoring body.

The inspired headline is something we all hope to write. But it should be examined from all aspects to make sure it is not grabbing attention just to grab it.

Body-copy style has changed a great deal over the years. Most of it has become conversational, punchy, pithy. An ad for the British Health Education Council shows a visual of a silhouette of a man with a cigarette in his mouth, the smoke curling up into his nose. The conversational headline reads, simply: "If only." The engaging body copy continues: "Nobody has ever smoked an entire cigarette . . . Breathing other people's cigarette smoke doesn't just get up people's noses. It gets down their throats and into their lungs . . . And if you don't smoke, but live with people who do, we hope you'll put this advertisement where they can't miss it. Right under their noses."

To some degree body copy has become an approximation of the spoken delivery in broadcast. Pauses, leaders, and one- or two-word sentences such as "Don't laugh," "Take heart," "No," or "It's easy" all attempt to force the eye of the reader into the rhythm of spoken speech. This is all to the good, I think. I always try to imagine a reader facing me when I write print copy. That way, this less personal medium becomes more personal.

The Subhead

Subheads or crossheads, boldface lines of type like the one just above this paragraph, summarize the thought to come. They immediately make long-copy ads more reader-friendly, as will small illustrations inserted so the type wraps around them in a format called a "rebus" ad.

In addition to the words, the inventive use of typography can also enhance the impact of print. Think of the times you have noticed just one person in a crowd. Your ad is there on a crowded page. What about it will set it apart? A typeface can speak volumes about you and your cause. Serif types such as Times are more traditional, more factual. (The new NASA logo went right back to serif type, as if their rockets had suddenly sprouted biplane wings and struts.)

Sans-serif types such as Helvetica project a modern and utilitarian feel. Leading, spacing, paragraphing, flowing type around visuals, and grouping type into shapes are all techniques to lead the reader into a rhythm you want, and to make reading the body copy fun.

And the following admonition may sound elemental, but it's amazing how many times I've had an argument with an art director on the subject: *Make sure the type is readable!*

Compressing type into an unreadably small size, or reversing type on a black or dense background, is a little bit like eliminating the mix on your broadcast track. If you can't hear it or understand it, or in the case of print, read it, you'll ignore it, no matter how artful the layout.

KEEP "OUT OF HOME" ADVERTISING SIMPLE

Most print ads do not present a moving target; but "out of home" or outdoor advertising, particularly on billboards adjacent to a highway, *has* a moving target . . . the target audience moving along the highway at sixty-five miles per hour.

The best single thing I can suggest for outdoor is keep it simple! Choose a message that can be instantly grasped by high-speed drivers on a freeway. Southern California routinely does it best, perhaps because it's such an automobile-driven area.

Transit cards on the outside of the bus or train reverse the high-speed situation. You may be moving, but more likely you are standing still, and the ads are flashing by. The same principle applies: *Keep it simple!*

The Trapped Target

A different dynamic is in place when it comes to transit advertising *inside* subway cars or buses. Here the target is trapped, staring at your message for long periods of time, on average about twenty-two minutes.

Long, serious copy is quite appropriate here. Strap-hangers are newspaper readers. When they glance up at your card, the momentum shouldn't change. Too much shock or cuteness can wear thin in the twenty minutes the average transit passenger is forced to stare at it.

Because the audience is a captive one, taste is a far more sensitive issue here. There have been a number of incidents in which a movie ad that was acceptable in magazines has been pulled down by an embarrassed transit authority. Criticism from riders cradling kids in their laps for long stretches and forced to stare at some gory or suggestive scene (such as one of the shocking PETA posters) or questionable language can have a negative effect on your campaign.

Use All Dimensions

Outdoor was thought of for many years as a "flat" medium. But its best practitioners are those that have expanded it to all dimensions. Break out of the borders, and your message will jump out.

Two of the best outdoor cause ads I have seen were produced by the creative team on the Massachusetts Tobacco Control Program:

- A bus poster displayed two crayoned arrows, about fifteen feet apart, pointing up at the bus windows. "If someone were smoking here," read the headline by the first arrow, "someone could get lung cancer here," read the other, finishing the important thought about the dangers of secondhand smoke in an enormously involving and thought-provoking way.
- A set of highway billboards on a major commuter route into Boston was changed every two weeks to create an almost animated progression. The first, on a nasty dark-red background, displayed the headline, "These are your lungs after 15 years of smoking." "Okay," says the smoker driving by every morning. "Another typical scare ad from the cigarette nazis!"

  But two weeks later the same board had a healthy pink section in the middle of the nasty red. The headline had been changed to "These are your lungs after you quit smoking for 6 months."

  After seeing this billboard the drive-by smoker will realize that there's a little hope for reversing the trend if they quit. Maybe

IF SOMEONE WERE SMOKING HERE.   SOMEONE COULD GET LUNG CANCER HERE.

FIGURE 6.1 *The Massachusetts Tobacco Control Program.* This bus poster used bus seats as a life-sized demonstration of the dangers of secondhand smoke. *Courtesy of the Massachusetts Department of Public Health.*

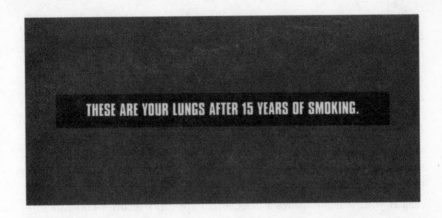

FIGURE 6.2 *The Massachusetts Tobacco Control Program.* This billboard, the first in a series of four posters that changed weekly, depicted a diseased lung improving over time after a smoker quits. *Courtesy of the Massachusetts Department of Public Health.*

FIGURE 6.3 *The Massachusetts Tobacco Control Program.* The second billboard in a series of posters that ultimately showed a pink, healthy lung. *Courtesy of the Massachusetts Department of Public Health.*

they'll be a little curious to see the next change. And change it did, depicting the lung two years and finally five years after quitting, when the whole board was a healthy pink. This billboard actually created anticipation about the next change for the driver who passed it every day.

The progenitor of this type of outdoor was "Watch this space" and the current generation of savvy outdoor creatives continue to animate this no-longer-static medium.

SYNERGISTIC PRINT

As you execute your cause campaign, consider other print options such as brochures, flyers, point-of-purchase cards, bill stuffers, and direct mail. The latter is a very specialized field, with some specific techniques that have been developed over years of trial and error by specialty agencies. If your cause requires a direct-mail appeal, I recommend subcontracting that aspect to a group of specialists.

With all supplemental print, you should never forget the synergistic effect of prominently featuring your campaign theme, logo, typeface, and graphics. To be readily recognizable as part of *your* effort, the family resemblance should be strong. If the target audience has responded favorably to any piece of your campaign, say, a television spot, it will be reassured that this brochure is from the same source.

If your cause has a limited budget, to maximize it you should use all the supplemental help you can get. These synergistic reminders of other parts of your campaign can affect or enhance the extra retention you get from involving your target as a "co-creator" in radio and print, the hot media!

7

RESEARCH

The Science That's Often an Art

Research can be both a blessing and a curse. If it is carefully designed and intelligently interpreted, it can be an essential tool at three distinct points in the process of creating your campaign. The curse of research (particularly qualitative research) is that it *is* an interpretive science. And that interpretation is sometimes suspect. Often a client will suspect that qualitative research is being manipulated by an agency to sell a concept the agency has affection for. Legendary advertising pioneer David Ogilvy said it best in *Ogilvy on Advertising*: "Research is often misused by agencies . . . as a drunkard uses a lamppost—not for illumination, but for support!"

But having acknowledged that, I have still always found strategy or rough-concept testing early in the process to be an essential tool for a creative team wading into a cause project.

Qualitative research generally comes from a series of focus groups or mall intercepts. At a second point in the process, after the advertising has been produced, but before it airs, it can function as an excellent disaster check to make sure you are doing no harm.

Finally, as we saw in Chapter One, an objective evaluation of any cause campaign may be essential to its survival. It can provide proof that you have been effective in accomplishing your goals. And quantitative evidence of that accomplishment may be essential to the life or death of your campaign, both in achieving continued funding by public agencies or private donors, *and* in achieving PSA placement by the media.

LEARNING TO LOVE RESEARCH

During my early years in the business, the research department and I were often at war with each other because the researchers seemed to be trying to reduce our creative "art" to a kind of Newtonian science.

I can remember very clearly storming into the office of an account executive who had arranged at some expense to give the members of my creative group a seminar. It was conducted by an outside researcher who, by means of some arcane "sweaty skin" technique and a quantitative analysis of hundreds of commercials, had established a code of unbreakable "laws" that would, if followed, create effective advertising. What was worse was that the account executive had invited our principal client to attend that presentation.

One of those laws was that the client's name *must* be mentioned in the first seven seconds of the spot. Imagine the number of involving commercials that would have been killed by strictly adhering to that rule!

"Geez, you're the worst focus group I've ever seen."

FIGURE 7.1 © The New Yorker Collection 1998 Robert Mankoff from cartoon bank.com. All rights reserved.

Fortunately, Procter and Gamble, a company not known for far-out creative, had just achieved an all-time record on a post-production recall score for a commercial for Puritan Oil. The riveting actor John Houseman gave a twenty-three-second treatise on how to control cholesterol. He didn't mention the product until the *last seven seconds*, but he had been so compelling in his narrative that consumers were leaning toward the screen, breathlessly waiting to be told the solution to their cholesterol worries. I showed that to the account executive and pleaded that we consider the laws to be *guidelines* that could be breached, perhaps at some risk, and not set in stone. I convinced him that to do otherwise would stifle the production of exciting advertising.

I pause as I write this, since *this* text may seem to some to be a book full of rules. But like that wise AE who altered the status of the researcher's laws, I will offer them as guidelines only.

David Ogilvy, who was often unjustly reviled by young advertising turks as a fussy creator of lists of rules, responded as follows to that charge in *Ogilvy on Advertising:* "I hate rules! . . . I may say to an art director 'research suggests that if you set the copy in black type on a white background more people will read it than if you set it in white type on a black background.' A *hint* perhaps, but scarcely a rule." So consider this volume a source of *hints*.

Qualitative research, as I have said, can be an imprecise science. The first and most obvious way to tighten up the procedure is to be very sure you have a first-rate facilitator or group moderator, and that he or she asks the right questions.

ASKING THE RIGHT QUESTIONS

The classic and somewhat ancient illustration of asking the right question is a street-intercept survey of New York newspaper readers reportedly done many years ago. "What newspaper do you read?" asked the interviewer. The responses would indicate that the *New York Times* far outsold the tabloid *New York Daily News*, when in fact the exact opposite was true (a situation that has changed in recent years).

The interviewers were briefed and sent out again. This time they asked, "Which newspaper did you *happen to read today?*"

This time the responses were much more in line with the real marketplace situation. The dynamic here was quite simple. Most respondents the first time out did not want to admit to some yuppie interviewer accosting them on the street that they regularly enjoyed the lurid stuff in the blue-collar tabloid. But after the question was changed, they were allowed to assume a casual relationship—the interviewer might take away the impression that "today I just happened to picked up a copy of the *Daily News.*"

IN AND OUT OF FOCUS

Focus groups are even more vulnerable. A group of strangers is put together in a small room with what is obviously a one-way mirror across one wall, and a video camera whirring in the corner. They are asked to expose their true thoughts about a whole range of personal issues—all the more so, if your cause is dealing with addictions or sensitive medical conditions.

Normally, they are put at ease with a series of innocuous opening questions. A focus group guide employed by the Partnership for a Drug-Free America starts out with an introduction and warm-up, designed to put the respondents and facilitator at ease with each other. This usually includes a description of the one-way mirror, the people behind it, and the fact that any tapes of the conversation will only be used for internal review. It never fails to surprise me how soon a group will forget all about the anonymous folks behind the glass.

Then the moderator asks a series of "lifestyle" questions, like these suggested by a Partnership's questionnaire:

- What are the kinds of things you do for fun? With peers, parents, groups, etc.?
- Who are the most important people in your lives?
- Why are they important?
- Who do you look up to?
- How would you describe yourself?
- What are your goals?
- What one thing has happened in the past year that has had the greatest impact on you?

Then the discussion moves on to the subject of drugs. It starts out fairly generalized, and then gets increasingly specific:

- When I say the word *drugs* what comes to mind?
- Why do you think people use drugs?

- What do you believe are the risks of using drugs? (Vary by type of drug.)
- What is the one biggest risk to you personally?
- What are your sources of information about drugs?
- What do you think would help you to resist peer/social pressure to take drugs?

Then a group of storyboards or rough commercials is shown, and the respondents are probed for comprehension and reactions:

- What is the main idea this commercial was trying to communicate?
- What else are they trying to tell you?
- What is your overall reaction? Do you like it, or dislike it?
- Was anything confusing? Unbelievable?
- If you were to describe these commercials to a friend, what would you tell them?
- Is there something the commercial could have told you that would have been more meaningful to you?

Sometimes focus group respondents are asked to rate or grade the commercials, although results of this should be taken with a grain of salt. A commercial that is not the best liked may still work best for your cause. The life or death of a product or service commercial is more likely to depend on winning a focus group "popularity contest," because if consumers don't like your spot, they probably won't buy your product. On the other hand, a cause effort that is a little unsettling (and therefore perhaps not the best liked) but makes them *think* may be your most effective piece of advertising.

Most people in focus groups want to help. They're frankly a little flattered to be valued for their opinion. The trick is to separate the truth from the "eager to please" comments.

More often than not, there will be one or two "opinion leaders" who are in love with the sound of their own voice. If given their head by the moderator, they will start to lead the group into rubber-stamping *their* opinions. There will always be a few timid souls around the table who are afraid they'll look stupid if they disagree with the vocal minority.

All of these very normal human attitudes can be dispensed with quickly by a skilled facilitator. And that *must* be done. Just as with hiring a first-class director for your commercials, you must be certain your research group (whether it is an in-house department or, as is more common these days, a subcontractor) does not stint on finding and paying for the best available moderator. And by all means, resist the temptation to do it yourself. (Scratch some copywriters, and they will probably tell you they think they could do it better than the professional facilitators. I am not one of those.)

When they're questioned adroitly, people will tell you the truth— if you are willing to listen . . . and believe. Don't be surprised if the response is often counter to your own pre-group judgment! Be willing to be humbled by the people around the table. I can say that after more than thirty-five years of sitting behind that one-way mirror, I can pretty well spot the truth-tellers. I hope you will develop your own instincts in less time.

Whatever you do, don't skip those sessions. The more you attend (and you'll have to sit through some boring ones), the more finely tuned your instincts become. After a while you'll start to pick up on body language and something the kids still call "vibes." You can't get these from simply listening to the tapes or watching the video. Usually the camera has zoomed in to the speaker, ignoring the restless shifting and eye-rolling of the people across the table as they react to one another's testimony.

And one tiny point about that infamous one-way mirror. Keep it down back there! It's amazing how soon the boredom of long stretches of hearing the same preliminary setup by the moderator will turn a serious group of advertising professionals into unruly sophomores! A distinguished and admired (but somewhat loud) agency president was seriously embarrassed when the interviewer excused herself and came back into the client booth to report that all his caustic comments about the low IQs and dowdy appearance of the ladies around the table were being quite clearly overheard in the interview room!

As an example of how unexpected the cause focus-group dynamic can be, I was surprised several years ago by a group of blue-collar, three-pack-a-day smokers in Massachusetts. The Tobacco Control agency was exposing them to a body of anti-smoking advertising produced in other states in the hope of selecting several commercials to flesh out the Massachusetts campaign during the months before we had the opportunity to build a library of our own.

Probably the single most famous anti-smoking spot produced during an extensive and generally successful cause campaign in California portrayed a group of supposed tobacco executives lounging around a smoke-filled boardroom trying to deal with the corporate crisis of losing 1,100 customers each day.

"Actually, technically, they die!" chuckles the pig-faced "Chairman." But we've got to replace them, he says, and then adds: "So forget about all that heart disease, cancer, emphysema, stroke stuff. We're not in this business for our health." The slimy "executives" chortle and slap their thighs as the name of the sponsoring body comes up in the closing titles. This is the surefire hit of any gathering of anti-smoking activists. I've seen it get standing ovations at medical and public health conventions. The strategy is obvious: these slimeballs in the expensive suits are exploiting the smokers for profit, killing them, and laughing about it! So don't trust the tobacco industry.

And yet *our* exploited smokers absolutely hated it. Furthermore, they hated *us*! We had replaced the California logo with a Massachusetts Department of Public Health title. And the consensus was that *our* well-intentioned group was the one laughing at the poor smoker, *not* the ugly, manipulative tobacco merchants.

This was a totally unexpected result from some qualitative research, yet I completely buy it. Remember, with a cause focus group, you may be dealing with the psychological defenses of an addicted population, whereas a packaged-goods group may be concerned with nothing more weighty than the "real barbecue taste" of a bag of chips.

Another surprising response to the "Boardroom" spot came from teenagers, admittedly the toughest target. Common sense had led the agency to the conclusion that nobody would have been more repelled than the kids by an establishment group portrayed as manipulators of the young. And yet, almost unanimously, in group after group, they seemed unmoved by the spot. Their attitude was often expressed like this: "Hey . . . it's a legal product! They're in business to make money any way they can, so good enough for them!"

How youth attitudes have changed since the '60s and '70s! But even then kids held the erroneous belief, still articulated by almost any group of teens, that "advertising doesn't affect what I do anyway!" This often comes from a group in which at least one kid is wearing a piece of Marlboro or Camel "gear," usually a T-shirt or a hat.

I'm happy to report some spots that were shown to adult smokers, those that expressed real understanding of the difficulty of quitting and gave empathetic tips, were enthusiastically embraced.

So, how did the "Boardroom" spot get aired for so long in California if it was such a turn-off to smokers? Clearly, that agency must have done its own research as well. There is a possibility of a geographic anomaly, that the more sophisticated California smokers got the message of cynical manipulation by the tobacco industry and were motivated to take steps to resist it, whereas Massachusetts smokers simply blamed the sponsoring body. This theory was supported recently by a new study funded by several state anti-smoking programs and conducted by Teen Research

---

Boardroom

| EXECUTIVE: Gentlemen, gentlemen. | The tobacco industry has a very serious multibillion-dollar problem. We need more cigarette smokers, pure and simple. | Every day, two thousand Americans stop smoking. And another eleven hundred also quit. Actually . . . technically . . . they die. |

| This means that this business needs three thousand fresh new volunteers every day. | So forget about all that heart disease, cancer, emphysema, stroke stuff. We're not in this business for our health. | *(All laugh)* |

FIGURE 7.2 *The California Department of Health Services.* "Boardroom" is one of the most famous anti-smoking spots ever satirizing tobacco industry cynicism. Yet heavy smokers in Massachusetts hated it. *Courtesy of California Department of Health Services.*

Unlimited (discussed in more detail in Chapter Ten). What it means is that with qualitative research, a predictable result is not always possible.

THE "BEAUTIFUL CHILD SYNDROME"

When it comes to risky behavior like use of drugs or tobacco, if showing teens how they are being manipulated by others is *not* a surefire deterrent, what about dramatizing the health risks? If it's done skillfully, this *can* be effective. And qualitative research can help sharpen that approach. It can certainly tell you when you've crossed the line. But there's an interesting youth syndrome that should be kept in mind when pursuing this avenue. When I was doing research many years ago for the National Institute of Mental Health anti-drug campaign, a psychiatrist at Yale University described a youth attitude he called the "Beautiful Child Syndrome." Middle-class parents, he said, are encouraging children to believe in themselves so much that we seem to be creating generations of "beautiful children," who consider themselves immune to the dangers of adolescence. "*Other* kids may get hooked on tobacco or drugs," says the beautiful child, "not me!" And this attitude prevails today, as revealed in focus group after focus group.

The threat of tobacco-caused *death* was revealed in research in Massachusetts to be such a remote idea to any but the most fearful child that it had very little impact. Some kids in a focus group I attended even said that since they fully expected cancer to be cured by the time they were thirty, the cancer risks of smoking were far outweighed by how cool they think the act of smoking is today. Ironically, every time there's hopeful news on the cancer cure front, more kids are lulled into that position!

However, as we will see in Chapter Ten, when confronted in ads by the *physical disfigurement* smoking causes young and beautiful people, they could be rattled, and possibly reached.

REACHING THE KIDS

As arguably the most difficult to reach target for any cause advertising, kids are also the most difficult group from which to get trustable information. In most instances, you are going to turn the pursuit of qualitative research over to experienced researchers. But how they do what they do may be worth a few paragraphs here.

Just how do you get kids to tell the truth in a focus group? Sid Furst, a veteran researcher and moderator (who used to have the neatest research facility in New York City, nestled up under the steep eaves of the attic of the Plaza Hotel), for years did all the youth research for Sony and Columbia Records. He told me he knows a few techniques for getting useful information from kids, but warns, as do most researchers, that this is a tricky area.

"You have to really work the group," he says. "Don't be a *moderator*. Invent a situation and retire. Listen, but let them explore the dichotomies. The direct, or cognitive, approach doesn't work. They don't want to be fooled. They're very suspicious of your role. A direct, institutional approach is wrong. Sometimes a totally negative approach is best.

"You *can* get teens to talk like crazy, and share their personal experiences, if you can disarm their paranoia. Many of them believe that what the adult world tells them is not true. The institutional norms are not their norms, and to them, they may not represent the truth. Adults tend to forget the intensity of teens when they're into a subject. Their neurology is different."

Sid also says there's no reason to look for very young facilitators because once they sit in that chair, they're part of the establishment. The best moderator is one of any age who can virtually disappear and let the group do the work.

THE CHAT ROOM AS FOCUS GROUP

Anyone who wants to know what kids are thinking and how they express it should check out some of the chat rooms on the Web. On-line research is definitely the next big trend, and a number of companies are pushing out into that exciting frontier. True anonymity is a plus, especially with kids. Because of this, confirmation of demographics becomes a crucial issue. The mechanisms to reward the respondents, however, with premiums such as CDs, or "Internet bucks" redeemable for merchandise, are already in place.

Home telephone polls are far less reliable than in-school questionnaires, and the results are always questionable. There is the unconscious fear that a parent may be listening in. The parental influence in the home seems to be felt even when parents are physically absent. Surprisingly, school is neutral territory, and the answers given there tend to be more truthful. Whether this same rule applies to on-line research remains to be seen, although my hunch is that the Internet carries with it a perceived cloak of anonymity. The bottom line to all this is that teen research can be, like teen advertising, very tricky. And misapplication of the results can easily lead you down the wrong path. Once again, you must ask the right questions.

THE MONGOOSE AND THE RATS

There is, in research circles, a classic tale of misapplied research. The Hawaiian Islands concluded that importing the Indian mongoose was the perfect solution to the infestation of rats, which had immigrated on visiting ships and multiplied to the point of threatening the island's sugar crop.

Research consisted of putting a mongoose, famous for killing the dangerous cobra, in a cage with rats and observing that, sure enough, it efficiently killed and ate the rodents.

The surprise came when the snarling little creatures were released on the big island of Hawaii, and the rat problem persisted. Despite all the positive research, one fact had been overlooked. The mongoose hunts by day, while the rat is nocturnal. So the predators were asleep when the rats were out gnawing on the sugarcane, and then woke up hungry and began to hunt and eat—not the safely sleeping rats, but lots of island chickens and endangered birds.

Intelligently conducted research with positive indications had produced disastrous results because one important question had not been asked. Even extensive, well-structured research can sometimes deliver the wrong results when, despite intelligent and sincere efforts, a key question is omitted.

Because the typical cause target is so complex, your research team must closely examine the deeply rooted psychology of each of them, and couch some questions that might never find their way into a standard product or service focus group. You must find for these people, who may be denying or unaware that they have a problem, the questions that will elicit their equivalent of the rat's nocturnal habits.

Also, try to couch some questions that strike at the tone and style issue. A discussion of the effects of heroin might have uncovered the disconnect in the Partnership for a Drug-Free America's "Frying Pan" spot. (See figure 9.8.)

RESEARCHING THE VOTER

Two campaigns that were developed in support of voter initiatives that are not strictly cause efforts (although one led to a well-funded cause campaign) are included as case studies here because they so precisely depended on research. More and more, politicians are depending upon qualitative research in developing not only their election advertising but almost every word they utter. And voter initiatives live or die by it. This has led to the development of some innovative techniques, which certainly have some application to cause efforts.

Shortly after I left Saatchi & Saatchi and started consulting, I was put in touch with a very persuasive New York businessman who was searching for a media consultant for an organization he had helped to found, U.S. Term Limits.

Thanks to some very successful voter signature drives, some form of term limitation question was on the ballot in fourteen states in 1992. Some of these initiatives, such as the one in California, sought to limit the terms of state legislators, some sought to limit the terms of U.S. representatives and senators from their states, and some sought to limit terms of all elected officials.

The thrust of the effort was to oppose the concept of the career politician, one who returns to the legislature, term after term, growing fatter, lazier, and more corrupt (all apparently proved by extensive evidence gathered by U.S. Term Limits).

The term limits movement had been nourished by growing cynicism on the part of the public about those in political power, and a realization that campaign-funding practices (the obvious root of much of the corruption observed) would never be reformed by long-term incumbents feeding off the benefits of that funding.

This was the type of campaign normally handled by a political media specialist, but the businessman who came to me thought it might be better served by an advertising generalist with some experience in cause campaigns. This was a political issue, clearly, but it was also a cause. And it was possible to utilize many of the cause advertising appeals to market this idea to voters.

During the same election year I noted with interest that in Massachusetts an initiative was being put forward to fund an anti-smoking effort through a voter-mandated 25-cents-a-pack tax on cigarettes. The prime mover behind the effort was an old friend, Dr. Blake Cady, at that time president of the Massachusetts division of the American Cancer Society. So even though I did not actively participate in that effort (one initiative was plenty), I watched it with great interest. Passage of the cigarette tax initiative led to the Massachusetts Tobacco Control Program for which I subsequently consulted.

Increasingly, initiatives are the source of funding for cause campaigns. Voter initiatives seem to be proliferating. But this is a trend decried by some political analysts.

In *Paradise Lost*, his widely praised book on the impact of voter initiatives in California, Peter Schrag characterizes California's latter-day populism as a parody of the system of checks and balances written into the U.S. Constitution, a mechanical device that's supposed to spare the individual the bother of any sort of political engagement.

Peter, who also happens to have been my college roommate, wrote what was probably the most biting criticism of the term limits movement as an editorial for the *Sacramento Bee*, where he served as editorial editor for many years. I took some pleasure in sending him "pro limits" material as well as spokespersons for his editorial board meetings, but neither of us convinced the other to change our positions.

THE TERM LIMITS CAMPAIGN

Effective initiative campaigns and cause marketing efforts have a number of things in common. Their appeals must be such that they tap a strong reservoir of emotion in the voter, and these emotional "hot buttons" are best determined by some very sophisticated research.

To design research for U.S. Term Limits, I called on Maria Falconetti, a fellow soldier from the Saatchi & Saatchi team that handled the Tylenol crisis. Maria is now president of the innovative research firm The Sherman Group Worldwide Inc., practitioners of a proprietary technique called the BUY© Test, a creative variation on the tried-and-true research technique of concept sorting. For U.S. Term Limits, Sherman used an adaptation of the BUY© Test called the CHOICE© Test.

In my preliminary meetings with the U.S. Term Limits committee I realized that nearly everyone had a different favorite reason why limitation was a good idea, and when these were compiled, we wound up with a list of about thirty different benefit statements, i.e., reasons to vote for term limits.

We boiled these down to sixteen, and they were printed on separate pieces of paper. These were then placed in front of individuals who had agreed, for a small stipend, to interrupt their shopping and sit with interviewers in cubicles in malls in four geographically disparate initiative states.

First, participants were read a statement that persuasively expressed the arguments *for* and *against* term limits. The statement ended with a strong "anti" message that might persuade them that term limits were a bad idea. Then, we tried to find the argument that would bring them back into our camp.

The statement was as follows (with blanks filled in with the ballot numbers of the initiative in the state in which the research was conducted):

ARGUMENT STATEMENT

On your ballot in the November election will be an initiative called Proposition _____. If passed, it will limit your U.S. senators to two terms, or twelve years, and your U.S. representatives to _____ terms, or _____ years in Congress. It will also limit the terms that your state legislators can serve to _____ terms, or _____ years.

People who favor this initiative point out that the president and most governors are already limited. However, your U.S. senators, U.S. representatives, and state legislators are not. And they have many things to help them make a lifelong career out of their office: huge staffs, free mail, and easy access to special interest money, to help them fend off any serious challenge.

Supporters believe that this limit initiative will create a new breed of senators, congressmen, and legislators from all walks of life, who will serve their voters for a limited time, and then return home to live under the laws they made, just as the framers of the Constitution intended.

Opponents of the initiative say that it will cause the U.S. senators and congressmen from your state to lose clout, that they will no longer be able to stay in office and achieve seniority, and that federal projects and funding will be funneled to other states that do not have similarly limited legislators. They point out that if you don't like the job incumbents are doing, you can just vote them out, and that Proposition _____ removes experienced members of Congress without a vote of the people, whether they are doing a good job or not.

Respondents were then asked a series of questions and instructed to sort a group of statements in order of their importance in supporting or opposing each question. While the actual questions asked are proprietary to the Sherman Group, they range from merely eliciting an expressed interest, to learning something new, to actual advocacy. This way, the most persuasive statement can be statistically isolated, and in the case of term limits we had two clear winners.

Some statements that seemed persuasive to U.S. Term Limits staffers but were discarded based on the research were:

- "Term Limits will return our government to what our Founding Fathers intended: representatives and senators as citizen legislators who serve a brief term and then return to private life."
- "Term Limits will mean that your representatives represent you, rather than the entrenched bureaucracy."
- "Term-limited representatives and senators will move quickly to change the self-serving seniority system in Washington, D.C. So, with term limits, committee members will be appointed on merit, not just length of service."
- "Term Limits will guarantee that your representatives and senators give their full attention to the issues you care about, instead of running for reelection the day they take office."

There were two winning statements that were fairly close to each other statistically:

- "Term limits will help cut out corruption in government. Statistics prove that the longer legislators are in office, the more they become involved in unethical activities like check bouncing, savings and loan payoffs, and post office abuses."

- "Term limits will give you a wider choice of candidates. It will open the doors of government to everyone who wants to run for office, including women and other minorities who have been excluded."

Both of these "winners" may seem almost absurdly obvious in hindsight. They were clearly among the first things we discussed pre-research. But it was interesting how many U.S. Term Limits staffers favored the more philosophical arguments such as the "Founding Fathers" rationale.

Maria Falconetti wisely pointed out that the first of the winning concepts had no "end-end" benefit, so in effect it still didn't answer the question, "What's in it for me?" Factual or historical statements, she added, were always less motivating. Accountability to constituency and an end to corruption seemed to be on everyone's mind, so it was decided to add an "accountability" component.

We ultimately decided to go with two different strategies. The "corruption" strategy ran in most states, and the "wider choice" strategy was executed for specialized buys in minority areas and women's media.

The "corruption" strategy was also the least polarizing. It took an emotional anti-corruption position (an end benefit) and we added an end-end benefit (this is how to get the legislator to pay attention to the issues you care about). We explored a number of theme lines written to this strategy, and selected the one that played, we believed, to voter frustration over powerlessness to influence government. It was emotionally direct, and in consideration of our target, down-to-earth: "It's something you can do!" A second "empowerment" strategy ran in limited markets.

The TV spot was customized by tagging with state-specific initiative numbers and trafficked to advocacy groups in each of the initiative states, who would then buy and place the media. The radio spot, written to the same strategy, utilized a "talk radio" format and included specific in-state "caller towns" for a true local feel. The advertising was well-received, and the initiative passed in each of the fourteen states in which it was proposed.

The limitation on national congressional and senate seats was declared unconstitutional by the Supreme Court a few years later, but the limitation on many state legislatures stuck and succeeded in dismantling many in-state dynasties, most notably in California.

CONGRESSMAN VO: I solemnly swear to support . . .

ANNCR VO: There is no limit to the number of terms a congressman can serve. So most just keep getting elected . . . *(Sfx: Tape rewinds)*

and re-elected . . . term after term. *(Sfx: Tape rewinds)*

The fact is the more they serve the more they represent special interests. The more they represent themselves.

(Sfx: Money bag drops into hand)

Last year, congress voted itself a 40 percent pay raise. This year you can stop all that

by voting yes on Prop 164.

Vote for term limits. It's something you can do.

FIGURE 7.3 *U.S. Term Limits.* "Pay Raise" was a voter-initiative commercial customized with different tags for fourteen different states. The initiative won in all fourteen. *Courtesy of U.S. Term Limits.*

THE MASSACHUSETTS TOBACCO INITIATIVE

A similar emotional voter disposition was detected by political strategist John Marttila and his partner Tom Kiley in Massachusetts when they did planning research on behalf of the proposed Massachusetts Tobacco Control Program, which was to be funded by an additional 25-cents-a-pack tax on cigarettes.

Seventy-five percent of the citizens of Massachusetts were non-smokers, and they expressed strong dislike of the tobacco industry, seen as masters of greed and deception. If this could be tapped into, the researchers figured the initiative was winnable, but they also realized the tobacco lobby was ready to pour an obscene amount of money into the state to block its passage (as it turned out, about $7 million!). Far from being naïve, the tobacco operatives determined that if it was positioned right, *they* might tap into the same distrust of government that motivated the term limits proponents.

The tobacco group hired an affable and popular former state senator named Jack Flood to be its spokesman. Flood appeared in some clever and quite cynical commercials pointing out the unique plank in the state constitution which states that any tax money, even when it's earmarked by the voters (as this was, for anti-smoking education) must be still voted on every year by the legislature. "And you know what your legislators will do with that tax money once they get their hands on it!" was the essential message of this jolly former member of that untrustworthy group.

The cynicism behind the campaign was confirmed when, a year after the tax was approved, the tobacco industry sent ten lobbyists to the state capitol to urge legislators to divert that money to a list of other "worthy causes" (i.e., anything but tobacco control), assuring that what they predicted in their ads would actually come true!

To Respond or Not to Respond

There were, according to Tom Kiley, many internal arguments about whether or not to answer the claim in the tobacco company ads. This was a typical debate, since all political advertising seems to be getting more and more negative. To respond or not to respond to attack ads becomes a crucial strategic decision during every campaign.

Political experts seem to agree on at least two principles:

1. If you're the big guy, and the unknown candidate (or cause) is attacking you, ignore it. It's hard to do, particularly if his barrages are scurrilous. But you only make the invisible guy important by answering.
2. Don't get into an argument you can't win.

In the opinion of Marttila and Kiley, trying to oppose the "you know what those sneaky legislators will do with your money" argument represented an unwinnable task, especially in light of the anti-government cynicism that showed up in all research. And for the cigarette tax proponents to reference that issue, even in rebuttal, helped the other side. Their research even suggested that the arguments weren't very persuasive to voters, as long as they were left unchallenged.

Kiley and his opinion researchers advised that the excise tax on cigarettes should be positioned not as the latest scheme of an overly intrusive state government, but as a practical, grass-roots effort, in concert with some very trustable health advocates, to protect the well-being of Massachusetts citizens.

It was suggested that the tobacco industry should be isolated as the sole opponent, identified as the group paying a "front" of spokespersons for "individual freedom" to speak out against the initiative. When a "Who do you trust?" choice was framed in the research between the claims of the American Cancer Society and those of the tobacco industry, the margin was 85 percent to 9 percent in favor of ACS.

Throughout the research process, Kiley insisted that the interviewers hammer the initiative. They used the arguments that had already been espoused by the opposition, such as "even if the funds are earmarked by the voters for anti-smoking education and programs, the legislature will use the revenue however it wants," and "if the increased tax is passed, people will just drive to other states with lower taxes, thus taking away business from Massachusetts." These arguments were put forth as if the interviewer were tobacco's advocate. But none of the arguments by themselves were seen to have a powerful effect on voting intentions.

Voter research also helped in writing the actual initiative language. It was discovered that, while there was little difference in support for measures that would mandate a tax increase of 15 to 25 cents, support sharply dropped off for a tax above 25 cents. Also considered a repressive measure by respondents was an "ad valorem" proposal to keep the state tax at one-third the price per pack, so that if cigarette prices were to go up, the state tax would go up, too. This idea was abandoned in drafting the initiative, and the tax proposal was kept at a flat 25 cents a pack.

Boiling It Down to a Simple Idea

The ultimate campaign was classically simple. The single idea of the strategy was: on the issue of protecting our kids from cigarettes, who do you trust?

The spot, written and produced by Marblehead Massachusetts political advertising specialist Ken Swope in conjunction with Marttila and Kiley, was quite simple. It showed a sea of actual cigarette packs, laid out on an eerily lighted "sweep." "Here's who's spending millions of dollars in Massachusetts to defeat Question 1 on election day," said the announcer. The commercial talked about the success of the similar California proposition that deterred kids from starting to smoke. It then showed the pristine logo of the American Cancer Society. "Here's who's sponsoring Question 1. . . . So, who are you going to vote for? It's about saving lives." Purposely omitted from a sponsoring list were some militant anti-smoking groups such as GASP (the Group Against Smoking Pollution) and the insurance industry, whose support for the initiative would be seen as motivated by business self-interest. All were ardent supporters of the proposition, but research showed they were viewed negatively by the public.

Incidentally, the photographing of actual product logos (i.e., actual store-bought packs) without permission, particularly in an ad trashing the manufacturer would under most circumstances be a strong no-no. When asked about that, Tom Kiley just smiled and said that if they'd come after him, he would have said simply "ok, we'll take it off after the election." Also, he had a strong hunch that the tobacco lobby did not wish to engage in a litigious brawl with the "good guy" (the ACS), which would most certainly result in additional airings of the spot on newscasts.

The pro-initiative forces had only about $250,000 to spend, and they elected to wait and buy a blitz of about seven hundred gross rating points for the ten days just preceding the election.

ANNCR VO: Here's who's spending

millions of dollars in Massachusetts

to defeat Question 1 on election day. Here's why:

When California voted

for a 25¢ increase in the cigarette tax, people stopped smoking at twice the national average. And a lot of kids never started.

Here's who's sponsoring Question 1. The American Cancer Society.

So, who are you going to vote for?

Question 1. It's about saving lives.

FIGURE 7.4 *The Massachusetts Coalition for a Healthy Future.* "Packs" was a voter-initiative spot supporting a proposition to fund the Massachusetts Tobacco Control Program. It ran for only one week at 4 percent of the weight of opposition advertising by the tobacco lobby. The proposition passed. *Courtesy of the Vote Yes on Question One Committee.*

The initiative passed, and the Massachusetts Tobacco Control Program was up and running. With the exception of that annual review by the legislature, it has never looked back.

In these two quite different initiatives, term limits and tobacco control, smartly designed research revealed the psychological underpinnings of the target consumers, and the strategy and tone of the advertising played directly to them.

QUANTITATIVE RESEARCH

In most cases, as the creator of a cause campaign, you will find yourself in the position of having to justify your expenditures to a legislative body or a board of directors. Unfortunately, unlike a product campaign, you usually don't have anything as precise as monthly sales figures with which to monitor your effectiveness. And the achievement of your probable goal of *changing attitudes* is much harder to measure accurately. Attitude changes in a cause target should lead to constructive action by that target. That is the goal of most cause efforts. Verifying those attitude changes and actions is the third point at which research can play a significant role in cause marketing.

The Massachusetts Tobacco Control campaign constantly pursued proof they had achieved their goals. If they couldn't produce evaluative evidence, they knew their funding could be reduced or cut off, which was, as they were to learn, the strategic goal of an aggressive tobacco-industry lobbying effort.

They did have figures showing a reduction in cigarette-tax revenue, a drop of 35 percent. But that admirable success was offset by their less-than-thrilling impact on reported youth smoking. They *could* claim that the state's teen smoking numbers were slightly down (minus 10 percent among eighth graders), while the national trend among teens was significantly up (35 percent).

And they did seem to be reaching *preteens* with their message. Teen smokers, as we have noted, are not generally receptive targets for establishment-produced "anti" advertising of any sort (smoking, drugs, gambling). But if the campaign had been as effective as they surmised in "inoculating" the very young, maybe a respectable percentage would resist the peer pressure and anti-adult attitudes that kick in about age twelve along with all those raging hormones. Because of this, they predicted much better teen numbers in the years to come.

In fact, in July of 1999, the Center for Survey Research found an in-state decline in smoking of 24.4 percent among fourteen- to seventeen-year-olds. Not what they had hoped for but probably enough to hold their own against the special interests. And their opposition was formidable. A fascinating document came to light during Minnesota's lawsuit against the cigarette manufacturers, as reported in the *Boston Globe*. The Tobacco Institute memo, dated December 3, 1992, stated "the list of potential projects to which the funds might be dedicated is almost limitless in a state as financially strapped as Massachusetts . . . so are the potential groups of allies. By targeting the initiative monies to appropriate channels . . . we can expect to pick up support of groups such as the state Board of Education, teachers unions, school nurses . . . and perhaps the League of Women Voters. We are leaving no stone unturned." In other words, they would pressure legislators to do exactly what they predicted they would do in their cynical anti-initiative campaign—divert the money to *any* other cause but tobacco control!

TRACKING THE TARGET

The Massachusetts Tobacco Control Program also did a large tracking study. To be valid, a tracking study must start right away, preferably before any of your advertising is aired so as to establish a benchmark. Then you test unaided awareness of your ads. In its most simplistic form, the study asks, "What ads have you seen recently?"

After a couple of years, the Massachusetts campaign was remembered, and, unaided, mentioned at levels right up there with Pepsi and Nike. So they were visible and they were recalled. But how persuasive, or more important how *effective*, were they?

For most cause campaigns, the most important measurement is a change of attitude. Most cause advertisers with limited budgets will be restricted to qualitative research to measure effectiveness. Data collected in this environment may be trustable or, depending upon the facilitator, it can lead to some incorrect conclusions. Two focus groups will deliver the opinions of about thirty people. These opinions can hardly represent the attitudes of thousands within your target group accurately.

If you have a large budget, most specialists will tell you that quantitative research is the only way to go. Jacqueline Silver, for several years a research consultant to the Partnership for a Drug-Free America, told me that when it comes to selling copy to government officials who oversee and will ultimately fund their efforts, producing quantitative research is essential. "The government is used to going randomly door-to-door to get data," she says. "They don't trust data from recruited groups or mall interviews."

Jackie and her team put together a program she describes as "state of the art," that has become, in her view, the last word in drug research. They did a national study in public and parochial schools that produced a huge projectable probability sample, using six to seven thousand self-administered questionnaires (to avoid bias and ensure anonymity). Collecting this data was, they felt, essential to achieve funding, and more important, to ensure that media outlets would take them seriously since all media was donated in the early days of the Partnership. In addition to getting data from schools, they also tracked an adult "parent" sample.

She and her researchers developed some quite innovative techniques, particularly when it came to young kids. The large sample helped them predict and track both attitude change and behavior. Individual drugs were separated out, and attitudinal data was collected on each. This data was then supplied to Professor Lloyd Johnson of the University of Michigan, who compared it with trends he had noted in data he had been collecting since 1979, and created a projectable sample. A key measurement for the Partnership was risk perception for individual drugs by the kids in various age groups. The trends were moving down and seemed directly tied to the media effort.

Questionnaires were simple, usually multiple-choice in format, with a "paste the sticker" option for the youngest groups. Examples of these questionnaires are found in Appendix C and Appendix D.

Jackie advises that for any large government-funded effort, you *must* have evaluative research, and it must be endorsed by recognized experts. This is important to the funding providers and to the media, particularly in terms of getting PSA allocations. As these slots are becoming increasingly scarce, there has to be some evidence presented to the media outlet that the space is not being wasted, that there are tangible results.

While conducting their initial research, Jackie and her staff were told to stay away from the inner city (to avoid the stereotype that drugs were only a minority problem) and address the increasing drug use in middle America. Later, as drug use in the country at large declined, they were instructed to probe inner-city schools, which they did, with some surprising results we'll discuss in Chapter Nine.

Unfortunately, most cause groups do not have the financial resources for such massive studies. Their evaluation must come from a combination of a more detailed version of qualitative groups or one-on-ones, and anecdotal or even statistical measurements of success—increase in volume of recyclables, for example, or decrease in incidents of forest fires, decrease in traffic deaths from not wearing safety belts, even website or hotline "hits," or private contributions to cause groups.

SPECIAL POPULATIONS

When it comes to special populations, such as minority groups within your community, standard qualitative research may not be enough. You would be strongly advised to subcontract to a minority consultant for that portion of your effort.

For the Massachusetts Tobacco Control campaign, the advertising agency hired an energetic African American–owned company called Media Investment Group. I had naïvely assumed MIG's staffers would merely translate our basic anti-smoking message into language that was appropriate to the state's African American population, cast good role models, and warn us off of any unintended breach of political correctness. The strategy given to them was the same as one of the strategies for the general population. It was designed to urge parents to protect their kids from the known dangers of smoking. In fact, we foolishly assumed that further strategy research was not required.

The first copy presentation was disappointing. In fact, several of the executions appeared to be off strategy. Sitting in the meeting, something occurred to me. They were *fighting* the strategy. And the reasons were related to the community they were targeting: the Black neighborhoods of Massachusetts, the community we had hired them to reach.

Put succinctly, the strategy had assumed that parents placed smoking high on the list of dangers to their children. They just needed to be reminded of the dangers, and they would act.

After we convinced MIG it was okay in this instance to change the strategy, that it was in fact why they were onboard, they pointed out that,

with all the other dangers on the streets of the inner city, smoking was
hardly even on the radar screen. It was not even considered a serious threat.
So steps had to be taken to warn and convince parents of the reality of
smoking's impact on the health of their children before the desired action
could be promoted. With the strategy adjusted to their keen understanding of the market, new copy was written and approved quite quickly.

Personal Knowledge

Ajibola Osinubi, the CEO of MIG, feels passionately that you must
have an intimate personal knowledge of the minority community in
order to make a meaningful impact. Otherwise, he says, "your ads will
be ineffective, and you'll hear complaints from the people that you don't
know what you're doing. They'll say the work was done by outsiders, and
somebody put a Black face on it!"

This also applies to research. Ajibola tries to stay away from
recruited samples. His people do random mall intercepts, controlled by
a few screening questions. Storyboards for all his spots are tested before
production. And here again, he insists on interviewers from the community. "With the African American community, they know if you're
from New York or New Jersey, not from here. They may just tell them
what they think they want to hear. Not the truth. The result will come
back skewed."

Two other factors came up strongly in MIG's research into its community and knowledge of the neighborhoods we were attempting to
reach: the sense of community in the inner city, and the resentment of
years of exploitation. Based on this, MIG developed a very impactful
spot with the theme line: "There are strangers coming into your neighborhood . . . watch your back!" The "strangers" mentioned are actually
billboards and point-of-purchase displays showing happy, successful
African Americans smoking.

Incidentally, the creative director for much of that inner-city
tobacco industry advertising was a talented art director named Norman
Black who had worked on my team at Grey for the NIMH anti-drug
campaign. He left for a career-building spot with the tobacco agency.
Recently he did some soul-searching and volunteered to do his own mea
culpa spot in the Massachusetts "Truth" campaign, in which he admits
targeting the inner city for his menthol tobacco products, and in which

he says a profound "I'm sorry I had anything to do with it." It's a pretty effective slap at the industry because Norman speaks with authority. He's been there and done that, creating strategies the industry has always pretended never existed.

The Massachusetts Tobacco Control team also hired a local Hispanic agency to prepare a spot based on the Latino population's sense of the importance of family. It showed what appeared to be a family reunion, but with an air of sadness. We realize at the end that it is actually a gathering for the burial of a favorite uncle who died of lung cancer. "Cigarettes—they bring your family together" is the ironic tag line.

Another Boston Latino consultant, Juan Mandlebaum of Geovison, produced an excellent spot that made use of a Hispanic iconic phrase:

Day Dream

VO: When I was little, my parents taught me the safety rules:

never talk to strangers; stop, look, and listen. If my parents knew then what I know now there'd be another rule: cigarette

companies are out to get you. Watch your back! They're strangers who come into our neighborhoods with smiles

and promises, spending millions to get us to start smoking. Let's warn our children: this stranger is a killer.

FIGURE 7.5 *The Massachusetts Tobacco Control Program.* "Day Dream," written and produced by the African American agency MIG, exposed minority targeting by the tobacco industry. *Courtesy of the Massachusetts Department of Public Health.*

"Por Favor, No Fume" ("No smoking, please"). The theme line for his spot about the dangers of second-hand smoke to your family became "Por Amor, No Fume" ("For love—of your family—don't smoke").

Geographic Differences

So if you need to reach special populations and your budget can stand it, it makes a lot of sense to hire minority advisers. And they should preferably be from your own geographic area. There is no monolithic minority group across this country.

Many years ago I learned that the hard way when we designed some anti-drug billboards for the Latino community for the National Institute of Mental Health. We had a striking billboard for Black neighborhoods in which a young Black man was shown shooting up (an image I would never use today). The headline said, "Untogether," pure street talk in those days for a really messed-up person (uses of *together* later moved into mainstream hip jargon).

I gathered some kids from New York's Puerto Rican community and asked them to give me a comparable Spanish phrase that would be seen as a put-down of the addicted heroin user. They agreed on "No es nada!" ("He is nothing.")

We put these boards up across the country. Suddenly the account administrator at NIMH was called on the carpet at the Nixon White House. It seems the administration had received an irate communiqué from a Mexican American cultural group protesting the depiction of drug use with a headline they read as "*It* is nothing!" Furthermore, they complained, it was obviously a Puerto Rican model (it was).

A bad situation was somewhat mitigated by a press event in which officials of the government and the Southern California community tore down the offending billboard. I learned later that the irate letter from the Hispanic group to President Nixon had insisted that he *punish* the parties responsible for this offending campaign!

In some cases, your primary campaign spots and ads can be simply translated into the language of various prominent ethnic groups within your community. In the greater Boston area we have both large Portuguese and Chinese populations, with media serving each. Translations of radio spots and selected print ads were examined by consultants from each community, and were deemed to be appropriate.

But once again, make sure your translators are thinking like advertisers. The most famous translation gaffe in history was reportedly when Chevy introduced the *Nova* in Puerto Rico. It's not to hard to figure why Islanders were not flocking to their dealers to look at the car whose name ("No-va") when spoken in Spanish proclaimed it "doesn't go!"

Talking the Talk

There's another important executional consideration that should be noted here. Dialogue written in street talk, or "Black English," can carry a ring of reality in commercials directed to the Black population, particularly young people. Just as when talking to kids about drugs, I always believed you'd better be up on the latest street terms. Otherwise you

Family Reunion

| VO: We always wanted | to hold a family reunion | I never thought there were so many. |
| It's so sad we got together for this reason. | It's so sad he didn't quit smoking. | Cigarettes—they bring your family together. |

FIGURE 7.6 *The Massachusetts Tobacco Control Program.* "Family Reunion," produced for the Latino media in Spanish as well as English, tapped in to the importance of family in Hispanic communities. *Courtesy of the Massachusetts Department of Public Health.*

may be seen as an unknowledgeable establishment "suit," and you may adversely affect your communication. Another sound reason to have a good minority consultant on board.

But I was surprised when some minority members of the Department of Public Health strongly objected to what had seemed to me to be a very entertaining and quite hip radio spot, produced by MIG, featuring a Black stand-up comic "talking the talk" at a comedy club. It was their judgment that the portrayal of African Americans in a commercial sponsored by a state agency should be positive and aspirational, rather than "trash-talking," even if it was an accurate mirror of the way members of the target community speak to each other.

Our solution in Massachusetts was to walk back the language a bit. We examined the script literally word-by-word, leaving in some expressions that were deemed to be authentic but not offensive. The final tape was extensively researched, and universally well received within the community.

Just as we discussed the extreme difficulty of authentically talking to the addicted target in Chapter Three, "talking the talk" to minorities and avoiding missteps may be one of the toughest assignments you ever undertake. If you make some cultural errors, you will do your cause more damage in minority communities than if you had chosen not to target them at all. Remember, first do no harm.

The by-product of a lot of years of exploitation in these communities is a deeply held suspicion of the establishment. As worthwhile as your cause and motives may be, make one mistake and you will not only be ignored, you could experience strong opposition. So hire the best *local* minority consultants you can find, let them do the research with appropriate "from the neighborhood" recruiters and moderators, and take the time to do it all right.

Here again, qualitative research can help you avoid mistakes, and if you can afford it, quantitative attitude measurements, like those done by the Partnership for a Drug-Free America, can be invaluable aids in achieving continued funding and free media placement.

8

MEDIA

Spending Smart to Reach the People

You've designed an impactful campaign, and you're very pleased with the way it's turned out. Post-production qualitative research has confirmed that it resonates strongly with your target. Now comes the $64,000 question. How do you reach the people? This is a crucial juncture for all cause efforts. In fact, it's a subject that should have first come up very early in your planning stage.

The most emotional and persuasive cause campaign in advertising history will fail if it cannot be placed, at reasonable weights, in front of its target audience. There are many routes to achieving this objective. You may be fortunate enough to get placement or endorsement by the Advertising Council. You may be able to leverage a modest budget into placement by your local or regional Broadcaster's Association as an NCSA (non-commercial sustaining announcement). You may have a very persuasive media liaison person in your organization who will get extensive free PSA placement. Or you may decide you have to use paid media to effectively and precisely target your audience. This will require securing a substantial budget.

We will discuss all these traditional ways to get your cause message out in the next few pages. We will also discuss some less conventional ways to reach your target. "Earned media" is what political specialists call PR coverage (as opposed to "paid media"). Since this is a text on advertising, I will leave the specifics of mounting an effective earned-media cause campaign to others, although I will touch on a few of the principles to keep in mind so that *all* your marketing efforts seem to speak with the same voice. I will also touch briefly on some of the new media, principally the World Wide Web, and spend a paragraph or two on cooperative ventures with community-spirited corporations (usually called "cause-related" media), which can help expand your reach without shriveling your budget. But first, let's get into the technical side of conventional media planning.

I was surprised to learn early in my career that media is not an exact science. When I first started in advertising, the media group was usually on a separate floor and trotted out to give their pitch during new business presentations. Usually they relied on lots of charts and graphs and databases full of numbers, and I ignorantly put them all in the same category as accountants—number crunchers with pocket protectors.

The truth of the matter is that good media buyers are a lot looser than that. They are the closest thing to modern-day horse traders that we have in advertising. This flows from a simple fact: every magazine, every network, every local commercial radio station or TV channel lives or dies by the amount of pages or on-air minutes they fill with ads. If a publication issue approaches press time and the ad page count is down, or the week's broadcast schedule has some holes in it, their salesmen are always ready to deal. And while this might seem, on the surface, to have little to do with cause marketing, it actually has a lot to do with it.

It used to be that every broadcast media outlet was required to allocate a percentage of its airtime to public service ads, to be considered favorably for license renewal. This requirement was abandoned in 1996. While most broadcast and media trade organizations continue to devote a percentage of airtime to PSAs, that amount is small and dwindling.

Alex Kroll, a former chairman of Young and Rubicam and chairman emeritus of the Advertising Council, estimated in a 1998 speech that the average time devoted to PSAs in prime time on each network in 1997 was five seconds a night! The local media situation was somewhat better, but not a lot. Although the council's Coalition for America's Children campaign received an estimated $3 million of free airtime in eight months in 1997–98, 75 percent of that was between the hours of eleven P.M. and six A.M.!

The Advertising Council does an excellent job of persuading the media to run its campaigns, and estimates it still receives more than a billion dollars in donated time and space a year. But this is still largely television in the wee hours, billboards on side streets, or ads in the back of magazines. The real difference between getting stuck next to the infomercial at three A.M. and running in prime time is having a good media horse trader in your camp. Don't think your spot will be aired just because you send it out in an attractive package to every station in town.

Steve Dnistrian, public affairs director of the Partnership for a Drug-Free America, gave me another set of disheartening statistics. Due to broadcast deregulation, the national store of PSA availabilities dropped precipitously in the early '90s. Where they had once been able to secure over $300 million in annual donated time thanks to the reputation and persuasive powers of Partnership chairman James Burke, this figure was suddenly reduced by almost two-thirds. Significantly, this reduction in anti-drug messages coincided with a softening of anti-drug sentiment and the first rise in drug use in ten years. This made it necessary for the Partnership to forge yet another partnership with the federal government in order to be eligible for government monies for paid placements.

So if you have some money to spend on a paid schedule, so much the better. Any number of things can also enhance your media position. These include making the buy in advance, committing all your money to one station in return for a specified number of free "bonus weight" spots, or buying a brief but concentrated schedule for a bargain rate in a normally fallow media period such as the weeks after Christmas (when retail stores have depleted their advertising budgets).

Richard Weinstein, a media executive at Arnold Advertising, tells me that the ability to bargain is increased by the number of media outlets in the city where you're buying. The more outlets you have, the more competition. Richard also points out that, although an early buy can get a good rate, if you have a feeling the market may get soft about the time you want to run your campaign, it might be smart to wait. And some media outlets, principally newspapers, have a public service or nonprofit rate; appropriate tax proof may be all you need to get the favorable price.

MEDIA-SPEAK

But before I go any further, let me define some of those puzzling media terms. (I am indebted to Ken Roman and Jane Maas's excellent text, *How to Advertise*, for helping me translate some of this exotic vernacular.)

Just like your creative strategy, the media strategy must begin with the target. Demographics are crucial to this analysis. A good media analyst knows fairly predictably what times, for example, the thirty-five- to fifty-year-old, married, middle-income, high-school-educated male sits in front of his TV set and what he will be most likely to watch. This is based on data collected mainly by four large media research firms, Nielson for TV, Arbitron for radio, Simmons for magazines, and Scarborough for local newspapers.

Having defined your target, your next step is to estimate how many times he or she will see your message. CPM, or cost per thousand, is the first thing your media buyer will determine. It is a gauge of the relative efficiency of a certain placement. But it is only a starting point. It is the cost of *potentially* reaching a thousand homes. If you paid $500 for the spot and it reaches half a million homes, your CPM is $1 ($500 divided by 500). But you could be reaching a thousand dogs and cats, lying in front of the glowing but unattended TV. You must always ask cost per thousand *what* because cost per thousand only measures cost, not effectiveness.

Next, you must narrow the definitions to start to look for your target. "Reach" is the number of homes that have the opportunity to be exposed to your message at least once. It is sometimes expressed as a "cume," or unduplicated audience. A plan that gets to eight out of ten homes has a reach of 80.

"Frequency" is the number of potential exposures your target will have to the message. It's usually expressed as an average (heavy viewers will see it more often, light viewers less), and reach and frequency are generally measured over a defined period of time (usually four weeks).

The next thing to take into consideration is the "rating" of the program in which your spot will run. If four out of ten homes are tuned to that particular program, it has a 40 rating. "Gross Rating Points" (or "GRPs") are the total of all rating points for a given campaign schedule. It is also a component of reach and frequency. The formula is $R \times F = GRP$. A plan that delivers an 80 reach and a 16 frequency for four weeks achieves a GRP of 320 per week (actually a pretty good number for effectively reaching your target).

Translated into English, what that means is that 80 percent of your target audience has a good chance of seeing your spot four times a week over the course of a month.

I have had some disagreement in the past over GRPs with some experienced practitioners of political advertising for whom 1,000 GRPs in the final few weeks before an election is not unusual. As a TV viewer, that kind of weight usually breaches my annoyance barrier shortly into the schedule.

The resulting sea of political ads every election year is, in my opinion, one of the things that is helping to turn off the electorate and reduce voter participation in elections. Not to mention how much it is driving up the cost of running for office. Severe reform of campaign finance laws, perhaps including providing a limited amount of free media to all legitimate candidates is, I believe, sadly overdue. But that's a subject for another book.

If you have a strong, intrusive spot, 200 GRPs is the minimum viable plan, and 300 to 350 GRPs should be perfectly adequate. One thousand GRPs is likely to bankrupt you and send your target screaming into the night, shouting "Enough!"

By all means, even if you are the administrator of a small campaign, if you are *buying* your airtime or ad space, consult a professional media expert. Every major market has a number of good freelance practitioners, and of course, every medium-to-large agency has an experienced media group on staff. You need their horse-trading ability. You need their clout. You need their personal relationships with the space salespeople at the outlets.

Convincing that media rep of the important public benefits of your cause can often produce some miracles at the end of the trade. Careful dealing can also extend the scope of your campaign with bonus spots. These are additional free placements, usually on a "one for two" or "one for three" ratio, with an extra free spot thrown in for each two or three purchased. But Richard Weinstein warns you should identify—and stay away from—"sweeps" weeks, when TV stations are heavily promoting their shows. And you should also avoid political season, during which stations are required to make space available to candidates at the lowest rate, leaving very little inventory for your media buyer to strike a deal for.

The Partnership for a Drug-Free America, with $195 million now appropriated by Congress for paid placement, is still asking the broadcast media to match this amount dollar for dollar in broadcast and print exposure, so the organization could receive nearly $400 million annually in media space for its messages. However, the shrinking PSA allocation pool will make this hard to achieve.

THE NCSA ROUTE

Recently a nonprofit organization for which I consult signed a deal to contribute approximately $40,000 to the New England Broadcasting

Association. In return for this amount, which went toward the operating expenses of the Association, member stations and cable systems contributed $160,000 in actual placements of the organization's PSA in a category they call the non-commercial sustaining announcement (NCSA.) The stations logged each spot as a donated PSA, while their trade association received a cash infusion toward operating expenses.

The sponsoring organization was given performance vouchers, listing actual on-air placements of the spot, which ran over a period of approximately three months. Here again, however, the client had no say over placement, so precise demographic targeting was not possible. Other broadcasting associations in other markets offer similar deals for NCSAs, including Florida (www.fab.org) and Texas (www.tab.org). Inquiries should be addressed to the individual state broadcasting associations, and a list of linked websites for those groups can be found at www.broadcast.net.

The principal users of the NCSA media route are government agencies. A limited number of charitable organizations may also apply for NCSA status. Obviously the NCSA gets priority handling by a broadcast outlet, because of the financial support to the state or regional broadcast association.

As with many things, going the NCSA route is a trade-off. If you have, say, $50,000 to spend, are you better off *buying* 300 GRPs in a week or four to five days (a modest "blitz"), or should you put yourself in the hands of an association for placement in the time slots its member stations couldn't sell, even if you end up with a greater number of ads running over a longer period of time?

If you want to startle your target, raise a new issue, or have an impact on an upcoming vote or decision, then the "blitz" is probably better. If you are manning a hotline related to an issue or problem that may suddenly occur or be discovered, such as depression or gambling addiction, then you may be better going for the four-for-one deal over a longer time period.

Most of these situations relate to campaigns where there's a designated media budget. But don't discount the emotional leverage of your cause in gaining maximum cooperation regarding bonus spots and placement. If your cause is cancer prevention, for example, and the public service director of a TV station has a close relative suffering from the disease, you may be surprised at the favorable placement your message will receive.

OTHER OPTIONS

If you are preparing a campaign for a cause that has virtually *no* money, there are several routes you can take.

A very effective recruitment campaign for the all-volunteer New York City Auxiliary Police has spots produced in donated facilities, some at cable-access channels, for virtually no money. The energetic and persuasive campaign director, Morty Dubin, a television commercial producer and also an inspector on the volunteer force, simply calls individual radio and TV media outlets and makes a strong personal case for the importance of the effort. Airing of the spots is always followed up with an official department letter of thanks, to be filed with the station at license renewal time. Once again, due to the awareness of the need to expand law enforcement capability within the city, Morty usually gets a sympathetic ear at the stations.

One caution here: if you are submitting a spot for pure PSA airing, be sure it is an entertaining or gripping message. It is a fact of life that no matter how worthy your cause, program directors and traffic managers at broadcast stations do not want anything on their air that will bore or turn away their audience. So try and make your message as zap-proof as you can! And also be sure to submit your commercial, or at least your copy, to the station far enough in advance of the proposed air dates so that it can run through normal clearance procedures. You certainly don't want to have an experience like that of the Friends of Animals described in Chapter Two.

Let's say you have an issue that's national in scope, that cries for network placement and national publication as well as airing on local outlets, but you still have a limited budget. Then you need the Advertising Council.

THE ADVERTISING COUNCIL—THE "MOTHER SHIP" OF CAUSE MARKETING

The Advertising Council was born in 1941 at an urgent meeting called by the Association of National Advertisers (ANA) and the American Association of Advertising Agencies (AAAA). They wanted to explore ways to reverse the growing negative image that business, and particularly the advertising business, had carried with them following the Great Depression.

The keynote speaker was James Webb Young, a creative vice president at J. Walter Thompson. Young asserted that the answer was not
to do advertising to defend advertising, but rather to do advertising in
the public interest, in support of causes that could impact the public
good. Young was certain that applying the powerful tools of persuasive
communication, learned and fine-tuned by advertising agencies during
years of moving products and services, to the curing or easing of society's ills would do more to improve public perception of the business
than anything defensive. Conference attendees overwhelmingly agreed,
and the idea of the Advertising Council was born.

Just three weeks later, Japan bombed Pearl Harbor, and the proposed Advertising Council became the War Advertising Council. In
cooperation with the Office of War Information, it produced hundreds
of advertising units, worth an estimated $13 million a year. The ads dealt
with such crucial wartime concerns as recruiting, war bond sales, con-
servation and recycling, volunteerism, V-Mail usage, home gardening,
security ("loose lips sink ships"), Red Cross blood donation, and so on.

This was an impressive start, and it allowed the Council to sort out
some policy issues right at the outset. To create the ads, it turned to the
professionals at the many AAAA member agencies. In addition to preparing ads to be signed by service branches or government agencies, these
advertisers were also urged to write and buy space for their clients based
on strategies and fact sheets supplied by the War Advertising Council.

The most famous of these "brag ads" was for the New Haven Rail-
road. Headlined "The Kid in Upper 4," it was designed to explain how
those delays so annoying to regular riders were actually due to the rail-
road's priority of moving troops, consisting mostly of scared kids like the
one featured in the ad's Norman Rockwellish illustration.

Other large companies noticed the positive PR New Haven
received after the Office of War Information ordered this ad to be
run in newspapers nationwide. This led to some inevitable abuse as
other corporations tried to wrap themselves in the flag—most notably
tobacco mogul George Washington Hill announcing in his ads (with
all the fanfare of an important troop deployment) that "Lucky Strike
Green has gone to war!" Soon after it was decided that while their ads
would continue to be prepared under the auspices of an AAAA advertising agency, with the cooperative supervision of a campaign director from the client sector, the ads would be signed only by the Ad

Council on behalf of the nonprofit organization for whom the ad was primarily speaking.

By 1945, an estimated $100 million annual dollars in free space and time was being provided for War Ad Council ads, and shortly before his death President Roosevelt requested that the work of the Council continue. This request was strongly endorsed by his successor, President Truman.

War No More

In 1947, with Smokey Bear tromping the forest and campaigns well under way on behalf of veteran's programs, the American Red Cross, and Community Chest (later the United Way), the War Advertising Council became just the Advertising Council. The advertising profession was firmly convinced it could best retain the goodwill of the public by doing the public good. And many advertising practitioners, myself included, started to feel a new sense of pride in the importance of their profession. My second Ad Council campaign was a "cold war" series, produced through Doyle Dane Bernbach for Radio Free Europe, themed "The Iron Curtain Isn't Soundproof." It won me my first Clio.

Clearly, for an emerging small-to-midsize agency, the ability to have a hugely visible Advertising Council campaign on its client list and new-business reel is a formidable plus. And as one might expect, since there are only forty major Advertising Council campaigns in any calendar year, there is a waiting list of agencies standing ready to work on each of them. For most of them, the result of joining that select roster is well worth the wait.

GETTING AD COUNCIL ACCEPTANCE

Applications to be selected as one of the national council campaigns are only accepted from private, nonprofit 501(c)(3) organizations, private foundations, government agencies, or coalitions of such agencies and organizations. They must be made in writing to the Advertising Council, 261 Madison Avenue, New York, NY 10016-2303.

To achieve national campaign status, your cause must be national in scope and pass a rigorous review process. In 1994, the Council instituted an interesting and extremely innovative policy change in which campaigns, once disparate entities, would be more "horizontally" integrated to support a single umbrella theme. That year, the Council began a ten-year commitment to America's children. Smaller groups such as Children Now and the National Action Council for Minorities in Engineering were accepted to sponsor national campaigns under this theme.

As future umbrella themes are adopted, a small national organization that might have considered itself unable to compete with, say, the Red Cross or the United Way may well qualify, so filling out an application is certainly worth the time and effort, and it could not hurt to stay in contact with the director of proposals at the Advertising Council. The Ad Council staff actively explores opportunities to partner with appropriate groups on as many as four to five new campaigns per year. Major campaigns are taken on for a minimum of three years. A copy of the Ad Council major-campaign application documents is included in Appendix A.

It should be noted that profit-making entities, trade associations, nonprofits that have not achieved 501(c)(3) status, and individuals are not eligible. Campaigns that promote products, industries, particular religions, or that seek to influence legislation or raise funds for their sponsors are also generally not accepted.

From my personal experience, although this is not stated in the official Advertising Council material, which they were kind enough to supply for this book, campaigns that may be seriously controversial, or ads that contain content not likely to be considered in line with public sentiment, are unlikely to receive council campaign status. Efforts promoting abortion counseling or drug needle exchanges, for example, however worthy they might seem to the sponsoring organizations, are unlikely to be considered because they may stray too far from the standards the Ad Council's Stacy Hammond describes as "generally accepted American values."

Similarly, campaigns opposed to the use of legally sold and advertised products, such as tobacco or snuff, would probably not be accepted by the review committee. The Ad Council is run by and for the business establishment. This is not meant as a criticism of the organization or its accomplishments, which are impressive. But if your cause is on the cutting edge, you might check with them before devoting long hours to a formal request.

I would also note that the Ad Council is obviously more prone to taking prudent risks than it was when I met with them to present some fairly hard-to-watch anti-drug spots in 1969. A very moving AIDS-prevention campaign that promotes the use of condoms is a clear example of this. (See figure 11.8.)

BOY 1: Well, I used to think that the baby just comes out from the mother cause she ate a lot.

GIRL 1: My dad used to tell me I came from a cabbage patch.

BOY 2: They tell me what not to do, and they know I'm probably going to do it. GIRL 1: My parents always, like, stutter . . .

GIRL 2: My dad's kind of scared about that. GIRL 3: My mom hasn't really talked to me. GIRL 2: He thinks that I'll, you know . . . GIRL 1: I couldn't talk . . . it's . . .

BOY 3: My dad, he's, umm . . . too embarrassed about, about umm . . . about talking about it . . . about sex.

FIGURE 8.1 *The Advertising Council/The Kaiser Family Foundation/Children Now.* "Parents" was a national campaign under the Advertising Council's "Commitment to America's Children" umbrella campaign. *Courtesy of the Advertising Council.*

Even though the airtime and other media space is donated to major national campaigns, there *is* a financial commitment for the sponsoring organization, and bootstrap organizations may not be able to meet that commitment. To be considered for national campaign status, a cause is required to demonstrate its ability to contribute a minimum of a million dollars to the Advertising Council over the three years of its campaign, or approximately $300,000 per year to be applied to production of materials by the partner advertising agency, plus $36,000 to cover Ad Council administrative functions. This amount may be adjusted upward in years to come.

Equation

(Music up & under) ANNCR VO: It's really quite simple.	The more advanced math you take, the better your chances at a better career. With courses like algebra,	trigonometry, geometry, and calculus, you'll choose from a wider range of more interesting jobs. If no one

has explained how the power of math can improve your future, demand that you be told.	Call NACME,	they'll tell you.

FIGURE 8.2 *The Advertising Council/The National Action Council for Minorities in Engineering.* "Equation" was a national campaign for a relatively small cause group under the Advertising Council's "Commitment to America's Children" umbrella campaign. *Courtesy of the Advertising Council.*

The return on this investment is estimated to be worth an average of $25 to $30 million annually in donated media value alone, not counting the value of the volunteer hours applied against the campaign by the volunteer advertising agency and council staff. So the return on your money can be nearly one hundred to one!

The Endorsed Campaign

If this is still too rich for your cause's blood, but you have produced a local PSA campaign in one of the top ten markets, or have a cause campaign that is locally produced but has national relevance, you can still receive some considerable benefits if you are accepted by the Advertising Council as an endorsed campaign. Fairly strict criteria must also be met for these efforts, but the financial commitment is considerably less.

The endorsed or bulletin campaigns that have passed review are listed in the Ad Council's bimonthly bulletin. The listing includes a brief overview of a cause's campaign and a description of available materials, including information on how those materials can be obtained. The cost for each bulletin listing today is $1,000, or $5,000 for six listings during one year. This is in addition to a $250 application fee.

Although endorsed campaigns cannot carry the Ad Council logo, the endorsement of the organization undoubtedly carries great weight with media public service directors and traffic managers. With the overwhelming number of valid cause ads coming in the mail every day, an Ad Council endorsement gives you an edge in your selection for PSA placement. If your cause is accepted as an endorsed campaign, you can rent some Ad Council distribution lists at a nominal rate, giving you another invaluable tool in distributing your materials.

So whether it be through the Advertising Council or the force of personal persuasion, it is possible to reach the people with your message for very little money. The key to its acceptance is the worthiness of your cause and the artfulness of your message.

ALTERNATIVE MEDIA

There are some other techniques to reach your limited target that have very little to do with what has traditionally been known as mass media. Don Peppers, a very smart former account executive with whom I worked at Compton Advertising (when it was still Compton) has developed a large body of materials and seminars in support of a concept he stumbled on almost by accident in 1990 that has since made him something of a marketing visionary.

While most of his peers were still extolling the virtues of mass marketing, Don and his partner, Dr. Martha Rogers, predicted a sharp turn in the media highway. As they tell it in their book, *The One-to-One Future*, Don had been asked to fill in at the last minute for the media director of his agency at a marketing conference in Toledo. His subject was new media technology. Since he had only three days to prepare and could not begin to immerse himself in the esoteric statistical media issues he thought the audience was coming to hear, he wisely elected to step back and instead view mass marketing from a philosophic mountaintop.

After a quick overview, he concluded that the new techniques and technology on the horizon might well eliminate the underlying basis for mass marketing itself. This made for a somewhat shocking address to a group of mass media experts. Very few people back then foresaw the slump of network ratings and the gross inefficiency of spraying mass messages across the widest possible group of people. While less visionary advertisers were lining up to pay millions for a coveted media slot in the Super Bowl or the Academy Awards, Don asked his audience to imagine the day when, with a punch of some phone digits or the click of a mouse, thousands of individuals would connect, one-to-one, with entrepreneurs and marketers.

Any cause campaign that simply puts its energy and resources into the traditional media misses some very cost-effective tools to reach the target. And the depth and value of that relationship with each member of your often hard-to-reach target, if nurtured and refined according to Pepper and Rogers' principles, can be far more valuable than a random connection via any of the mass media.

Of course, direct mail was a precursor to, and early employer of, the principles of one-to-one marketing, and it's still going strong. Massively detailed databases deliver target prospects to direct-mail marketers, together with very sophisticated demographic profiles.

Now the World Wide Web is spreading like a giant tent, and entrepreneurs are finding it a surprisingly cheap marketing route, with a much better chance of making that personal connection with the desired targets. Why? Because those targets have already initiated a dialogue by clicking on a Web banner or reading an E-mail instead of deleting it. So they are partially qualified prospects already.

Susan MacMurchy, a talented former colleague, who through her company Big Blue Fish regularly advises sports marketers, high-tech firms, and nonprofits on such matters, suggests that a website may be a very low-cost media vehicle to reach the right cause target with some in-depth information. And if your desire is to offer, say, treatment centers, "quit tips," the latest medical information, or links to compatible sites, the economies of scale are enormous. Just remember to pick your domain address carefully, with an easy-to-remember key word or phrase. Even if it is not totally retained by those who see or hear it in your ad or commercial, a good search engine will deliver you to the prospect days after their exposure to you through mass media.

There are a number of national providers that can get you started at a surprisingly low monthly cost. There may of course be a provider in your area that can give you a little more personal service.

Costs will vary according to how much you want to accomplish with your site. Things like bandwidth and memory come into play here, and you should probably go to a website designer or producer for guidance in these matters. Be sure your site is maintained twenty-four hours a day, seven days a week, and that you have a back-up server in case your primary goes down. You need a clear understanding and a signed agreement with the ISP (Internet service provider) regarding service level, compensation for down times, and the ability to dial up your site from remote locations.

Despite its many pluses, a website should not be your *only* media outlet. You should still do general advertising to establish your image, and announce the availability and address of the site. As with all media, be very sure your graphics, logo, language, and theme lines are rigidly policed as they are translated to the site.

And just because it is the Web doesn't mean it has to be static and amateurish. Tasteful limited use of motion, animation, 3-D graphics (if you can afford to have them designed), and interesting links to other "hot" sites can give off subtle signals that you are serious about your cause and are manned by professionals, not well-meaning amateurs. However, just as with a good ad or commercial, simple is usually better. And you can put brilliant, involving copy on the lowest-cost, least-technical site.

Susan MacMurchy offers the following advice to clients designing websites:

- Design your site to draw people deeper into it once they have logged on. For example, you can place a teaser page (sometimes called a "splash page") ahead of the home page. This teaser should be as interesting and motivating as a good headline for a print ad.
- Since your site is a way for interested parties to find out about you before they reveal themselves, prepare it as thoughtfully as you would an annual report.
- To ensure repeat visits, regularly update your site. Unlike an ad or commercial that you can walk away from once it's trafficked, your site needs constant care and attention. Constantly changing promotions, cross-promotions with other sites, premiums and gifts, and recipes or helpful hints will keep the hits coming. Design your site to draw visitors back repeatedly and to inspire them to explore, buy, or donate while they're there. Web designers call this making your website "sticky."
- A regularly updated news ticker across the bottom of the page can keep the public informed about your cause's activities. You should also include a file of all your organization's press releases, and news stories or links to press sites with information related to your cause.
- Be sure your site is easy to access and loads quickly. Don't include so many intricate graphics and photographs that your site visitor loses patience staring at blank pages.
- Make the site easy to navigate. It should be well organized so visitors can logically get to the areas they want or link to other sites.
- Every graphic and section of copy should be consistent with the image advertising you are doing off the Web. Visitors must know that this is truly *you*, not some similar sounding group or copycat with less worthy motives.

Banner ads are valuable commodities. Your organization may have a strict policy against any commercial tie-ins. But if, for example, your cause is the preservation of wildlife, your respondents are presumably animal lovers and owners. A banner ad linking them to a respected pet supply or pet food manufacturer could pay for the creation and maintenance of your site. Or you could barter: your banner in their site for theirs in yours.

At the very least, you could trade linking banners with causes or nonprofits with similar goals or interests. People logging on to the partner site could then link to you, and vice versa.

Web "communities" will offer to build free sites and help get them out to search engines. The catch is that they want you to link with retail sites, selling everything from books and CDs to golf equipment. Every quarter you get a check representing commissions on merchandise sold through a referral from your site. Some of these retail sites may be totally counter to your cause's charter, but links to booksellers for pertinent books or CDs may feel okay. And the price is right.

For examples of cause-related sites, check out Join Together (jointogether.org), a Massachusetts site devoted to issues of substance abuse, tobacco, and gun control; the Massachusetts Tobacco Control Program (quitnet.com); or the Massachusetts Council on Compulsive Gambling (masscompulsivegambling.org). They offer a wealth of information, including quitting tips, treatment center locations, current news stories on related issues, and links to dozens of other sites. None of these referenced sites has a solicitation capability, but the Partnership for a Drug-Free America (www.drugfreeamerica.org) does.

The Ad Council has started making Web banners available with some of its best-known icons—McGruff, Smokey, etc. Convincing sympathetic corporations or organizations to place your banner on their websites (with your logo, slogan, artwork, or icon) could expand your coverage for very little. It should, of course, be a linked banner, so that a mouse click will deliver the prospect to your site.

With the explosion of the Internet and other related media we are witnessing a phenomenon of change almost as significant as the one that occurred in the late '40s when the flickering TV tube first moved into a place of prominence in many of America's living rooms. We are quickly approaching a quiet but certain revolution in the uses of media, undreamed of when Marshall McLuhan first opened our eyes with his radical analysis. The smart cause marketer must keep a watchful eye on the hourly changes in this world. True to that principle, I will keep this chapter and other related subjects updated on my own website at www.causemarketer.com.

EARNED MEDIA

Cause marketing is a natural for earned media. Whatever your cause, there is bound to be a widespread reservoir of sympathy and positive feeling within your community, or for that matter, throughout the country. Therefore, favorable PR is far easier to come by than for a commercial product or service, or even a political candidate or voter issue. Treatment for compulsive gambling, smoking cessation programs, and litter control can all get good coverage on the evening news and in the pages of urban dailies and national magazines.

Whether you handle your PR in-house, or give it to a specialist, the key PR people should be members of your team in good standing, participating in all strategy and briefing sessions.

While the language of your PR strategy may vary somewhat, the key elements should be the same: target, objective, principal idea, support points, and particularly tone and style. Whatever the event or story, try to make sure your campaign theme lines, logo, and central benefit are prominently featured. Here again, it is a case of synergy. All your PR should remind people of the advertising; all visual and verbal hints should trigger a recall of your advertising messages. Tone and style are important here as well. If yours is a serious appeal, a newsworthy but frivolous event would be as wrong as a humorous commercial.

CORPORATE CAUSE-RELATED MARKETING

Another way to greatly expand your coverage on a limited budget is via a corporate co-sponsorship of fund-raising and image-building events or media advertising. *Time* magazine estimates that corporations spend more than $500 million a year for the right to sponsor various social programs. Obviously, it must be an appropriate marriage for your cause, with a corporation whose goals and culture are compatible with yours. Some nonprofit boards frown on any seeming commercialization of their issues. However, after careful scrutiny of the corporate entity, cooperative events can be effective fund-raising and image-building routes. As we have already noted, this is generally referred to as "cause-related marketing."

Causes from AIDS to breast cancer to the environment to literacy have embraced corporate entities such as Avon and Nike for support in such events as bicycle rides, walk-a-thons, swims, and so on. Seed money, premiums, and cooperative advertising can all be derived as more and more corporations seek the "good citizen" status such events confer. Again, caution must be exercised to ensure a company with a reputation for shady practices is not trying to buy respectability or political clout by embracing your cause for its halo effect. Some very worthwhile arts organizations in New York City discovered this the hard way when, as reported in the *Non Profit Times*, Philip Morris, their generous benefactor over the years, leaned on them to use their influence to lobby against stricter City Council anti-smoking regulations. To add insult to injury, in late 1999 Philip Morris, characterized by *Business Week* as the "most reviled company in America," traded upon several of their cause-related associations (such as their support for battered women's safe houses and food programs for the elderly) to clean up thier image in a series of beautifully produced commercials signed "The People of Philip Morris. Working to make things better." Whether these will resonate with the public (they certainly help employee morale) remains to be seen. My supposition is that they may backfire. When you make an altruistic claim you had better be sure it is in synch with your image. J&J was able to say "trust Tylenol" because it was made by a company people truly did trust. This is certainly not the case with these warm and fuzzy portrayals of what many Americans consider an "evil empire!"

On a more positive note, cooperative corporate promotions with "clean," compatible companies can be particularly helpful to nonprofits with limited budgets. Donna Gittens, CEO of Causemedia, a Boston communication firm specializing in cause issues, divides her company into two divisions: one devoted to preparing the kind of social-marketing campaigns to which most of this book has been devoted, the other to bringing corporate entities and nonprofits together for cause-related events or larger-scope campaigns.

Donna, who for many years was public affairs director at a major Boston TV station, says evaluation of these efforts is particularly important inasmuch as the corporate partners in the effort are used to getting—and will expect—tangible proof of the effect of their product advertising.

If the marriage is compatible, this can be a win-win arrangement wherein nonprofits get well-funded exposure, which may include paid advertising favorably placed by their corporate media buyers, and corporations get extensive favorable PR for their embrace of worthy causes. Employee morale is enhanced, and corporate status as a good citizen of the community is ensured. It has been found that corporations professing to support, for example, the environment or education have much more consumer credibility if they have recognized nonprofit partners.

So with a conventional or perhaps more innovative media plan in place, your cause campaign will be ready to go. And our how-to section is complete.

In Part 2, we will look at some familiar cause marketing at work and examine the history of two of the most prolific cause advertising producers: the Partnership for a Drug-Free America and the Massachusetts Tobacco Control Program. I'll also offer my top ten list of cause campaigns. And finally, I will set down some conclusions and cautions that I hope will inform *your* journey into cause marketing.

PART 2

CAUSE MARKETING AT WORK

9

THE PARTNERSHIP
FOR A DRUG-FREE
AMERICA

The Cause Colossus

The best-funded and most widely seen cause campaign in the
United States, and possibly the world, is the Partnership for a
Drug-Free America. I remember its roots very well. As creative director on one of its predecessors, the National Institute of Mental Health
campaign, I was invited to lunch with Dick O'Reilly, who was planning
the Partnership. He was looking for advice. Quite simply, based upon
my very difficult and unsatisfying experience with a similar campaign,
I advised him not to do it.

Sadly, I never saw him again. Dick wisely ignored my advice and
collaborated with Phillip Joanou, a board member of the American
Association of Advertising Agencies (AAAA), to create the Partnership
with a grant from the AAAA. A short time later, Dick reluctantly went
on a white-water rafting junket sponsored by a Midwestern agency,
seeking to recruit board members for his cause. The junket went terri-
bly sour, resulting in the drowning deaths of eight top marketing and
advertising executives, among them, a former client of mine and an
account executive I knew quite well at Compton. Also killed was Dick
O'Reilly.

The tragically dropped flag was eventually picked up. I was
encouraged to read that a man I admired greatly, James Burke, retired
chairman of Johnson & Johnson, had agreed to head the Partnership.

JAMES BURKE AND TYLENOL

Burke and I had a brief but charged association when I wrote and supervised the Tylenol advertising that helped lead to the recovery of that brand from two frightening product-tampering incidents. Burke personally took charge of the effort, and I felt his decisions were always courageous and wise. I clearly remember sitting in his office after the second incident with a small group from the agency as he pushed a handful of strange-looking capsules toward us.

"This is the best tamper-proof capsule my people can come up with," he said. Some of the capsules had ugly brown sears where attempts had been made at heat-sealing them. "I can't be 100 percent sure with any of these modifications that our product won't be used to kill more people. So gentlemen, unless we can do better, we may have to go out of the capsule business!"

And he did it shortly thereafter. At the time of the tampering incidents, Tylenol capsules were the largest selling and most profitable Johnson & Johnson product. J&J took a $100 million dollar pre-tax write-off against Tylenol losses in 1982, the year of the first tampering incident.

Framed on a wall in Burke's J&J office was a corporate credo, the original principles of which were set down by the son of one of the founders of the pharmaceutical giant, Robert Wood Johnson. It stated in clear terms that, although the company was dedicated to returning profits to its shareholders, the well-being of its customers would come first, above everything else. Burke, who had updated it in a series of executive meetings, practiced the principles of that credo every day of his tenure at J&J, and made sure all his associates did as well.

I wrote a commercial within twenty-four hours of the first Tylenol tampering news report, but Burke insisted on holding it until some massive research indicated that the public was waiting for a message from the company. Halloween was coming up, and he was concerned about provoking copycat killings. He also didn't want to "fling down the gauntlet" to whomever had done this.

He had some support from the greater marketing community. Professor Lipstein of the NYU School of Business was quoted in the press as saying, "The only thing they can do is withhold advertising and reduce public awareness. If they could hide under a rock and hope it all goes away, they would."

Advertising pundit Jerry Della Femina said ominously "A flat prediction I'll make is that you'll not see the name Tylenol in any form within a year."

We at the agency argued that the incident was heavily in the news anyway, and that the public was waiting to hear from the company in their own words. I agreed to eliminate any inflammatory language (an earlier version had said things like, "this insane act damages all of us."). Our qualitative research, directed by Compton researcher Maria Falconetti, showed respondents a rough taping of the spot I had written for J&J medical director Thomas Gates. We asked research respondents if they thought it appropriate for the company to pay for airtime to run this kind of announcement. Mr. Burke was deeply concerned about "selling too much." The results produced remarkably strong numbers, particularly in the "intent to purchase" response. Even 85 percent said it was entirely appropriate to buy time for this message, a number Maria called "extraordinary." So we ran the spot and some print, and the recovery was also "extraordinary."

Within a year of the first incident, Tylenol's share of the analgesic market, which had dropped to 18 percent, had recovered to 28 percent. This recovery was guided by a strong man who cared more about the well-being of his consumers than the bottom line, and did the appropriate research to be sure he was right before he aired any advertising. Part of what the research told us was that the brand had a very positive image. Our advertising and J&J's reputation had created a situation where we held the consumer's trust. As one research respondent put it, "If a terrorist puts a bomb in your Ford and it blows up, you don't stop buying Fords!"

In a strange way, the Tylenol campaign became a cause campaign. And in my view, this boded well for the Partnership under Burke's stewardship, even though I still had concerns about the possibility of the group making serious mistakes due to the size and complexity of its undertaking.

Burke was elected chairman of the Partnership in the spring of 1989. He inherited a three-year-old consortium that had, despite limited funding, produced more than thirty TV commercials, sixty-four print ads, and fourteen radio messages, all of them produced pro bono by top agencies, and widely exposed in airtime that had been willingly donated by all three major broadcast networks and a number of cable networks.

At the time he accepted the position, Burke said his Tylenol experience allowed him to talk to the media in ways others couldn't because he had the media's trust. I can attest to that. Burke's open-door policy with the press, in which he provided complete access and virtually total disclosure of every step taken to deal with the crisis, has become a classic Harvard Business School case study. (Unfortunately, his example was sadly ignored in subsequent corporate disasters such as the *Exxon Valdez* oil spill.)

EARLY PARTNERSHIP SPOTS

A few of the Partnership's early spots, produced before Burke's arrival, were examples of the kind of thing I feared the Partnership would attempt when I had that lunch with Dick O'Reilly. One was the spot called "The Burbs," with its toking teens, which was discussed in the Introduction.

There were also some very positive efforts among those thirty spots. Several attempted to dramatize the disdain in which some of their peers held the pot smokers. That drug was properly separated out and specified, and its use was realistically portrayed. One spot, although it did portray a nonspecific "all drugs" analogy, showing a young woman diving into an empty swimming pool, had the plus of appealing to the "tempted to experiment" teen in a fairly honest fashion.

ENTER THE WHITE HOUSE

In 1998, the White House Office of National Drug Control Policy announced it would provide $195 million annually to buy media for an anti-drug campaign, and the task of creating that advertising was awarded to the Partnership. Due to the aforementioned shrinkage of PSA availabilities, the Partnership needed government dollars to buy media placement. The trade-off was that the political policymakers would henceforth play a stronger role in the Partnership's efforts. It should be noted here that the Partnership receives no government money for its role in supervising the campaign.

Having experienced firsthand James Burke's respect for consumer research, I was also curious about that aspect of this well-funded effort. Thanks to a former colleague, Barbara Feigen, research director at Grey

*(Music up: "The neighborhood"
from the motion picture
Poltergeist.)*

 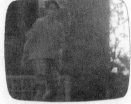 

Statistics show that 46 percent of
all kids who smoke marijuana

are inner-city youth.

Guess who the other
54 percent are?

FIGURE 9.1 *The Partnership for a Drug-Free America.* "The Burbs" was intended as a wake-up call to middle-American parents to get involved with their kids. It may have had the unexpected negative outcome of normalizing drug use to kids. It broke the cardinal rule of not showing drug use, by showing kids smoking pot. *Courtesy of the Partnership for a Drug-Free America.*

(Music underneath)
(Dialog overlaps)
TOMMY: Whoa, look at . . .

GIRLS: Tommy, he's so stoned.
TOMMY: This is totally . . .
happening.

GIRLS: Look what's happened to
him.
TOMMY: You know I look like . . .
GIRLS: . . . such a mess.

TOMMY: Yeah, this weed is
definitely . . .

GIRLS: Gross. Ever since he
started smoking pot, he's gross.

TOMMY: Like, everybody's
doing it.
GIRLS: and it's so uncool.

TOMMY: They're really into
me. They think I'm so . . .

GIRLS: out of it. He's
really out if it.

FIGURE 9.2 *The Partnership for a Drug-Free America.* "Perceptions" contrasted the self-image of a kid who thinks he's cool with the negative perceptions of peers. Showing marijuana smoking may be mitigated by the girls' put-downs, but it might still be a turn-on. *Courtesy of the Partnership for a Drug-Free America.*

Advertising, I was put in touch with Jaqueline Silver, who was a Partnership research consultant for several years.

Candid, funny, and smart, Jackie has been involved with cause research probably longer than anyone in the field. She told me she was present at the birth of the Ad Council's "Just say no!" spots. (She urged them to add "Just" to take the edge off the finger-shaking tone of the originally proposed: "Say no.") She also confirmed that the campaign had indeed originally been targeted to 10-year-olds and under.

When the Partnership was founded, Jackie was asked to work with them, and was part of the committee that decided early on that the only

---

Pool Party

(Music up and under)
(Sfx: Drumming sound throughout)
ANNCR: Doing drugs is like being on top of the world.

(SFX: Talking in background throughout) Everyone says so.

Everyone seems to be having one dandy old time. Hey, it's part of growing up . . . or is it?

Just think about this . . . before you go and do something you've never done before,

you just better know what you're jumping into.

(Music out)

FIGURE 9.3 *The Partnership for a Drug-Free America.* "Pool Party" was a cautionary exploration of the thought processes of teenagers contemplating drugs. It was an "all drugs" spot, but the truthfulness of tone may have overcome that negative. *Courtesy of the Partnership for a Drug-Free America.*

possible approach to a cause problem as vast and multifaceted as drug abuse was to adopt the McDonald's strategy of providing many different messages for many different people.

Burke insisted on extensive research, and as noted in Chapter Seven, the Partnership produced a massive national projectable probability study.

The research provided the organization with the crucial insight that, when it came to drugs, parents were still the most trusted source of information. Thousands of kids and their parents were interviewed, separately. Most of the parents assumed the principal influence on the kids in the areas of drugs (and other destructive or risky behavior) was other kids, peers, and the media. The kids said they would most likely listen to parents and grandparents. Almost all the parents interviewed were astonished when confronted with this.

There was also a large disconnect between kids, who reported their parents rarely spoke to them about drug abuse, and parents, who claimed to have discussed it a lot. Thus was born the "Talk to Your Kids" campaign, an effort in which I strongly believe. The theory is similar to one we applied to a campaign for the Massachusetts Council on Compulsive Gambling: if you try to materially change the attitude of the user or even the contemplator in your advertising, you may fail, but it's quite likely that you *can* successfully appeal to the family or a loved one to intervene.

Let's examine three of the recent "Talk to Your Kids" spots. The first, called "Girl/Interview," is excellent because, as we have discussed, it meets people where they are; it reflects the real world of viewers. The kid is great. Also, to make a point, she is very young but extremely bright. It is obvious, however, that her caring parents have omitted the subject of drugs from their otherwise comprehensive cautionary discussions with her. The next two, "Any Way You Can Talk" and "Carroll O'Connor" are, in my opinion, less effective: the first because it seems to ridicule parents, the very people you want to reinforce, and the second because of its rough, punitive tone.

Since I assume all these were written to the same strategy, I wonder what the tone and style section contained, or, if they were written to a creative brief, whether any such section was even included. If that section contained language like "real, empathetic," as the first spot clearly is, then the other two could not have been properly written to it. The "hip-hop Pop" of the "Any Way You Can Talk" ad would have to have been specified "humorous, ironic," and the O'Connor spot would have to have included "tough, hard-hitting," or something similar. It is obvious that the humorous spot was just meant to be intrusive, in the hope that laughing at the inept parents portrayed would help viewing parents feel more confident ("I couldn't do any worse than that!"). My reaction is that of the older brother in the commercial who shakes his head in disbelief. I am also puzzled as to why at a time when the unfairness of drug laws is under public attack, the only real fact presented to the kid is that marijuana can "lead to prison."

Research consultant Jackie Silver disagrees with my negative assessment that the Carroll O'Connor spot was too punitive. Based on her analysis of responses from many teens, Jackie believes that, deep down, kids welcome a strong intervention. "I wish my parents had done that," was a common response. *Whatever* parents do to get involved, Jackie says, is better than no intervention at all. The Partership's Steve Dnistrian strongly concurs, saying that spot has gotten a lot of positive response from parents. That acknowledged, I still feel that the compassionate, real tone of the "Girl/Interview" spot is much better.

These three presumably strategically linked spots constitute a good example of the importance of tone and style, and how ignoring or leaving out that consideration can make a key difference to a cause effort. As impactful as they are, the second two may be much less effective because they strike an off-putting *tone* for parents—their target audience. If research showed that only a small minority of parents reacted negatively, then the spot should run. If, however, a more significant number reacted that way then it should be re-thought. Because of the strong performance by O'Connor, this is a perfect example of good advertising for a bad "product" (a strategy that has an off-putting—or no—tone and style section).

Jackie Silver reports that when drug use in society at large began trending down, the Partnership was asked to mount a massive inner-city effort as a Phase II research project. It was carried out in New York City, and then replicated in other urban areas like Chicago and Los Angeles.

This Phase II research provided the Goodby Silverstein Agency with a brief to do what is arguably one of the best cause spots ever produced. The advertising community awarded it and one other Partnership spot the Grand Effie in 1994 as the most effective ad campaign in

INTERVIEWER: What would you do if a stranger talked to you?

GIRL: I wouldn't talk with him

'cause he might be bad. INTERVIEWER: Very good. And what would you tell someone

playing with matches? GIRL: I would tell them not to play with them because they might start a fire.

INTERVIEWER: Wow. How come

you know so much? GIRL: My mommy told me.

INTERVIEWER: Oh. And what did your Mommy tell you about drugs? *(Girl is silent.)*

ANNCR VO: Your children are listening. Are you talking?

FIGURE 9.4 *The Partnership for a Drug-Free America.* "Girl/Interview" is the most appealing execution of the "Talk to Your Kids" series, featuring a perfectly cast kid—young, bright, very real. The copy is on target and the tone just right. *Courtesy of the Partnership for a Drug-Free America.*

(Sfx: Dad cracking knuckles)
Son . . .

your mother and I have
to talk to you.

MOM: It's important.

DAD: Marijuana.

(Sfx: Rap music clicks on)

DAD RAPS: The wacky weed,
it is bad.

Of this I know, believe your
dad. Remember this,

it's your decision, but marijuana
can lead to prison.

ANNCR VO: Any way you
choose to talk to your kids about
drugs is a good way.

Call for a free brochure.

FIGURE 9.5 *The Partnership for a Drug-Free America.* "Any Way You Can Talk" is a very broad example of the "Talk to Your Kids" strategy, with a tone that might be offensive to the target—parents. *Courtesy of the Partnership for a Drug-Free America.*

America. It showed an African American boy cutting through some back lots on his way home from school, mainly, we learn as the spot unfolds, to avoid the dealers on the corner. Included in the voice-over, narrated in the kid's voice, were these thoughts: "My teacher tells us 'just say no'. Policeman says the same thing. They should walk home through here. 'Cause the dealers don't take 'no' for an answer." The voice-over (now in the voice of a strong, kindly mentor) adds: "To Kevin Scott and all the other kids who take the long way home. We hear you. Don't give up!" (See figure 11.4.)

Since I was not the target for this ad and hadn't seen any of the research, my mistaken assessment upon first seeing it was that it seemed simply to say "go out of your way so you don't have to just say no!" I

Carroll O'Connor

| CARROLL O'CONNOR: This is Hugh. This is my son. | He started on drugs when he was sixteen. | When his life became confused, unreal, |

| filled with horrifying hallucinations, he ended his life. | Get between your kids and drugs any way you can . . . | if you want to save the kid's life. |

FIGURE 9.6 *The Partnership for a Drug-Free America.*   "Carroll O'Connor" is also a "Talk to Your Kids" ad, movingly produced but rough! The punitive tone may have worked for some but probably also turned some away. *Courtesy of the Partnership for a Drug-Free America.*

did feel it scored high on the "first do no harm" scale, but I completely missed its strategic and especially its tonal brilliance.

It turns out that this approach was precisely what the massive inner-city quantitative study showed was needed. Going into the study, Jackie Silver admits her staff also started from a mistaken assumption: that inner-city dealers, with their jewelry, cars, and girls, were largely viewed by neighborhood kids as glamorous figures, "Robin Hoods of the 'hood" if you will!

Their research questionnaire contained questions like: Does this describe someone who sells drugs? (Check yes or no to each statement):

- has many friends
- is scared all the time
- uses drugs
- dies young
- goes to jail
- is a good friend
- is scary
- gets respect
- is lonely
- has lots of girlfriends or boyfriends

A follow-up was "Does this describe a girl who hangs around with someone who sells drugs?"

- has many friends
- scared all the time
- has nice jewelry and clothes
- has babies young

Other questions (all multiple choice) were:

- What would you do if someone you know gives you drugs?
— walk away
— try them
— tell Mom
— fight the person

- Agree a lot, agree a little, don't agree at all?
— I would like to try marijuana to see what it's like.
— It's hard for a kid to say no to drugs around cool kids who are using drugs.

Also included were some questions that went to the mentoring idea, such as: Answer yes, no, or I don't know to the following.

- I have an adult to talk to about my problems.
- I wish I had an adult to talk to about my problems.

and:

- How much do you learn about drugs from your parents or grandparents?

A version of this questionnaire for second and third graders used pictures and asked the kids to attach a sticker to the answers they picked. (A copy of these surveys is in Appendix C.)

As it turned out (despite the research team's pre-survey assumptions), although some kids still viewed drug dealers as peers who might even be a source of employment as runners and lookouts for the younger ones, a surprising number were very leery of the dealers. They would go out of their way to avoid them, but were afraid that they would be viewed as uncool or cowards by their peers. Viewed from this perspective, "Long Way Home," which is quiet, supportive, and aspirational, is perfectly targeted. It makes a hero of the young non-user, and helps create and reinforce good feelings about avoiding drugs. It is precisely in line with the principle articulated in the previous chapter, namely that "it recognizes the situation as it exists, and gives encouragement . . . rather than telling people how they *should* behave."

Recently, the Partnership produced a return of the "This is your brain on drugs" spot. The reaction to the *original* spot has always been somewhat mixed. Some young people think it's cool. Others put it in the same category with "Just say no!" Satiric T-shirts have appeared on the street emblazoned with the phrase, along with some hip "R. Crumbish" artwork of a freaked-out brain.

The advertising press obviously thinks it was an outstanding spot. *Entertainment Weekly* listed it as one of the ten best commercials of all time, and a group of industry executives selected it as one of the fifty best commercials ever for *TV Guide* (along with the "Crying Indian," one of only two cause commercials selected).

The basic problem I have with it, and I'm certain it's largely due to the pressures applied to the campaign by its government and "establishment" backers, is the same one I faced years ago doing an anti-drug campaign for the National Institute of Mental Health. The government position at that point in history was that all drugs are equal and equally dangerous. In other words, "all *drugs* will fry your brain. Period."

I'm certain some still consider that an appropriate stance. But an anti-drug message won't resonate with teens if it is expressed as "all drugs are equally dangerous." Like it or not, every high school kid will tell you they have classmates who regularly smoke pot and are high-functioning, productive students. They may be heroes of the football team or officers on the student council, and they use pot, a "drug," and their brains certainly aren't "fried." Here again, a deft and admittedly very strong analogy obscured what might have been a truthful portrayal of the dangers of

---

Any Questions?

Is there anyone out there who still isn't clear about what "doing drugs" does? Okay. Last time. This is your brain.

This is drugs.

This is your brain on drugs.

Any questions?

FIGURE 9.7 *The Partnership for a Drug-Free America.* "Any Questions?" ("This Is Your Brain on Drugs")—whether you love it or hate it, it's the most famous Partnership spot. Strong, intrusive, but it suffered from the "all drugs are equal" idea. *Courtesy of the Partnership for a Drug-Free America.*

specific drugs. So once again, some kids could convince themselves that the establishment didn't have a clue!

Jackie Silver disagrees with my position. She feels it was a great spot for its time, perhaps one of the best anti-drug messages ever. "Remember," she says, "at the time it was done, there was a high usage of drugs. *Indiscriminate* use of all drugs. Kids wandering the street, stoned out of their minds!" She's not so sure, however, that producing the return was a good idea. Today, she points out, kids know a lot more, and the drugs should be segmented out.

SEGMENTATION

Partnership PR Director Steve Dnistrian assured me that the group has become very aware of the need to segment the different drugs. So in that respect, the return of "This Is Your Brain," produced and aired by the now government-funded Partnership in 1999, has taken a positive step in addressing this specificity issue by identifying the dangerous activity as "snorting heroin."

The casting is great, the young woman is cool. But she then proceeds to smash up her whole kitchen, symbolizing, apparently, the destruction of family and home that can follow the drug abuse. However, heroin, although certainly carrying the risk of debilitating addiction, delivers a relatively soporific high. To have the spokesperson behaving violently, like a crackhead or an amphetamine user, may send a very mixed and apparently uninformed message.

When I mentioned the spot to Dr. Shaffer, he said he had assumed it was about snorting cocaine. When I pointed out that it was for heroin, he said, simply, "That's a mistake." Even Jackie, who was not involved with that spot, told me she thought it was an anti-coke commercial. Here again, a detailed discussion of the tone and style strategy section, in which "violent and intrusive" (which seems to be the tone of the spot) might have been examined and discarded as wrong for the drug in question, could have helped this.

This ad is an instructive reinforcement of the overriding power of tone and style. Even though the woman says "heroin" *twice* in the spot, Dr. Shaffer, Jackie Silver, and I all assumed after a few exposures to the commercial that it was for cocaine. Three fairly sophisticated "insiders" made the wrong assumption, based on the violent tone and imagery. I must assume many of the kids it was targeting made the same mistake.

This is your brain.

This is heroin.

This is what happens to your brain . . .

after snorting heroin.

(Sfx: Pan hitting counter)

This is what your body goes through.

It's not over yet.

This is what your family goes through!

And your friends! And your money! And your job!

And your self-respect!

And your future!

Any questions?

FIGURE 9.8 *The Partnership for a Drug-Free America.* "Frying Pan" is a dramatically produced commercial that specifies heroin as the drug being abused. However, its violent imagery seems inappropriate for a drug with a passive high. The wrong tone may hurt its credibility. *Courtesy of the Partnership for a Drug-Free America.*

And then, once they realized heroin was the subject, they would have been puzzled or turned off. Quite often in a cause commercial it's not *what* you say, but *how* you say it that is retained.

Should a possible problem with this concept have been flagged in the Partnership's massive research effort? Probably. Maybe it was simply a matter of not asking the right question. In fairness, I should mention that I showed this spot recently while speaking to a group of college students, and the majority thought it quite effective. They all caught the heroin mention, and felt the "smashing up the family" analogy was okay, and that the sultry portrayal of the young girl was consistent with "someone some heroin users might be hanging around with."

Anti-Marijuana Efforts

The increase of pot use continues to be the most daunting problem for the Partnership's client body, the White House Office of National Drug Control Policy. Despite overall drug-use decline, youthful use and tolerance of marijuana continues to rise, with Partnership tracking studies indicating that teen reporting of "widespread use" was up from 46 percent in 1993 to 59 percent in 1996.

Dr. Lloyd Johnson of the University of Michigan, a man Jackie Silver describes as the principal drug-use researcher in the world (he has been gathering massive amounts of data since 1979), concluded in the June 1998 *American Journal of Public Health* that lifestyle factors alone can't account for the recent changes in marijuana use. He and his colleagues, Gerald Bachman and Patrick M. O'Malley, did a detailed analysis of data from a large annual nationwide survey of high school seniors by the Institute of Social Research, funded by the National Institute on Drug Abuse. They concluded that attitudes about *specific* drugs, as well as the perceived risks and social disapproval of use, are among the most important determinants of actual use, and that young people *do* pay attention to information about the risks and consequences of drug use when it is presented in a *realistic* and *credible* fashion.

In response to this data, the Partnership has wisely mounted a large, segmented anti-pot campaign, which I feel is much more in tune with targeted kids than any previous effort on marijuana. In addition to making it very clear that the Partnership has segmented the effort, the best thing is that the ads portray kids and their thoughts and anxieties *very* realistically and credibly. I assume this came right out of the research. One of these spots, "Cafeteria," uses a research finding similar to one we jumped on in Massachusetts for one of our anti-smoking efforts: that most kids assume a lot more of their peers are using the drug than actually are. Revealing this can be an extremely simple yet powerful tool for kids to use in resisting peer pressure to smoke pot. The preteen spot ends with "Maybe we're not as different as we think." And one aimed at teens concludes, "The average kid thinks everybody smokes it, but the average kid doesn't" over a title that says "4 out of 5 kids don't smoke pot." It's reverse peer pressure, pure and simple.

Another spot, called "Moment of Truth" is a '90s answer to "Just say no!" and I think it's quite successful. Derived from research into the thought processes of kids, it dramatizes what many of them are really going through. The tone of this spot, although light, is just fine. In a much more realistic way than in the past, it helps arm kids for their "moment of truth." It recognizes the reality of teen pot use, obliquely references the fact that it's not as widespread as they might think (many of the kids in the spot are on the contemplating kid's side), and the end line, "don't want to, don't have to," is a very nice un-slogany slogan.

Less successful is a series of testimonial "talking heads." The "beautiful child" may see the speakers as losers whose experiences don't apply to them. An exception is a spot called "April," in which a teen's low-key, dead-on testimony should ring true with its target, other female teens.

The most successful spots in this anti-pot campaign continue to be those that, to use Howard Shaffer's language, "meet people where they are and take them to where they may not want to be, rather than telling them where they *should* be."

Once again in 1999, the trend seemed to be reversing itself, with trial use declining from 44 percent in 1997 to 41 percent, while awareness of the advertising increased by 41 percent.

Harder Drugs Are Easier to Fight

Segmenting out the various drugs has made the Partnership's task a great deal easier. The severe and life-threatening dangers of harder drugs, which may have been ignored by kids when they were lumped together

(Sfx: Party music)
POT HEAD: Here . . .

(Sfx: Clock stops)

BOY VO: Oh, man, I knew this was gonna happen.

I don't want to smoke pot, but I can't just say no. I wanna hang with these guys, they're my friends.

What if . . . my parents find out? What do my parents know?

What if I cough, I'll look weird. If I don't I'll look cool. No I won't. I'll look stupid.

If I smoke I could lose it. If I don't I could lose my friends.

AHHHH!

BOY OC: No thanks.

POT HEAD: Cool, man.
(Boy sighs)

DON'T WANT TO? DON'T HAVE TO.

Partnership for a Drug-Free America®

BOY VO: Don't want to? Don't have to.

(Sfx: Party music)

FIGURE 9.9 *The Partnership for a Drug-Free America.* "Moment of Truth" is a reasonably accurate dramatization of what a kid faces in school today. A "Just say no!" for the '90s. *Courtesy of the Partnership for a Drug-Free America.*

with less dangerous drugs, can be dramatized with great impact when they are isolated in segmented spots.

The dangers of meth and heroin are dealt with in a very dramatic and realistic way in several spots, one of which, a spot called "911," I have included here.

Inhalant sniffing or "huffing" is a particularly insidious danger to kids, because "good kids" who might be reluctant to go to a dealer for illegal substances, but who are still curious, can find a high right under their sink. And they're given permission to think that if the products are sold at the supermarket, they certainly can't be *that* dangerous.

These frightening findings were revealed in what Jackie Silver called a "classic strategy study." The very sudden transition from what

---

April

APRIL: When I was high on pot

I was flirting with this guy and I didn't even know who he was.

I didn't know his name. And we were—we ended up having sex with each other.

And I felt like, why am I doing this to myself? What's going on with me?

I felt very ashamed and I felt embarrassed.

I felt dirty.
APRIL VO: Marijuana, it won't get you nowhere.

FIGURE 9.10 *The Partnership for a Drug-Free America.* "April" was the best of the "Personal Experiences" anti-pot commercials. The spot featured a young woman who was very believable, as was her dialogue. *Courtesy of the Partnership for a Drug-Free America.*

911 OPERATOR: This is 911 Operator 224. What's your emergency?

GIRL *(On phone):* We need an ambulance, oh my god, my boyfriend, he's gonna die! OPERATOR: Okay, please try to calm down.

GIRL: He's unconscious, he's bleeding, he's covered in blood. OPERATOR: I need to get some information from you, okay?

GIRL: Okay. Hurry. OPERATOR: Okay, where are you? GIRL: At the corner of 17th and Main.

OPERATOR: An ambulance is on the way. Stay on the line. Tell me what happened. GIRL: He just started freaking out and fighting things, and he

put his fist through the window, and now he's bleeding. OPERATOR: Okay, was he using any drugs? GIRL: Yes. OPERATOR: Do you know what he took?

GIRL: Oh, some speed, meth I think. OPERATOR: Okay, how much did he take? GIRL: I'm not sure.

OPERATOR: We got an ambulance going over there right now. GIRL: Please hurry . . .

FIGURE 9.11 *The Partnership for a Drug-Free America.* "911" is a grim reminder of the possibility of an overdose. It is an inexpensive production with only voice-overs and titles, but it worked very hard. *Courtesy of the Partnership for a Drug-Free America.*

appears to be a mild high, a pleasantly fuzzy feeling, to a heart-stopping or brain-damaging incident is a danger the Partnership decided must be explained, particularly to younger kids. This is done brilliantly in one of the Partnership's best spots, "Drowning" (see figure 11.5). The "Spoon Feeding" inhalant campaign is equally strong.

AGING ROCKERS AND RISING STARS

The Partnership, in association with the Musicians' Assistance Program, a music industry group, has recently produced a series of commercials using rock musicians as celebrity presenters.

Spoon Feeding

VO: Remember when your son
was a baby?
MOM: Here you go.

VO: Well, now it can all come
back to you.
MOM: Just one more bite.

VO: All he has to do is sniff glue,
paint, or household cleaner
to get high.

MOM: That's a good boy.

VO: After all, not all kids who do
inhalants die.

Not your kid? Inhalants are
damaging somebody's. Talk to
yours now.

FIGURE 9.12 *The Partnership for a Drug-Free America.* "Spoon Feeding" showed inhalant dangers from the point of view of parents. The surprise revelation is very strong. *Courtesy of the Partnership for a Drug-Free America.*

It should be obvious from earlier remarks that I would be dubious about the credibility of this approach, because of the point of view I heard expressed so many times in focus groups ("If you pay them enough, they'll say anything") and the real danger that one of your stars could be involved in a public drug bust.

Several of the spots (most are shot by music-video directors, and the MTV style pervades the pool) *are* effective. I admit having to rely on the expertise of my daughter Carol Burnham, a music industry pub-

Kiss

(Music)

PAUL STANLEY: I've seen what drugs can do to people. If it doesn't kill you, it'll kill your soul.

ACE FREHLEY: Drugs are nowhere and I'm talking from experience.

PETER CRISS: I've probably been through everything, done everything, took everything, and I can sure tell you that drugs are no way to go.

GENE SIMMONS: Don't lose your friends. Don't lose yourself. Don't be a fool. It's no way to rock.

(Music up)

FIGURE 9.13 *The Partnership for a Drug-Free America.* "Kiss" was perhaps the least effective of the spots co-produced with the Musicians' Assistance Program. It featured "yesterday's band," whose members seem to be functioning nicely despite confessed former drug use. *Courtesy of the Partnership for a Drug-Free America.*

licist, and her husband Hugo Burnham, a former member of a popular
rock group who now manages young bands, for help in identifying the
personnel in these spots. They also offered opinions as to their relevance
and credibility among the teen record-buying public.

We all found least effective a spot with aging members of "Kiss,"
in makeup, intercut with vital performance shots. Under all that face
paint they look pretty healthy. When one member confesses taking
"everything" and declares "drugs are no way to go," I can hear the kids
shouting, "Oh sure! You're still doing great. Maybe I can take everything and slide, too!" This "confessional" by an aging but wealthy group
runs the risk of being greeted with scorn by kids. But once again, Steve
Dnistrian disagrees, insisting fans know Kiss lost millions while its members were struggling with drug addiction.

I was moved by the testimony of Troy Nowell, widow of Brad
Nowell of the group Sublime. She's a very young and attractive mother,
and their son Jake, whom she is holding in her lap singing little nurs-
ery rhymes, is adorable. Heroin killed the father, and the effect is very
moving. Both Carol and Hugo said Brad's tragic death was well-known
to kids and the spot would probably have some resonance. However,
both also felt that the didactic "Heroin kills!" statement hurt the otherwise credible tone.

They judged the spot with Lauryn Hill to be best. She seems very
sincere, and the spot and the low-key copy project an image of her as a
credible positive role model. The spot becomes particularly intrusive
since her sweep of the 1999 Grammy Awards. She is now a bona fide
superstar and, from what I can gather from my "experts," unlikely to fall
from grace. "Stay positive" is her credo, both in her work and in her life,
and her role model status probably lets her effectively break the "no
celebrity" rule.

As important influences on teen attitudes and opinion, the Musicians' Assistance Program undoubtedly felt this series of spots could
help burnish the industry's image, and several of the commercials probably resonate quite strongly with the teen target. However, I continue
to believe there's a real risk with these "clean and functioning" spokespersons. The minute one of them has a widely publicized fall from grace,
and the odds are that it can happen, then the kids will feel they've been
conned by the establishment one more time.

TROY: I'm Troy Nowell. I was married to Brad Nowell, the singer of Sublime.

Brad died of a heroin overdose.

Jake's been robbed of having a wonderful person be his father.

He regretted the day that he ever tried heroin. He regretted that he was a slave to that drug.

It got in the way of everything. Heroin gets in the way of everything. It stops lives.

It's such a waste. It really is such a waste. Educate yourself. Heroin kills, peroid. We miss him and we'll miss him forever.

Don't let anyone miss you. JAKE: A, B, C, D, E, F, G . . .

TROY: I'm hoping that he'll learn from his father's mistake. I'm hoping that a lot of people will learn from his father's mistake.

FIGURE 9.14 *The Partnership for a Drug-Free America.* "Troy Nowell/Sublime" is a Musicians' Assistance Program spot that should resonate strongly with kids because Sublime singer Brad Nowell's overdose was much publicized. The "Heroin kills" line may be too didactic. *Courtesy of the Partnership for a Drug-Free America.*

LAURYN HILL: I think you have to realize who you are as a person.

You know, who you are as a child of God, and that your potential is so much greater than any chemical substance.

You know, drugs they destroy people, they destroy lives, they destroy families.

You know, I'm soon to be a mother.

And these are things I think about.

Please stay positive and stay away from drugs

because, you know, there's no place—

no place positive you can get with that route.

FIGURE 9.15 *The Partnership for a Drug-Free America.* "Lauryn Hill" featured an excellent, no-nonsense use of a very positive role model. It was helped by Lauryn Hill's elevation to rock stardom via the 1999 Grammy Awards. *Courtesy of the Partnership for a Drug-Free America.*

SUCCESS STORY

If I had that lunch today with Dick O'Reilly would I still tell him not to start the Partnership? No. Certainly, the statistics which the Partnership has published are impressive. Cocaine use is down 77 percent, and there's an overall 48 percent decline in drug use since the Partnership first went on the air. It is an historic decline, and the Partnership can probably also claim credit for a part of the similar decline in crime.

Even teen drug use seems to have turned around. In a statement released by the University of Michigan in December 1998, Dr. Johnson and his colleagues reported that the troublesome trends seem to be reversing. Fewer eighth, tenth, and eleventh graders report using *any* illicit drugs, including alcohol. A 1992 study funded by Johns Hopkins University concluded that, even during a time of rising drug use, advertising had a deterrent impact on 75 percent of viewers who had not used drugs as well as many who had.

Jackie Silver believes this research also clearly shows that the decline is related to attitude changes among the young. "It's proof," she says, "that cause marketing *can* change attitudes."

Drug use is cyclical. As is smoking among the young. When the numbers are down, the various cause campaigns addressing that use will, understandably, claim credit. Declines in drug use can also be attributed in part to the opposing forces of incarceration and treatment. Since treatment, tragically in the view of Michael Massing, has been declining due to reduced funding, the incarceration route is clearly the ruling one. Whether an equivalent emphasis on treatment would have produced a similar or greater decline is hard to say. It certainly would have produced more rehabilitated citizens, as opposed to the damaged and bitter individuals the prison system is releasing. And, as part of another cyclical change, Jackie points out that treatment is coming back into favor, particularly within prison populations.

But to keep the trend curving down, the tendency to experiment must be addressed; here again, the Partnership must try to reach the younger kids. In fact, despite the decline in total drug-use numbers, use among teens was up again in the early '90s, about the time the Partnership campaign presence was reduced by declining PSA availabilities. As Steve Dnistrian points out, the media campaign is only 1 percent of what the government spends on all those prisons, interdictions, and yes, treatment ($17 billion). If a well-funded media campaign could reach young kids early, maybe they wouldn't need so much money for the rest (prisons, treatment, etc.).

I continue to believe the most significant discovery in the massive research applied against this segment by the Partnership is the relevance of parental mentoring. And this, combined with more sensitive and truthful spots aimed at the young, constitutes my best hope to "inoculate" the next generation of teens, and turn the curve down again.

REVIEW BY COMMITTEE

Creative work for the Partnership is done on a volunteer basis by a number of agencies. It is coordinated by an in-house creative-account team, and is reviewed on a regular basis by "a committee of the top creative directors in the business." About two-thirds of the messages submitted to the committee are rejected. Partnership executives say the committee combines the talent and energy of creative experts with varied backgrounds and philosophies to finally reach a consensus.

All of this sounds very good. But its very size and grandeur may create some problems for the Partnership. This is an ego-heavy group. They are all very busy at their own agencies saving accounts or trying to reverse downward market-share trends on their top brands.

This is not meant to imply that any of them would intentionally slough off a responsibility as important as this. But you are not going to get the concentration you would in a normal tightly held agency process. And you are not going to have the agony and introspection that this thorny subject may require. Jackie Silver, who has not been involved with the Partnership for a while, said she felt the strategies were becoming more and more general and open to interpretation.

In the last six years of playing a client role as a consultant to various government agencies, I have had the occasion many times to walk into a conference room and judge a lot of advertising. After many years as an agency creative director, I think my copy instincts are pretty well honed, and I can usually quickly pick out the best-constructed pieces of work. But the crucial choices were based on hard study of the strategies and the research that led to them. A charming, brilliantly written spot with dynamite visuals may still be dead wrong for the complex targets and objectives of a cause campaign.

The Partnership's blue-ribbon panel will certainly only approve copy that is well constructed. But it may not always approve the work that is best for the cause.

During the time I was at his agency Bill Bernbach was reported as saying that one of the worst things an advertising person can do is make a great ad for a bad product. The public will flock to buy it, then be disappointed, and won't trust you as much the next time you knock on their door.

By the same token, because of the talents and experience of the people reviewing it, all of the Partnership's work will have the look and feel of great ads. But if the "product," in this case the strategic approach to very complex issues, is wrong, the ads may do more harm than good. And the targets, particularly the kids, may not listen next time.

It's hard for me to know how well this complex review process actually works. It could be a very difficult way to put together a cohesive and consistent campaign. However, when asked about the importance of strategy during this process, Steve Dnistrian assured me that many, many concepts are rejected for being off-strategy. He also commented that he feels his committe works very efficiently for the most part. He did add, however, that getting a government sign-off on copy requires going through about twenty more layers of review!

The need to serve many masters and constituencies can create an unhealthy climate for any advertising campaign. A 1999 *New York Times* editorial took the Partnership to task for opposing the inclusion of youthful alcohol abuse in its overall strategy, noting that "The Partnership argues that an anti-alcohol message would dilute the anti-drug message . . . but some of the Partnership's members earn lucrative fees for promoting alcohol products." If segmenting and dealing with each drug in its own minicampaign is current Partnership policy, then a segmented effort dealing with teen alcohol abuse would hardly seem to be a "diluting" factor. In fact, publicity about the Partnership omitting alcohol, particularly if seen as bowing to pressure from its volunteer agencies with alcohol accounts, could make the organization seem hypocritical, and further enforce teen cynicism about the entire effort. Jackie Silver told me she felt the Partnership would never oppose a legal product like alcohol or tobacco. However, use of those substances by underage kids is clearly illegal.

I understand very well how the decision to omit alcohol might have been reached, but it does point out the difficulty of serving so many masters on a cause effort. A "drug-free America" seems on its face to mean a complete prohibition of all drugs. If alcohol (and even tobacco) were to be officially lumped in with the illegal substances, then the Partnership might be seen to be adopting a "pro prohibition" stance, and would certainly hear about it from contributing agencies that maintain lucrative beer and tobacco accounts. It's a PR nightmare, especially since Mothers Against Drunk Driving (MADD) went on the attack in 1999, attempting to affect campaign funding by lobbying sympathetic members of Congress. The group even accused the Partnership of accepting funding from the alcohol lobby (it does not). Via an amendment to the funding bill, MADD attempted to place underage drinking under General McCaffrey's purview, and mandate that half the Partnership's budget be applied to this cause.

It's not a new dilemma. In 1973, while serving as chairman of the National Coordinating Council on Drug Education, I wrote an article for *Reader's Digest*, "How to Protect Your Child Against Drug Abuse," which for a time was the magazine's most requested reprint. In the manuscript, I listed all drugs that kids might abuse, and their possible effects, including alcohol. When the magazine was published, some anonymous editor (probably to mollify the ad department) had eliminated the booze reference.

When two causes start feuding, it can only hurt the efforts of both. I believe that an appropriate stance for the Partnership might be similar to that embraced by the Massachusetts Council on Compulsive Gambling. Most of the council's funding comes from the state lottery and state racetracks. The group has never hidden this fact. Its stated mission does not oppose gambling, which it recognizes as an enjoyable recreation for those who partake in moderation. Its purpose is to oppose *underage* gambling and to provide understanding and counseling for those who are addicted.

By the same token, despite the severity of its name, the Partnership for a Drug-Free America could certainly embrace an anti-drinking (and yes, anti-smoking) stance for our teenage population. And it could very appropriately campaign against drunk driving (as, in fact, have many of the alcohol vendors represented by its contributing advertising agencies).

It is the Partnership's current position that a government-mandated inclusion of an anti teen-drinking mission could weaken it only in so far as it caused a dilution of media funds. In testimony before

Congress in June of 1999, before the funding change amendment was defeated, Richard D. Bonnette, the Partnership CEO, stated, "We wholeheartedly support the concept of developing a national advertising campaign targeting teenage drinking. Alcohol abuse is a huge problem in America, and plays an undeniable role in substance abuse among children and teenagers. . . . But it is not possible to target both effectively within the current appropriation." He also stated that changing attitudes about alcohol, a legal product, would be much more difficult than changing attitudes about illicit drugs.

Yes, the research needed to design an effective campaign against underage drinking would be a large and expensive undertaking. It would be an even tougher challenge than combating teenage use of tobacco, another legal product. Even though many kids have parents who smoke, most are trying to quit, or at least acknowledge its destructive effect on one's health. However, the ritual of nightly cocktails or wine with dinner exists in many responsible households, and the parental initiation of teens into that custom when they come of age is quite common. Clearly this is a very different set of circumstances from illegal drug use.

But the use of alcohol by kids is widely acknowledged to be a possible gateway to other substance abuse, and as such, it belongs in the Partnership's long-range planning. In fact, given the publicly recognized links to the alcohol industry through its contributing advertising agencies (however unfair any "quid pro quo" assumption might be), I would consider it important that the Partnership very publicly request an adequate budget to research and mount such an effort. Otherwise it is vulnerable to being labeled disingenuous by its critics.

STEADY IMPROVEMENT

Overall, the quality of the individual Partnership ads continues to improve. So whatever difficulties may be imposed by the size and scope of the operation and its need to serve many constituencies, the Partnership does seem to be fulfilling its original mandate.

Jackie Silver grants that, due to the size and scope and variety of opinions contributing to the production of hundreds of pieces of advertising, it should be expected some mistakes will be made.

"But if we can change one kid's attitude about drugs, even though we make mistakes with some commercials, then it's all worth it," she says passionately. I can't fault that. I can only fervently hope that as more learning is achieved, the number of mistakes can be lessened. I'm told they have produced over 600 units of advertising, so the box score is pretty favorable.

Fortunately, their's is a degree of complexity the average cause account does not face. And the other side of the coin is that there are massive resources available to the Partnership when it comes to research and media exposure, and it does possess the clout of a government effort when it comes to opening any and all doors.

In late 1999, the Partnership went in a surprising and very positive direction by producing a totally integrated TV, print, and website campaign on the "parent as mentor" strategy called "The Anti-drug." Possessing a very contemporary look and feel that seems designed to appeal to parents who lived through the '70s, the campaign uses intriguing symbols and very contemporary language. An example: "the most effective deterrent to drug use among kids isn't the police or prison or politicians—it's you. It's Truth, Honesty, Love, Communication."

The look, feel, and sound of the effort is the same across all the media, which is, in my opinion, a good thing. The print and TV ads lead to an excellently designed website (www.theantidrug.com) where clicking on the appropriate symbols (Truth or Love, etc.) reveals some very adroitly phrased capsules of advice. A parenting brochure can be ordered or downloaded, and parents are led by the hand into starting a rational dialogue with their kids in a fresh, non-threatening way.

The campaign is unified, smart, and I believe should be very successful. It is interesting to note that the campaign sponsor is listed as the Office of National Drug Control Policy, although the Partnership website can be reached through a link. I sincerely hope that this is the first of many new and mature media ventures by the Partnership and the ONDCP.

It will require the wisdom of a Solomon to keep this effort on track, and if anyone can pull it off, it is James Burke. While I may quibble over a few individual executions, it is remarkable that so much of it has come out well.

IO

THE MASSACHUSETTS TOBACCO CONTROL PROGRAM

Anatomy of a Campaign

Following the success of the term limits voter initiative and the simultaneous passage of the tobacco-control initiative in Massachusetts, I wrote a note to Dr. Blake Cady, welcoming him to the initiative winner's circle, congratulating him on the success of *his* voter campaign, and offering to help in any way I could.

He put me in touch with Dr. Greg Connolly, the man the state Department of Public Health had designated to manage the campaign. Greg asked me to serve on the agency selection committee, and ultimately to serve as his advertising consultant, which I did for the next four years.

I hope the following analysis of the campaign that evolved can be instructive to anyone planning a large cause advertising program, but particularly to agencies in the other states that are poised to mount similar campaigns funded by the tobacco industry settlements reached in 1999.

Tobacco-control advocate Greg Connolly is a remarkable man. He trained as a doctor of dental surgery, and in fact, still sees a limited number of patients. Like Dr. Cady (who is one of the area's leading oncologists), he got sick and tired of seeing the destructive results of smoking in those he was committed to keeping healthy. He went back to school and got a degree in public health, and then went to work for the Massachusetts Department of Public Health, specializing in tobacco issues.

Passionate, smart, articulate, Greg Connolly is very effective, and also occasionally controversial, in his dealings with the news media. As he has moved from gadfly to director of a highly visible program, he occasionally gets in hot water. Still, Greg has continued to be the soul of the program, and thanks to his boundless enthusiasm and energy, and tireless communication and strategizing with peers and colleagues throughout the world, he has become an internationally recognized leader in the fight for tobacco control. He also has become a much-in-demand international spokesman for tobacco-control issues. If there's a tobacco-lobby "enemies list," as some contend there is, he's certainly near the top, and probably proudly so.

His attacks on tobacco appear regularly in the *Boston Globe*, the *Wall Street Journal*, the *Journal of the American Medical Association*, and the *New York Times*. He has appeared on "Nightline," and he is somewhat famous for cracking up the "Today" show's very controlled former co-host Jane Pauley by referring to the tobacco-industry spokesman he was debating as "Mr. Butts," a knowing reference to the cynical industry "spokescartoon" drawn by Pauley's husband, "Doonesbury" creator Gary Trudeau.

He is also, as far as I'm concerned, an ideal cause client. He is a comprehensive source of the latest information, gathered formally from the public-health literature and informally via the Internet and the large and loosely organized international group of tobacco-control activists.

He will throw out a million ideas, and is self-aware enough to know that some are crazy but may contain the germ of a great concept. He is up-to-date on every bit of anti–tobacco-control advertising in the world, and is constantly parading it before people in his ad agency to get opinions and advice, and to challenge them and push them into doing something better.

But for all his passion and creativity, he is usually content to let the marketing experts he helped hire bring their skills to bear on the problems before them. He challenges them, but he listens. And when they perform well, he is a delightful cheerleader for their work. He is also able to step back and examine the work, and draw savvy conclusions about it. He is constantly shaping his philosophy of using the media smartly to combat tobacco use, and many of his conclusions I have found useful to include in this book.

Also crucial to the early success of the campaign was the exceptionally patient and supportive commissioner of public health, David

Mulligan. David retired from the department in 1997 and was replaced as commissioner by former American Cancer Society activist Dr. Howard Koh.

CAMPAIGN KICKOFF

While the campaign would ultimately become a multi-pronged effort, with many separate mini-campaigns tied together by similar language, typography, and sponsoring-body identification, it was agreed at the outset that it had to speak first to the voters. They had defied the predictions of many pundits by passing the tobacco-control initiative against a well-financed effort by the tobacco lobby. And they had been waiting for what must have seemed a very long time to see the fruits of their vote.

The voting public had no interest in, or understanding of, the fact that it had taken six months to staff the campaign committee, run a fair and equitable RFP selection process, start evaluative and tracking research, and do all the qualitative planning research that such an ambitious campaign demanded.

It was decided to immediately produce a "launch" campaign which, in essence, acknowledged the bold step the voters of the Commonwealth had taken, reinforced the urgency of the problem, and thanked the citizens for their support. In a way it was to be a dramatization of our long-term marketing strategy.

In the letter inviting RFP finalist agencies to prepare their final oral presentations, one instruction was to create an introductory campaign theme line. Houston-Effler, the winning agency, came up with a very intrusive one: "It's time we made smoking history!" I suspect it was viewed as a short-term introductory line, but it was so well embraced it stayed in place on virtually all our advertising for the first six years. Okay, okay, we talked earlier about a "no puns" policy. But this is one of those "brilliant" puns with an aspirational spin. And the kids seemed to like it a lot.

A series of inspirational TV spots were boarded, employing masses of kids and a gospel-flavor track that thanked the people of the Commonwealth for their support and then laid out our objectives. Producing the commercials required a long and elaborate shoot. Hundreds of schoolkids had been bused out early in the morning to an abandoned air-force hangar at Hanscomb Field outside Boston to stand by for their appearance as "the youth of Massachusetts."

At about three o'clock in the afternoon, after working many hours to get the spokeskid's narrative just right, we still hadn't gotten to the rest of the kids, who were shuffling and grumbling in a tent off to one side.

Sensing a possible revolt from a group that had no understanding of the arduous nature of a film shoot, I grabbed a bullhorn and stood on a folding chair.

"I guess you must think we're the most disorganized group of people in the world," I started. There was mumbled agreement. "But you've got to understand . . . we're taking a lot of extra time to get this just right. We need this to be every bit as good as the cigarette company ads!"

"No!" shouted a twelve-year-old African American kid, his eyes dancing. "You've got it wrong. It's got to be *better*!"

Launch

VO: Last November the voters of Massachusetts took a stand. They looked at the facts. They weighed the costs, the human costs. And they passed a cigarette tax. Too many have been hooked, too many have died.

Too many kids have grown up believing what the tobacco companies say. That smoking makes you attractive or cool. By voting for the tax they said enough. We care about our brothers and sisters. Maybe if they see that we don't smoke, they won't smoke.

We care too much to pass this on to another generation. To pass on something so deadly, so senseless. It's time to draw the line. It's time for a show of strength. It's time we made smoking history.
SUPER: It's time we made smoking history.
A message from the Massachusetts Department of Public Health.

FIGURE 10.1 *The Massachusetts Tobacco Control Program.*   "Launch" was produced to be a statement of goals for the campaign. It dramatized a report to voters who passed the program's funding referendum, and featured hundreds of kids and a gospel-flavored music track. *Courtesy of the Massachusetts Department of Public Health.*

During the most difficult and discouraging stretches of the campaign I would often see that kid's image and hear his voice. And it always made me smile.

The edited spots and some double-page print ads were trafficked heavily all over the state, coinciding with the kick-off event in Faneuil Hall that introduced the campaign to the media.

We then examined all the California-produced ads aimed at the adult smoker, hoping to find several that might be consistent with our early goals and allow us to flesh out our initial pool. Qualitative research showed that several of them resonated well with our targets. We selected and tagged them with our logo and theme line, most notably an animated spot titled "Cessation Man," which we felt (and the research confirmed) struck just the right tone of sympathy and understanding for the smoker contemplating quitting. These ran as a part of a second wave.

FIRST, THE KIDS

Since the thrust of the voter-initiative campaign had been that this was primarily to be an effort for our kids, we felt we had to go into production right away with some ads targeted at teens. Due to the limited time we had to do extensive qualitative research, our researchers weren't able to discover a "silver bullet" with which to approach that difficult group, but they did uncover some teen motivations that seemed to have leverage. At least I knew we were true to the principle of "first, do no harm."

Five spots were produced quickly. One, perhaps the most effective, was a spot aimed at teenage girls. Through the device of wrinkling and then unwrinkling a photograph of an attractive teen ("our only friend who smokes!"), the spots appealed to the vanity of young girls by pointing out the shocking fact that smoking will age them by creating wrinkles. This was a tangible illustration of the consequences of smoking. The campaign would return to the aging theme with much greater impact four years later in the very effective "Pam Laffin" spot.

Another, an "attractiveness" spot aimed at adolescent boys, presented a sultry teenage Uma Thurman lookalike telling hormonally challenged males "five things all guys should know," presumably to appeal to a babe like herself. The ad was illustrated by hip cutaways to old movie clips. The clincher: "nix the smoking."

A third, narrated by a very cool African American, takes place in a pickup basketball game. Our man says he loves "playing against a smoker . . . wheezing and coughing, colors changing in their face." The payoff? Pretty simple. "You smoke, you choke!"

Interestingly, I think in retrospect that those first efforts aimed at teens were probably among the best done by the state in targeting that illusive demographic, because they were "talking to them where they lived," about issues relevant to their daily lives.

Monica

| GIRL 1: This is Monica, and she's like, our only friend who smokes. GIRL 2: We're trying to get her to stop. GIRL 3: Yeah. | GIRL 1: We told her that smoking stinks up her hair. GIRL 3: She said she could fix it. Same with her breath and clothes. ALL: Gross. | GIRL 3: We told her smoking made her teeth yellow. GIRL 2: She said she could fix it. |

| GIRL 1: But then we read somewhere . . . GIRL 2: this really did it . . . GIRL 1: about how cigarette smoke gets, like into your skin | and causes permanent wrinkles. GIRL 3: So we told her. GIRL 1: She freaked. GIRL 3: Totally. GIRL 1: Then she quit. | GIRL 2: It was cool. GIRL 3: Really. GIRL 1: 'Cause now we don't have any friends who smoke. |

FIGURE 10.2 *The Massachusetts Tobacco Control Program.* "Monica" was a dramatic reminder of the tendency for smokers to get premature wrinkles, and was perfectly positioned for female teen targets. *Courtesy of the Massachusetts Department of Public Health.*

It should also be noted that it was the strong recommendation of the agency team that each teen spot be tagged with just the payoff line of *that* message, and that even the typeface and layout of each spot be different.

This obviously flies in the face of a major principle of this book, that of synergistically tying every piece of communication together. The agency made an ardent and interesting case that the appeal of each youth spot should stand on its own and not seem to be tainted (in the eyes of the teen target) by some "big government" theme line. Let it reach the kids and move them, they argued, before they realize it's "another of

---

Attractiveness

| OK. Here's five things all guys should know. | One, don't change into something different when we're around your friends. | Two, ring the doorbell, don't beep the horn. Three, hold the onions! |

| Four, there's an invention called the telephone—use it. And five, nix the smoking. | That yellowish teeth, cigarette stench thing—it's not working. | You guys getting this? *(Music up and out)* |

FIGURE 10.3 *The Massachusetts Tobacco Control Program.* "Attractiveness" took another pass at the teen target, this time males, who were let in on some secrets of attractiveness offered by an attractive young girl and intercut with cartoon and archive visuals. "Nix the smoking" topped her list. *Courtesy of the Massachusetts Department of Public Health.*

those state anti-smoking ads" and turn it off. Interesting, but in retro-spect I'm not sure it was correct.

We tried appealing to youthful activism in three spots that drama-tized true stories in which some kids made a difference: in my home city of Gloucester, where four kids got the city council to pass an ordinance banning cigarette machines; in Chicopee, where some kids got a mall to go smoke-free; and in Roxbury, where kid pressure got mom-and-pop stores to give up the practice of selling "loosies" (individual cigarettes for a price that kids who couldn't spring for a pack could afford).

Florida, as a cornerstone of its anti-tobacco campaign, organized their youth into "SWAT" squads to take on the tobacco purveyors in provocative ways, such as calling up tobacco advertising agencies and magazines that run tobacco ads. Our "youth activists" were a little

---

Stamina

(Sfx throughout basketball game) When I play ball, I love playing against a smoker.	*(Sfx: Cough)* Wheezing and coughing, colors changing in their face.	They can't even talk trash, they're so winded.

Don't know what these guys are thinking, man. The money players today? They don't smoke.	You smoke, you can't breathe. You can't breathe, you can't run. You can't run, you can't win.	Yo, you gettin' all of this? I'm not talking trash, man. I'm talking truth.

Figure 10.4 *The Massachusetts Tobacco Control Program.* "Stamina" has a strong appeal for any young athlete. It shows a hip young man talking some very contempo-rary talk. *Courtesy of the Massachusetts Department of Public Health.*

more constructive. Both efforts, while intuitively sensible, did not have a lot of resonance with the majority of the targeted kids. Florida officials did claim their ads resulted in getting kids energized to talk about the subject, and that they have significantly reduced teen smoking in their state.

Our next youth effort was aimed at six- to twelve-year-olds. It depicted, in action-adventure film style, the arrival of a "HAZMAT" (hazardous material) team at an ominous-looking industrial facility. You think they're going in to clean out a nuclear waste dump. Instead, they snatch a cigarette out of the mouth of the startled guard, while listing the toxic ingredients in that lethal cylinder.

Another approach to the teen market was suggested during some qualitative pre-strategy probing done in some wide-ranging focus groups. Several self-admitted heavy smokers in the twelve- to eighteen-year-old groups revealed they had been shocked to realize how deeply addicted they had become. Many teen smokers told us they were just smoking to be "cool" and sociable with their peers, and that they fully expected to quit when they grew into their twenties (the girls usually said "when they got pregnant"). Addiction was a foreign idea, and most were convinced it wouldn't happen to them. The one- to two-pack-a-day teen smokers were shocked to find themselves hopelessly hooked.

Our response to learning that was to design two spots spelling out the nature of addiction and how serious an impact it could have on their lives. One used the analogy of a kid underwater in a swimming pool, having to take his next breath (similar to the Partnership's "inhalant" spot, although none of the Massachusetts team had seen that spot when this one was written). The other portrayed the familiar picture of the poor, helplessly addicted schoolkid, shivering in the snow outside the no-smoking boundaries so he could feed his addiction.

Unfortunately, the "underwater" spot only ran a couple of times because of a post-production mistake. I thought the spot was strategically excellent, but during the shoot, I urged making some alternative takes with lots of motion in the water so no one would get the idea the kid was dead, but that he was in fact just holding his breath. The creative team cut it with the motionless takes for maximum impact, and the day after it premiered the commissioner got some angry calls from parents of kids who had drowned in swimming pools. A recut with the alternate takes solved the problem, but by then it was too late—the department had decided it was too controversial and shelved it. It is available, however, from the Centers for Disease Control. The strategy and photoboards for this spot are in Chapter Two (figure 2.3).

THE CAUSE AS "BRANDING"

The ad agency came to the Department of Public Health one day with a plan to try and emulate the marketing giants at Nike and Pepsi who know how to reach the teen market so well. Not only do they sell their sneakers and soft drinks on the basis of product benefits such as "air soles" and "authentic taste," but much more important, they sell them as image brands. When you displayed a Nike "swoosh" on your body or held a can of Pepsi, you were "labeled" in a cool way, like the product.

The theory sounded great. The execution was a little more troublesome to pull off. Much of branding is image. In establishing a youth branding campaign that emulated the Nikes and Pepsis of the field, the tone and style section of our strategy would be almost its most important plank. We had to look and talk "cool" to be sufficiently intrusive to be talked about in the study hall the next day. We might not do a lot of specific benefit proselytizing in the spot, but we would have to establish a mood and tone of voice that would make our smoke-free "brand" as readily embraceable as Joe Camel or the Marlboro Man.

The resulting spots were okay, and I think they amused the kids (satisfying the "first do no harm" requirement). But to truly establish a brand among kids through cool imagery and very little "sell," you'd better have a Nike-size budget. And despite the very generous budget we were handed, we couldn't even come close.

Our "Lung" spot from that campaign is also an example of the kind of "gross-out" effort that has formed the basis of much of an Arizona antismoking campaign that employs spit, urine, and other bodily fluids. "Didya see that ad last night where the kid actually coughs up a lung?" may have been heard around some Massachusetts school locker rooms. The consensus in Arizona is that the portrayal and description of the act of smoking in gross terms seems to be resonating with kids. A "taunting" line ("tumor-causing, teeth-staining, smelly, puking habit") to hurl at the smokers in your class may be a pretty good little weapon. On the other hand,

(Sfx: Doorbell rings)

GIRL: Hi, Mike.
MIKE: *(Coughs)* Sorry I'm late.
GIRL: Come on in.

GIRL: Everybody, this is Mike.
MIKE: Hello. *(Coughs)*

MOM: Hope you like pot roast.
(Mike coughs violently)

GIRL: Are you okay?
(Mike coughs his lung out.)
(Sfx: Splat)

MOM: A lung...

ANNCR VO: If you're not cool
already, smoking won't help . . .

(Dog barks)
And if you are cool, you don't
need it.

FIGURE 10.5 *The Massachusetts Tobacco Control Program.* "Lung," an attempt to create a cool "smoke-free brand," was designed to appeal to the "gross-out" side of the teen psyche. *Courtesy of the Massachusetts Department of Public Health.*

many teens into their "grunge" period may think that a smelly, puking habit suits them just fine!

Telling the Truth

Probably our most effective youth effort consisted of two graphic, truthful spots, one of which became a series. They were shot in stark black-and-white by award-winning Cambridge documentary filmmaker Erroll Morris (best known for his films *The Thin Blue Line* and *Fast, Cheap, and Out of Control*).

The first, "Cowboy," is a touching on-camera reminiscence by the brother of Wayne MacLaren, the former Marlboro Man model who died of lung cancer (see figure 11.6). During Mac MacLaren's emotional reminiscence of how proud he had been of his brother were intercut shots of Wayne in his white hat, a symbol of rugged independence (the Marlboro image), and a home video of him taken in a hospital room, bald from chemotherapy, with tubes coming out of most orifices. "Lying there with all those tubes in you, how independent can you really be?" asks Mac MacLaren at the end of the spot.

Incidentally, when the giant Marlboro Man billboards were pulled down throughout Massachusetts as part of the multi-state tobacco settlement, the Department of Public Health was offered the locations and put up a similarly designed board featuring Wayne MacLaren and the caption, "died from Lung Cancer." (At about the same time the more "in your face" California state campaign used its acquisition of the famous Sunset Strip Marlboro Man billboard to portray a similarly dressed cowboy with a clearly flaccid cigarette dangling from his mouth. "Impotence" replaced "Marlboro" in a similar typeface.)

A second commercial in the Massachusetts pool portrayed a puffy and disfigured twenty-six-year-old named Pam Laffin, who says "I started smoking to look older, and I'm sorry to say, it worked!" Intercut in this spot were pictures of a young, vibrant teenager. The smoking had led to emphysema, removal of a lung, and a lifelong regimen of medication that created "this fat face and a hump on my neck."

The "Cowboy" spot broke a rule about talking about death to these "immortal" kids, but the irony of the death of a corporate icon was not lost on them. And the disfigurement of a young woman not much older than them seemed to resonate very strongly. Pam made herself available for school and health-fair appearances, and these PR events, linked to the commercials had a strong impact.

We learned of the value of these PR events after school appearances by two lung-cancer victims, Janet Sackman and Bob Mehrman. They had been filmed and recorded to be part of our adult campaign, but due to their startling vocal disfigurement, also resonated with kids. Mehrman's radio spot (see figure 10.7) won the Boston Ad Community's "Grand Hatch" award for best commercial in show. As you read the copy, imagine the voice shifting from that of a mellifluous radio announcer to the "robot" sound of an audiovox.

Pam Laffin

| LAFFIN: I started smoking when I was ten because I wanted to look older. | And I got hooked. Cigarettes gave me asthma and bronchitis, but I couldn't quit. | I didn't quit until I got emphysema and had a lung removed. |

| I was 24; I'm 26 now. My medication which I'll take for the rest of my life, | left me with this fat face and a hump on my neck. | I started smoking to look older, and I'm sorry to say, it worked. |

FIGURE 10.6 *The Massachusetts Tobacco Control Program.* "Pam Laffin" is a difficult-to-watch testimony of a physically damaged twenty-six-year-old former smoker who "started to smoke to look older." It was intercut with young and beautiful images that resonated strongly with kids who may have started smoking for the same reason. *Courtesy of the Massachusetts Department of Public Health.* .

Radio Script

Client:	Mass. Department of Public Health
Title:	Bob Mehrman—"Past"
Merhman archive:	Good morning and welcome once again to Community Dialog. I am Bob Mehrman, Public Affairs Director . . .
Mehrman Archive:	This is Commonwealth Journal. I am Bob Mehrman, and this week . . .
Mehrman Archive:	This is Bob Mehrman. Thank you for joining us . . .
Mehrman (through electro-larynx):	This is Bob Mehrman today. I don't have that voice anymore. For 40 years I was a television and radio announcer up until the day they took out my larynx, because I had cancer from years of smoking. So never again will anyone hear me introduce a lovely ballad from Frank Sinatra or read the weather for a beautiful, sunny afternoon, or report the news from a distant land. Instead, you will hear my brand-new voice, which comes out of this device called an electro-larynx. I'm telling you how dangerous cigarette smoking can be. It can change your life and your dreams.
	As a broadcast announcer, my entire life I always wanted to have an unmistakable voice. It's sad how it finally came true.

FIGURE 10.7 *The Massachusetts Tobacco Control Program.* "Bob Mehrman," a radio spot, used audio juxtaposition of the strong radio voice of a former broadcast announcer and the electro-larynx production of the same voice now ruined by tobacco-induced disease. It received "Best of Show" at the 1995 Hatch Awards in Boston. *Courtesy of the Massachusetts Department of Public Health.*

The agency then did an extended series on Pam that got more explicit about her grisly search for a second lung transplant. A documentary about Pam Laffin was prepared from this campaign footage by the ad agency and has formed the basis for a school lesson plan in Massachusetts. Several other states have shown that tie-ins between advertising and school curricula increase the retention and effectiveness of a cause campaign many-fold. This is just one part of a coordinated effort within the various communities in the state. Working with local prevention groups, the goal is to "ground" the campaign and change societal norms across all populations.

It took five years to see a decline. During the period of increased smoking among teens nationally (35 percent), the teen smoking incidence in Massachusetts fell from 31.4 percent in 1993 to 24.4 percent in 1999. So, statistically speaking, they have bucked the trend. The youth

---

Janet Sackman

| JANET: You may get cancer but I doubt you'll get the truth from cigarette companies. | They keep saying you can't get hooked on cigarettes | even though many smokers who lose their vocal cords can't quit. |

| I'm Janet Sackman. I was a model in cigarette ads | and I convinced many young people to smoke. | I hope I can convince you not to. |

FIGURE 10.8 *The Massachusetts Tobacco Control Program.* "Janet Sackman" featured a cigarette model who got hooked and damaged her lungs and voice box. Once again, the juxtaposition of former beauty and physical impairment made for a strong message. *Courtesy of the Massachusetts Department of Public Health.*

numbers are part of an approximately 35 percent remarkable statewide reduction. This reduction represented a net loss of more than $1.3 billion for the tobacco industry.

Drawing Conclusions

I asked Dr. Connolly what he had learned over five years of trying to reach the youth target, and he drew a couple of conclusions: "while we can reach kids under twelve in a meaningful way, I almost think we should reduce our efforts in the twelve- to eighteen-year-old age group." He explains this is because "they are so resistant to any 'establishment' effort that we may promote smoking rather than prevent it." If this group is addressed it must be "in the direct, honest, truthful tone of the Laffin and MacLaren spots." Connolly feels that ads like these are "de-glamorizing, de-normalizing, and de-legitimizing" smoking and that while it will certainly take some time, some gains may be made this way.

Connolly also feels that the fifteen- to twenty-four-year-old group can be susceptible to these messages. "There's great incentive at that age to stop and they're not so badly hooked that they can't quit" he explained. The dangers to pregnant women are one well-known incentive. Another is the fact that smokers are often ostracized in the workplace, an arena that youths in this age range are just entering. As Connolly explained, members of the so-called Generation X "have a powerful incentive to try to quit. The boss walks by and sees them outside smoking and shivering, and says to himself 'there's a loser!' When young people realize this we have to be there to give them the tools to act on that incentive."

This is not to imply that the various state campaigns should give up on teens. In fact, many states are digging in their heels against another threat to teens from a surprising source.

Industry Ads

As part of its settlement deal, Philip Morris agreed to produce some spots against teen smoking. Built into the language of most of these settlements is a very specific prohibition against "personal attacks on or vilification of any person, company, or government agency." One of its large New York agencies developed a campaign called "Choice," aimed ostensibly at teen smoking. But of course, the cigarette giant pegged it all to personal behavior and freedom of choice, a tune it's played since the start of anti-tobacco lawsuits. The smoker has made a free choice, manufacturers say. Billions of dollars of advertising had no effect on that decision, just on which brands consumers chose to try.

The four-state study by Teen Research Unlimited (TRU) of Illinois, tested two spots each from California, Arizona, Florida, and Massachusetts, as well as the Philip Morris spots, with identifying tags removed. Without exception, the state spots did better. In fact, when asked to guess which spots were produced by a tobacco company, the kids identified the Philip Morris spots by an overwhelming margin.

While these industry spots were relatively persuasion-neutral rather than purposely bad, I am reminded of a scene in the satiric book by Christopher Buckley, *Thank You for Smoking*. The hero, a spokesman and PR specialist for a tobacco lobby, is finally sent by his industry employers to hire an ad agency. In a very prescient piece of plotting, Buckley imagines that the industry finally must buckle under to public pressure and produce some youth-directed anti-smoking spots. Despite going outside of New York to find the least creative shop he can, Nick, our hero, is presented with some effective advertising at the first creative meeting. He sets up a video conference with Sven, the agency Creative Director:

> "[We] avoided the whole health issue," said Sven, "and instead tapped into the adolescent's innate fear of being manipulated by adults. You didn't like it."
>
> "Right. Because it was effective."
>
> "It's gone. So now . . . we want to speak to them with the voice of despised authority . . . "
>
> "I like it already," Nick said.
>
> "Okay," Sven said. "Here we go." He pulled the board into video range. All it had on it was type. It said "Everything Your Parents Told You About Smoking Was Right."
>
> " . . . You know what I love about it?" Sven said. "Its dullness . . . kids are going to look at this and go 'Puuke.'"
>
> "I think," Nick said, "that I can sell this to my people."

All this would be worth a chuckle, if there weren't some disturbing trends behind it. Many states that are to be recipients of the tobacco-settlement money are asking why they should spend the money on home-grown advertising when there's "perfectly fine" stuff being produced by the tobacco industry.

Figure 10.9 shows one of the Philip Morris spots. They are very restricted in what they can address. While the "Choice" theme was expressed in what appeared to be "real kid" talk, the impact was predictably underwhelming with the teen research respondents.

It goes even further. Some state tobacco-control committees are hearing from their Republican governors on the subject. I have no personal evidence of a quid pro quo. However, I do know that while anti-

---

Choice (Bus)

INTERVIEWER: Hey guys, can I ask you a couple of questions?
GUY: Go ahead, all right.
INTERVIEWER: Have you ever tried cigarettes?
GUY: Nope.

INTERVIEWER: Why not?
GUY: I don't know, I just never wanted to, you know what I mean?
INTERVIEWER: Really?

GUY: Yeah, I mean some of my friends tried it or whatever, somebody'll have a pack after school, and you know, they'll smoke it or whatever.

INTERVIEWER: Do you think they tried it because other people were doing it?
GUY: Yeah, yeah . . . yeah, but that's dumb though, ya see what I'm sayin'?

. I mean the reason that it is dumb, not... they're dumb, but that's a stupid reason to do anything.

OTHER GUY: It's stupid as far as I'm concerned.
GUY: I feel ya, I feel ya.

FIGURE 10.9 *The Philip Morris Company.*   "Choice (Bus)" was produced as part of the states' tobacco settlement, and claimed "personal choice," rather than industry manipulation, influences young smokers. Industry attempts are under way to manipulate state governments to replace their campaigns with these spots, which tested poorly among teens in research conducted by Massachusetts and other states.

smoking ads were largely ignored by the tobacco industry, probably because they know their core market is already hooked, there has been a change that is causing them concern: they are losing some smoking-related illness trials. Most of these losses are in states where the jury pool has seen some anti-smoking ads, most of which have a strong anti–tobacco industry message.

With the exception of New Jersey, states with Republican governors seem to be the most ardent in closing down local campaigns. And according to the *Boston Globe*, the largest contributor to the Republican Governors Association, with a seat on its fund-raising board, is Philip Morris. The *Globe* describes Governors Association meetings as "fertile ground for lobbying Republican Party executives to get behind the industry's agenda."

This is a constantly evolving situation and demonstrates the difficulties that exist when a cause marketing effort goes up against a well-funded and well-connected industry.

Now let's get back to the other aspects of the Massachusetts multi-campaign campaign.

SECONDHAND SMOKE

The next area we attacked was environmental tobacco smoke, known generally as secondhand smoke. The emergence of evidence regarding environmental tobacco smoke as a cause of disease radically altered the anti-smoking landscape. Even many of the devout libertarians who opposed any tobacco control as being the work of "tobacco nazis" were brought up short by the idea that other people's poisons exhaled in their (and their children's) space could cause serious health problems. As the old saying goes, "I believe in your freedom, but it stops at the tip of my nose!"

The state of California has found considerable success devoting a lot of its anti-smoking cause effort to using secondhand smoke dangers as leverage to put nonsmoking regulations in place. In Massachusetts we decided we could not ignore this issue and designated one mini-campaign to the subject.

The tobacco-control agency designed a series of surrealistic spots showing some people exhaling clouds of smoke (photographed in an ugly, unseductive way that didn't break the "show no product" rule) and a spokesman talking about the 34 percent increase in your chances of getting lung cancer by being in the same room. The on-camera person,

Thomas Gibson (who aced the New York audition and went on to become Greg on the television series "Dharma and Greg"), says, "You know, there's a warning on cigarette packs for people who smoke. Where do you think they ought to put the warning for people who breathe?"

A scared little girl was used in the same format to bring the message down to protecting kids. And to raise the bar, in the third spot, it was slowly revealed that the female spokesperson talking about smoke getting in the body of "every single person there" is pregnant. "There are no exceptions," she adds as there is a flutter-cut of the fetus.

A spot showing a baby monitor with the sound of a baby coughing reveals, via type, that "every year 200,000 babies get sick from second-hand smoke." As a large male hand descends into frame and turns the

---

Warning

(*Music, sfx throughout: people inhaling smoke*) This is secondhand smoke.

It's what you breathe when you're in a room where other people smoke.

The same stuff you smell on your clothes goes into your lungs

and increases your risk of getting lung cancer by 34 percent.

You know, there's a warning on cigarette packs for people who smoke.

Where do you think they ought to put the warning for people who breathe?

FIGURE 10.10 *The Massachusetts Tobacco Control Program.* "Warning," one of three secondhand smoke spots, photographed smoke to appear menacing, not seductive. And yes, the spokesman was Thomas Gibson, before he became Dharma's Greg. *Courtesy of the Massachusetts Department of Public Health.*

annoying device off, the title becomes "but the tobacco industry doesn't want to hear it!"

The tobacco industry still denies the dangers of secondhand smoke even though disturbing new data from California confirms the greater incidence of lung cancer in waiters and waitresses working in smoking-allowed bars and restaurants. But the issue seemed to be motivating to citizens of Massachusetts, who, town by town, have passed increasingly stringent "no smoking" regulations for restaurants and public buildings.

QUITTING

The tone of the "quitting" campaign, aimed at smokers who were contemplating quitting, was very supportive and very knowing about the

Baby Monitor

(Sfx: Baby crying)    (Sfx: Baby coughing)    (Sfx: Monitor clicking off)

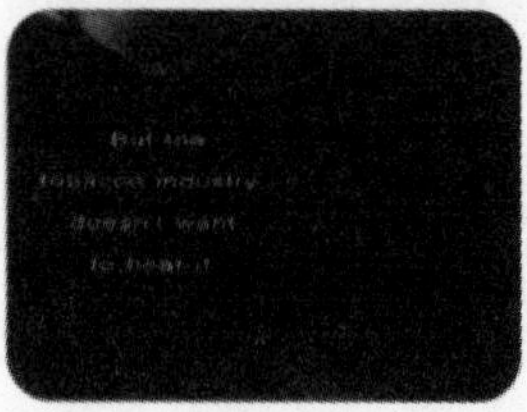

(Silence)

FIGURE 10.11 *The Massachusetts Tobacco Control Program.* "Baby Monitor" used sound effects and titles to dramatically present the effects of secondhand smoke on infants. *Courtesy of the Massachusetts Department of Public Health.*

trauma of quitting. It promoted the American Cancer Society–manned "Quitline" and offered quitting tips to smokers.

"Cigarette Pack" remains one of the best-received spots in the campaign because, once again, it's reaching addicted targets where they live. Smokers in focus groups told us that they had actually tried the "picture in the pack" tip.

A companion pool dealt with the promise of increased lung capacity, with two warmly exaggerated spots congratulating smokers who had quit, and paying off with "superhuman" displays of increased lung capacity.

Cigarette Pack

I know I shouldn't smoke. I've tried to quit a million times.

I know about lung cancer, heart disease, all that stuff.

I mean, they're listed right on the side of the pack.

It still doesn't make quitting any easier.

But I'm going to keep at it because the way I see it

if the reasons in the side of the pack don't get to me, the reason on the front will.

FIGURE 10.12 *The Massachusetts Tobacco Control Program.* "Cigarette Pack" was a strong, sympathetic portrayal of a "quitter," and demonstrated a viable quitting tip: slipping your child's picture into the cellophane on the pack. It resonated strongly with smokers and greatly increased traffic on the "Quitline," whose number was supered at the end. *Courtesy of the Massachusetts Department of Public Health.*

THE EPIPHANY

Many smokers have said during qualitative research sessions that there is a moment when smokers decide the habit has taken them over, that it is ruling their lives and making them slaves to something they decide they have to cut loose. Some said it happened in a car in traffic when a lighted ash fell into their lap and nearly set them on fire, or when a first date noticed the constant trips to the bathroom, or during the agony of a transcontinental flight with no chance to smoke.

They described it as an epiphany, and the agency designed three very warm, funny spots that exaggerated that moment but gained some rueful recognition from smokers. For the dropped-ash situation, there was a brutal parody of a beleaguered "Marlboro Man" (see figure 4.5). For the "first date" situation, the agency designed a ladies' room visit from hell, complete with screeching smoke detectors and spraying sprinklers. And for the trapped flier, the famous "Twilight Zone" episode was parodied, with a chain-smoking "demon" on the wing outside the plane's window.

LIGHT CIGARETTES

Research with smokers also revealed an alarming misconception that "light" cigarettes are actually safer, and therefore healthier to smoke, than regular brands. So those who were having trouble quitting believed that by switching to lights, they were at least minimizing the risk. In truth, that's another cynical myth perpetrated by the industry. The cigarettes are actually designed with little vents around the filter, which give them low numbers on the "smoking machines." But these vents are covered up in the course of normally placing the cigarette in the mouth, so the tar levels tend to rise right back to about where they are with regular cigarettes. And if they don't, smokers traditionally just suck harder until they get the flavor they crave and the tar they don't.

Research told us many smokers were delaying quitting by "tapering off" to lights under this specious reasoning, so some commercials were designed to tell them they were doing just as much damage with these as with regulars.

Again, gentle humor was used to make the point, a tone that qualitative research said was appropriate for that target. An animated skull and crossbones made the point about the dangerous extra puffing, and a spokesman with a vacuum cleaner demonstrated the "vents" fallacy.

YOUTH ACCESS

The state's youth-access strategy was covered in Chapter Two. This very successful campaign, which I believe had an impact on public opinion on this issue, resulted in the ultimate stiffening of local and state regulations regarding sales to minors.

Skull and Crossbones

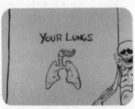

| SKULL: I gotta get me a new agent. I mean, I've been on almost everything that can hurt you, right? | Huh? So, how come I'm not on light cigarettes? Those are killin' smokers left and right | 'cause people are puffin' on them harder. Don't even know they're doin' it. |

| So they're suckin' in more tar and nicotine than the tobacco industry says they are. | Man, light cigarettes are deadly, and I should be right on the pack tellin' it like it is. | Hey, has this face ever lied to you? |

Figure 10.13 *The Massachusetts Tobacco Control Program.* "Skull and Crossbones" was a humorous animated spot revealing the risks of light cigarettes and the fallacy of switching to them as a "healthier" alternative. *Courtesy of the Massachusetts Department of Public Health.*

As mentioned in Chapter Five, "hot" and brilliant director Tony Kaye directed the basic spot (see figure 2.2). As we were shooting in a hospital in Somerville, Kaye, ever the improviser, convinced one patient with an audiovox device to "sing something" as the camera rolled. The man sang "Happy Birthday" and the footage was so compelling that, with some editorial ingenuity, we had another "anti-industry" spot. Incidentally, it won the Clio that year for best public service spot.

THE ANTI-INDUSTRY EFFORT

Four stark documentary spots in the series called "The Truth" dramatized the duplicity of the tobacco industry in its various activities to lie

---

Happy Birthday

  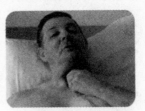

MAN (OC): *(Raspy voice)* Happy Birthday with the buzzer.

(Mechanical voice sings) Happy birthday to you,

happy birthday to you, happy birthday dear . . .

(Silence)

(Mechanical voice sings) . . . happy birthday to you.

FIGURE 10.14 *The Massachusetts Tobacco Control Program.* "Happy Birthday," an unexpected bonus spot, was created during shooting of another commercial when a lung-cancer patient with an electro-larynx was asked by the director to "sing something." The resultant "Happy Birthday" was turned into a strong anti-industry spot that won the public service Clio in 1996. *Courtesy of the Massachusetts Department of Public Health.*

and suppress information. The first two were confessionals by Patrick Reynolds, scion of the R. J. Reynolds Company, and Victor Crawford, a former tobacco lobbyist who died of lung cancer shortly after completing our filming. The third was by Janet Sackman (see figure 10.8), and the fourth featured Victor DeNoble as head of a tobacco company "addiction" research project employing rats. DeNoble had traveled to corporate headquarters to report his findings, and when he returned, his lab had been cleaned out, the rats killed, and he was fired.

In 1999, with the entire program under fire from the governor, the findings of the TRU research were released, with Dr. Connolly's comments about the "last place" finish for the Philip Morris spots. "Philip Morris can't do the kinds of advertisements that work best," Dr. Con-

---

Patrick Reynolds

REYNOLDS: Do you know what's in cigarettes?

No. Because the last thing the tobacco companies want is for you

to know how many poisonous chemicals there are in cigarettes. So they just don't tell you.

Not on the pack, not in their ads. I'm Patrick Reynolds, the grandson of R. J. Reynolds.

My family's name is printed on the side of 7 billion packs of cigarettes every year.

Why am I telling you this? Because I want my family to be on the right side, for a change.

FIGURE 10.15 *The Massachusetts Tobacco Control Program.* "Patrick Reynolds" presented the scion of the famous tobacco family, who regrets the damage caused by the deception of his family business. The commercial was shot in stark documentary style. *Courtesy of the Massachusetts Department of Public Health.*

nolly told the *Boston Globe*. "It's impossible for them to put a dying Marlboro Man on TV like we did."

To reinforce this, the Massachusetts campaign released a series of spots entitled "Where's the Outrage," which are about as anti-industry as you can get. They are also very current and very strong. (Viewers—and perhaps voters—are urged to access the www.getoutraged.com website). The site had received 300,000 "hits" by late 1999, with lots of outraged messages posted on the site bulletin board.

A sudden and significant validation of the embattled strategies of both the Massachusetts and Florida campaigns came in September 1999. Arnold Communications, the Massachusetts agency, joined forces with Crispin Porter & Bogusky, creators of the Florida program, along with several minority agencies to pitch a huge national anti-smoking campaign estimated at between $150 and $225 million in billings and targeted to the youth of America. This campaign was funded by the 1998 forty-six-state settlement and managed by the American Legacy Foundation, a group set up by the states to administer those funds.

Outrage

VO: The tobacco industry needs your children. It's an economic imperative. One business cycle winds down, another picks up the slack. It's nothing personal. It's just business. Minus a conscience.

SUPER: 3000 kids get hooked every day. Where's the outrage? It's time we made smoking history.
www.getoutraged.com

FIGURE 10.16 *The Massachusetts Tobacco Control Program.* "Outrage" was a strong anti-industry spot with a chilling and cynical voice-over. The visual, however, broke the "don't show product" rule. The website URL shown at the end is a source of anti-industry news and "insider" documents. *Courtesy of the Massachusetts Department of Public Health.*

Competing against ten of the largest American agencies, Arnold Communications and Crispin Porter & Bogusky based their pitch on work they had done in their individual states and that their research showed had resulted in a significant reduction in youth smoking. Both states had run youth campaigns headlined "The Truth." The Florida campaign focused more on youth activism, with its "SWAT" teams testing and taunting the industry, while the Massachusetts effort focused on actual testimony from repentant former tobacco employees and their relatives as well as smokers damaged by nicotine-related disease. However, the two efforts meshed amazingly well according to Arnold creative director Peter Favat, who took a lead role on the pitch.

It is likely that the national campaign will evolve from the melding of these two state efforts and, interestingly, will use tobacco company money (derived from the settlement) to expose the "truth" about devious industry efforts to lure new young customers. This anti-industry thrust is exactly the approach that industry lobbyists and Republican governors in both Florida and Massachusetts have reportedly attempted to undermine, both subtly and not-so-subtly. Hopefully, under the impetus of this national campaign, the state programs will return to their previous ardor and the bland industry-produced "Choice" spots will quietly fade away.

The Massachusetts campaigns have a 35 percent overall reduction in cigarette sales as their most impressive performance "evaluation." Given a cyclical model in which consumption goes up and down, and the fact that research "attitude" figures are sometimes suspect, this is a measurable decline in tax revenue. It represents a very significant accomplishment for this sometimes embattled cause effort.

After two years of unrelieved hard-hitting campaigns—from "Pam Laffin" to "Get Outraged!"—it was decided to celebrate the Millennium with a more optimistically toned group of spots in early 2000. These ads showed diverse groups of children laughing and playing under the theme "What if we raised a smoke-free generation?" It is, said Dr. Connolly, a way of "giving the people of Massachusetts a hug" after being "in their face" for so long. However, he promises they will be given reasons to "get outraged" again soon!

This temporary change of approach is a wise move. A campaign with the frequency of exposure and longevity of this state effort cannot deal solely in shock and human misery. As Dr. Susan Moeller states in her book *Compassion Fatigue*, prolonged exposure to such material will cause an audience to become simultaneously over-stimulated and bored. The next time we see one of those "tough" messages we will simply turn the page (or change the channel). Instead, advertisers must give their targets hills and valleys of outrage and optimism.

It should be obvious that I am strongly invested in this campaign. It is particularly satisfying to see it form the basis for an effort poised to reach out to youthful smokers across the country in a cause campaign second only in size to that of the Partnership for a Drug-Free America. It stands a good chance of continuing to push those tobacco consumption numbers down and to change personal behavior and even public policy. That's what a well-executed cause campaign is all about!

A TOP TEN LIST

*My Pick of the Best Cause Marketing
Campaigns and Why They Worked*

In this era of top ten lists, I see no reason not to join the trend, especially in a book dedicated to laying out principles that should guide you toward some degree of excellence.

I am sure there are other campaigns that sponsors or creators may feel belong in this chapter. If you want to offer suggestions, please E-mail me at rearle@causemarketer.com. If there's a second edition, we'll give them full consideration. I may also consider placing a "Cause Campaign of the Month" on the site.

As of my survey of the field today, here are my picks:

1. American Cancer Society: "Yul Brynner"

This commercial was one of the strongest pieces of cause advertising ever produced. It broke one of my rules by using a celebrity presenter, but it used that celebrity in a shockingly strong way, one that was *directly* tied into the essence of the cause. A beloved performer tells you that if you are watching him, he has died from the results of the activity the sponsoring organization is trying to prevent. No frills, no "addyness" just a voice from beyond the grave. And boy, do you listen to what he says!

2. The Advertising Council/The National Forestry Service: "Smokey Bear"

One of the most famous icons in advertising history, and Smokey has legs! I doubt if his original creators realized what a durable icon they

produced. One of the things I admire about this campaign is how innovative Smokey's handlers have been over the years; animation, jingles,
drama, scenic beauty have all played a role in keeping Smokey's messages fresh. But they have also respected and preserved his essential
qualities.

Smokey is simple, strong, straightforward. He's a denizen of those
woods you're visiting, and he cares about preserving them. Anyone who
grew up watching Bambi realizes how terrifying a forest fire can be. But
Smokey wouldn't run away. Smokey's strong. He'd stay and fight the
fire if necessary, but he'd rather have you douse it and cover it up so he
doesn't have to.

Yul Brynner

ANNCR VO: Ladies and
gentlemen, the late Yul Brynner.

YUL BRYNNER: I really
wanted to make a commercial
when I discovered that I was sick,
and my time was so limited.

I wanted to make a commercial
that says simply now that I'm
gone, I tell you, don't smoke.
Whatever you do, just don't
smoke.

If I could take back that
smoking, we wouldn't be talking
about any cancer.

FIGURE 11.1 *With thanks to the American Cancer Society.*

FIGURE 11.2 *Courtesy of the Advertising Council.*

An icon originally designed to engage kids, with the hope that they would influence their parents in a camping situation, Smokey crossed all the demographics, and now belongs to us all.

3. The Advertising Council/Keep America Beautiful: "Crying Indian"
The "Crying Indian" is dear to my heart and the second icon on this list. It's a strong, simple, durable, much lauded symbol, recognized by *TV Guide* as one of the fifty greatest commercials of all time. A detailed description of this campaign is found in Chapter Four.

4. The Partnership for a Drug-Free America: "Long Way Home"
This is not only the 1992 winner of the "Grand Effie," it is a great cause advertising spot, covered in some detail in Chapter Nine. The thing I most admire about it is that it grew straight out of the research (which delivered an unexpected finding). In every detail—language, tone, visual imagery—it seems to directly reflect the life and environment of the target. It is strong, reinforcing, real, and doesn't preach! And by simply reinforcing some attitudes young targets perhaps didn't realize would be supported by anyone, it has a stronger impact than anything that might have seemed like a lecture.

FIGURE 11.3 *Courtesy of the Advertising Council and Keep America Beautiful, Inc.*

5. The Partnership for a Drug-Free America: "Drowning"

This spot, also described in Chapter Nine, is a prime example of how information can be dramatically transmitted to targets that desperately need it. The imagery is surreal, but doesn't go over the top. Totally involving to the target audience, it dramatically holds their attention while communicating the hard facts about inhalants. This one could save lives!

6. Massachusetts Tobacco Control Program: "The Truth—Cowboy"

This spot addresses the real health consequences of smoking in a way that can impact both adults and children. It gets around the "immortal" teens' rejection of the "you'll get sick and die" argument because it shows the physical destruction of an icon that, admit it or not, they have admired and tried to emulate. The cool, macho Marlboro Man image was likely a factor in their decision to smoke. By showing a home video of the horrible disfigurement he suffered in his final days, the ad is an in-your-face reminder that the dangers of smoking are very real. And the use of that shot, together with his brother Mac's heartrending

BOY VO: My teacher tells us
just say no.

Policeman says the same thing.

They should walk home

through here.

'Cause the dealers don't take no
for an answer.

ANNCR VO: To Kevin Scott

and all the other kids who take
the long way home.

We hear you. Don't give up.

FIGURE 11.4 *Courtesy of the Partnership for a Drug-Free America.*

Drowning

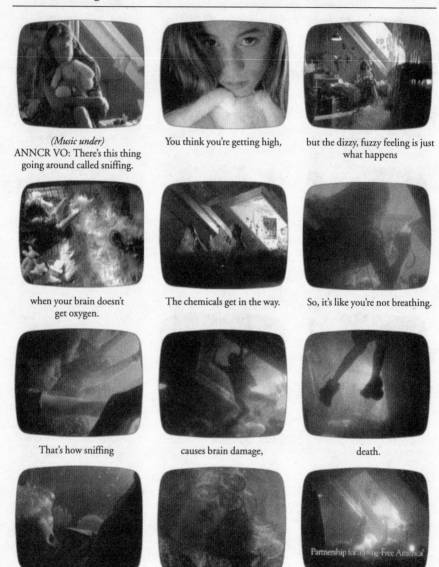

(Music under)
ANNCR VO: There's this thing going around called sniffing.

You think you're getting high,

but the dizzy, fuzzy feeling is just what happens

when your brain doesn't get oxygen.

The chemicals get in the way.

So, it's like you're not breathing.

That's how sniffing

causes brain damage,

death.

So when you think you're sniffing,

your brain thinks you're drowning.

And your brain is pretty much right.

FIGURE 11.5   *Courtesy of the Partnership for a Drug-Free America.*

narrative, turns the imagery that the tobacco lobby had spent millions to promote right back on itself.

7. *The Advertising Council/The Parkinson Foundation of Canada: "Puzzle"*

This is a fairly old campaign discovered in the Ad Council archives, but when it comes to mounting an appeal for people to seek information about a crippling disease, it's about as good as it gets. The symptoms of Parkinson's disease were clearly and touchingly portrayed. Employing the kid's puzzle as a "product demonstration" was simple but strong. The use of the child in the spot added just the right contrasting note. He slipped the puzzle pieces in easily, while the tremors of the old man's hand prevented him from doing so. The child's "helping hand" at the end as the voice-over gave the contact number for help was touching but didn't become banal.

The Truth—Cowboy

MACLAREN: I used to love cigarette ads—the cowboy on his horse, rugged, independent.

It was beautiful. Then the cowboy died. Got lung cancer from smoking.

His name was Wayne MacLaren, and he was my brother. I'm Mac MacLaren.

The tobacco industry used my brother in ads to create an image

that smoking makes you independent. Don't believe it.

Lying there with all those tubes in you, how independent can you really be?

FIGURE 11.6   *Courtesy of the Massachusetts Department of Public Health.*

Puzzle

(Music under)
ANNCR: Tremor in the hand, stiffness in the muscles, lack of coordination,

can make an adult more helpless than a child.

One in every two hundred Canadians

over the age of forty is hit by Parkinson's disease.

If you think it could be you, or someone in your family,

contact the Parkinson Foundation for help.

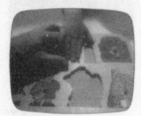

Because there is help.

(Music out)

FIGURE 11.7 *Courtesy of the Advertising Council.*

8. The Advertising Council/AIDSFILMS: "Vilma"

"Vilma" is a perfect example of the Ad Council's constant goal to keep up with issues that are important today. This spot was supplied by AIDS-FILMS, a nonprofit organization, and the sincerity and moving quality of the very real "Mom" makes it an extremely effective spot. Others in the series deal with the resistance of the "macho" male to condom use, and the deceptively healthy appearance of some people with AIDS.

9. The Advertising Council/The United Negro College Fund: "A Mind Is a Terrible Thing to Waste"

What a positive theme line! This is a campaign that could have become whiny, maudlin, or ultra "PC" in its appeals. Even the most moving grab for our sympathy might have had the unintended side effect of being dismissive or patronizing to the African American community.

Vilma

MOM: I have AIDS. And my baby has AIDS. My husband may have it, but he won't go to the doctor.

In the beginning, he wouldn't even talk about it. My mother helps us, but sometimes I think she's afraid.

Every night I kneel by my baby's crib and pray to be strong for him. Every night I pray that my baby won't die.

ANNCR (VO): Protect people you love. Use a condom.

FIGURE 11.8 *Courtesy of the Advertising Council.*

Instead, a strong, self-assured young man is portrayed, his head fading away, symbolic of the invisibility promising youth can experience if not educated up to their potential. His strong intelligence is taken for granted. The tragedy of wasting this intelligence and all the hope for the future it carries with it is characterized perfectly in the language. Even the subtle sound effect of the door closing as the head dissolves away is a strong but simple reminder of the consequences of ignoring this message.

A durable, long-lived campaign, and deservedly so!

10. The Advertising Council/U.S. Department of Transportation, National Highway Transportation Safety Campaign: "Crashing Glasses"
It would have been hard to beat this campaign's predecessor, a commercial entitled "I want to see Venice," in which a beautiful and promising

---

A Mind Is a Terrible Thing to Waste

ANNCR VO: There are people born every day who could make peace, cure disease, create art,

abolish injustice, end hunger. But if they don't get an education they may never get the chance.

A mind is a terrible thing to waste.

Send a check to the United Negro College Fund.

FIGURE 11.9   *Courtesy of the Advertising Council.*

young woman named Jenny was photographed to the accompaniment of an inspirational ballad. Then we were told that she died at the hands of "a lonely man driving drunk." (Note how the man was characterized in a sympathetic way rather than as a monster, so that targets could realize this might be them.)

But in its '90s successor, we are given a perfect symbolic graphic, glasses being clinked in the centuries-old rite of good fellowship between friends. Then in an instant, the camaraderie is turned into tragedy, and the shocking crash of the glasses directly reminds the viewer of the possible consequences of drinking and driving.

The theme line is perfect, not punitive or finger-shaking, just a direct expression of a concerned friend over the well-being of a companion.

Strong, simple, perfect tone, perfectly targeted.

Crashing Glasses

ANNCR: When friends don't stop friends from drinking and driving . . . *(Sfx: Car skidding and crashing)*

friends die from drinking and driving . . . .

(Sfx: Car skidding and crashing)

Friends don't let friends drive drunk.

FIGURE 11.10 *Courtesy of the Advertising Council.*

12

SOME CONCLUSIONS

My great-great grandfather, Absolam Backus Earle, was a Baptist evangelist who traveled the world "converting souls." My great uncle, Wilbur Deming, was a missionary in Asia, and his father, my great grandfather Minor Deming, was pastor at the Tremont Temple in Boston. *His* cousin P. T. Barnum used to loan him the circus tent for Sunday revival meetings when he was in town, which I always thought lightened him up quite a bit. One day my father, observing my devotion to cause marketing, commented that I was probably carrying on, in my own way, a long family tradition.

In drawing some conclusions about cause marketing with which to close this book, it has occurred to me that cause promotion does have a tendency to wrap itself in missionary zeal. I've heard that Puritan preacher Cotton Mather in 1721 used his influence and pulpit to promote a cause dear to him: urging the citizens of the Massachusetts Bay colony to get inoculated against a raging smallpox epidemic. But I'm not sure this kind of zeal in pursuit of a cause is always a good thing.

That is not meant to put down the sincerity of those who do this work. I believe total devotion to the cause by those who promote it will create the commitment and extra energy it takes to get the work done and placed before the public in a timely fashion.

However, there is a downside to excessive zeal: it can sometimes blind people to the practical techniques required to make things happen. It can make its practitioners resistant to criticism, no matter how constructive, and it can reduce their ability to step back and take a hard look at the work. Is the work good because the cause is just, or is it good because it is good work?

BAPTIST PLUS BARNUM

So the first conclusion I would like to leave with you is: Be a missionary if you must, but be a bit of a Barnum, too!

You may be very moved by the tragic story of Carroll O'Connor's loss of his son to drugs. You may almost want to say "amen" to his heartfelt plea. But is his sincere zeal the best vehicle for your message?

Because you are deeply moved by the subject, you may convince yourself that you are deeply moved by the ad. But it may not be the best message to reach the specific target that will give you the best result.

As an advertising professional, do all the smart things you would regularly do to sell detergent or a new SUV model. Do your research carefully; create a tough, smart strategy; cast and produce and place your advertising with all the skill you can muster. Then, if it also provokes a soul-satisfying emotion when you see it, that's a plus and so much the better!

NO CHICKEN SOUP

In this age of *Dummies* and *Chicken Soup* books, which seem to offer quick answers to everyone's problems, let me state that you will not finish this book and feel that you now possess the secret to effective cause marketing.

I wish I could fill this concluding chapter with an easily mastered list of rules that promise success, but I can't. In fact, I sometimes think the single best thing I can leave you with is a theme that I have repeated over and over: *this is the hardest type of advertising to do, bar none.* Do it badly and you may do your cause more harm than good. If you just stop and ponder that fact before you move ahead with your program, you will have taken an important first step in avoiding some of the easy pitfalls awaiting the practitioners of this difficult art. I'll take the theme a little further to a conclusion I'm sure you don't want to hear: *if you can't do it well, don't do it at all!*

But lest I end on too negative a note, let me extract a few of the principles I hope you will retain from this exploration, and list them here at the end. More of them, I fear, are in the category of things to avoid rather than innovative techniques to improve success. But if you pay attention to the principles on this list, you stand a much better chance of doing it right, of doing no harm and possibly doing some good.

THE SEARCH FOR GREAT RESEARCH

There is no advertising activity that requires any more sophisticated research than cause marketing. As agencies explore account planning and other researchers experiment with concept sorts, sophisticated and vast quantitative studies, and Internet research, I urge the research community to continue to push the envelope when it comes to cause work, particularly with an eye to analyzing and characterizing the psychology of the target market.

In an age of incredibly sophisticated computer-driven production techniques that allow advertising to be produced as thrillingly and efficiently as at any time in its history, many of the techniques used in research are still archaic.

The obvious conclusion is that no matter how well produced the advertising is, if the basic strategy and psychological appeals are off target, so, too, will be the advertising. And the fault will lie in the research.

So keep your eyes and ears open. Somewhere, I am convinced some young researcher out there is about to find a technique that will deliver the kind of data crucial for this type of marketing.

But until that savior appears, get the best researcher you can, and analyze the data very, very carefully.

NOTHING LESS THAN THE BEST

If you are pitching a cause account, put forward your best and brightest. Be sure your best people are involved, and that any speculative work is well researched and thought out. This is important work. And it may well lead to the most visible and praiseworthy pieces on your agency reel. I can't tell you how many new business pitches for a commercial account in which I have been involved over the years were clinched when the CEO learned that an admired PSA for one of his favorite causes was produced by the pitching agency.

THE SOLID STRATEGY

Whether you're with a "planning" agency, working with a creative brief, or still use the tried-and-true creative strategy, build it of solid bricks and firm mortar. Build it strong, build it carefully, get everyone involved to sign off, and keep it in front of you at all times.

Let's take a few minutes to return once again to that crucial guide. No matter where or how far you travel in your quest for the perfect communication of your ideas, stick your head up regularly, check out that crucial signpost, and make sure you haven't wandered too far afield.

The Target

Remember how different your targets are. Remember how different their psychology may be. Consider an elaborate "what do we know about them" section. And visualize the targets. Picture them right there in front of you!

Never, never co-opt something written for one very limited target for use on another. Remember the "Just say no!" debacle.

Also, if you are portraying your target in your advertising, make sure that portrayal is sympathetic, or at least empathetic. The portrayals of parents in the Partnership spots urging them to talk to their kids seem to be all over the place. I recently reviewed some spots from several different groups aimed at the loved ones of compulsive gamblers. The frustration of loved ones when they discover a family member has gambled away savings or a paycheck is usually severe. But when dramatizing this, the line between a sympathetic portrayal of that frustration and one that is mean and off-putting can be very thin. These, unfortunately, were mean. The worst thing you can do is have your target react to an unsympathetic wife or child in your thirty-second drama by saying: "That's not me. I would never behave like that."

Principal Idea and Desired Action

Principal idea and desired action are always intertwined, and more so in cause marketing. As I've said many times, in most product or service advertising, the action is obvious: go buy the product! In cause campaigns, it's a very different story. The desired actions can be many, some dead simple, some life-changing and complex:

- listen to us
- think well of us
- give money
- think before you hurt your environment
- volunteer
- get involved
- support change
- vote
- act
- think before you act
- warn your friends or loved ones before they act dangerously
- help your friends or loved ones get help
- talk to your doctor
- talk to your kids
- stay strong
- think about your actions and beliefs
- think about the consequences of your actions
- think about how your beliefs can impact others
- care about consequences
- make a resolution
- open your mind
- open your heart
- teach, mentor

Wow! And I could go on. Also there are some actions and reactions we *don't* desire:

- think we're stupid or out of it
- keep on doing risky things
- ignore what we say
- do the opposite of what we say

Almost none of these possibilities is considered when you're doing a product or service campaign. So, while you craft the best communication for your brand you can, what's the worst that can happen if you fail? The share goes down, the account leaves, you're in trouble. You'll bounce back!

On the other hand, if you ignore the complexity of these issues in a cause campaign, you may do some major harm. Major harm! But if you take your time, and take the extra effort to really get it right, you'll do some good. And that's no small accomplishment in today's world!

Tone and Style

I keep coming back to tone and style. It's so important because it's the oft-ignored factor that can really sneak up and bite you if you're not careful. Strike the wrong tone with these psychologically complex targets, and it's good-bye! And don't call again!

Consider every word of your promises, your benefit statements, your slogans. A positive tone of voice can help you win. Too negative, and you lose.

THE KIDS

Just when I was despairing in my ability to give you any cogent insights on the youth psyche, the excellent study by the TRU group in Illinois was commissioned by the four states who have taken the lead in anti-tobacco advertising: Arizona, California, Florida, and Massachusetts. The study, as noted, will be used as a defense against a growing trend in the tobacco-settlement states to use that money to run the bland and neutral campaign funded by the source of the settlements, the Philip Morris Company. And even though this was a tobacco-specific study, much of what we found could apply to any other approach to this puzzling demographic.

When it comes to talking to teens about smoking, the "grunge" approach of the Arizona program and the industry-exploitation campaigns in Florida and California seem to lag somewhat behind the approach finally settled on in Massachusetts: giving strong, tangible, true stories of the serious effects of smoking as told by real sufferers. Of course, none of the "winners" has been shown to be as effective with teens as the creators of those campaigns would wish. But all the state campaigns work considerably harder with the youth audience than the "Choice" campaign produced by Philip Morris. That was revealed to be too rational, too unreal, too boring!

I'm not sure I'm as ready to give up on the twelve- to eighteen-year-old group as is Massachusetts' Dr. Connolly. But I do agree that they are absolutely the hardest to reach, especially when it comes to risky behavior practices.

Jane Rinzler Buckingham, who did some of the early youth research for the Massachusetts anti-smoking campaign, notes how readily kids under twelve are to accept an establishment anti-drug, anti-smoking, or anti-drinking message. Kids that age are generally fairly docile and obedient and ready to listen to their parents, as the Partnership's research has shown (although I know some parents who might dispute that). But the minute those hormones kick in, reports Jane, they're no longer "ours." And establishing independence may mean acting directly opposite to the way we want them to act. They belong to their peers. And the "establishment" is often seen as the enemy.

This trend has been true almost forever. But the way it plays out could change in the next year. Or in the next state. If your mission is to reach kids, on the subject of tobacco, drugs, or whatever your cause, the best advice I can give you is to keep testing. And keep watching. And analyze the data very carefully. As the trends change, change your approach. Adolescents have always been an enigma, and they probably always will be. But we can't give up on them. They are a significant target for the cause marketer, and campaigns aimed at this vulnerable target are always going to receive the most public interest and support.

THE INDIRECT APPROACH

In the title of this book we promised to tell you how to use advertising to change personal behavior. But since there are enormous differences in the kinds of causes for which marketing is being done today, there must be very different approaches employed for each.

As we have seen in the chapter on the addicted target, a direct approach to this target may not be best. To reach the addicted gambler, for example, we have opted for an indirect approach by going to the family and loved ones who may be far more ready to recognize there is a problem for which treatment should be sought.

While I sense that certain camps within the Partnership for a Drug-Free America advisory group may still wish to mount a stern "thou shalt not" approach to all youthful drug experimentation, I continue to root for those who recognize the power of the parent and mentor as far greater than any ad, and solicit their participation through the mass media, while supplying guidance through other sources.

Experimenting with addictive substances or behavior cannot be effectively addressed just through short messages. But messages that approach the problem indirectly can accomplish a great deal. And once again our messages can set a tone, an attitude that may make our targets receptive to the more in-depth approach.

The hard line or moralistic approach, which says to kids things like "no sex until marriage" or "all drugs will lead to death, mental breakdown, and destruction of a family," ignore the nature of life today, and the youth perception of it. The peer group, probably the principal source of information on average teen opinion, is bound to contain high-functioning users of marijuana, and nice, polite, "future good citizen" couples who are sexually active.

Like many of those conservatives, I, too, wish the world were a more moral place, where most of life's decisions were painted in the black-and-white of right and wrong, as many of them were when I was threading my way through adolescence. But it is not, and no amount of wishing or proselytizing will make it so.

So do we wrap our messages to kids in a high moral tone they are likely to reject and, therefore, make every message from ours or any cause organization suspect?

Or do we accept the reality of the way things are? This means opting for messages which, for example, segment out and educate about the drugs that are most dangerous and misunderstood, such as inhalants or speed, and try to save *some* kids from their serious consequences. Do we, say, recognize teen sexuality and stem the spread of serious disease and pregnancy in that population by promoting "safe sex"? None of this precludes a strong pitch for abstinence, but each avoids the dismissal of the sponsoring body as a bunch of rigid moralists with little relevance to the real world.

We must meet people where they are. We cannot be disingenuous and describe their world as the world we wish it were. If we do, they will reject us. This is not advocating a soft approach to risky behavior. We must describe the dangers of these behaviors. But we must do it honestly, and not exaggerate them or lump all categories together.

While completely addicted targets surely are best reached indirectly, it may be possible to "soften up" addicted targets with some information that describes the source of their problem, be they social, chemical, or genetic causes, and reduces or removes their anxiety about self-perceived moral weakness. Spousal and child abuse, youth nutrition, and immunization efforts may also require an indirect approach.

DIRECT-APPROACH CAUSES

Fortunately, not all human behavior we wish to impact with our messages is so complicated.

The decision to carefully extinguish a campfire or properly dispose of litter, to become a mentor, to organize a neighborhood crime watch, to buckle a safety belt, to take the keys away from a drunk friend, or even to give to a cause like the United Negro College Fund or UNICEF can be the result of a direct, emotional, involving advertising message.

Even the decision to use a condom during sex, while it carries a bit more emotional and personal baggage, can probably be inspired by a fairly direct (albeit more psychologically crafted) message.

If these or similar goals are what your cause is all about, then you are fortunate, and the search for the right message will be an easier and less frustrating one.

But an important conclusion that I want to leave you with is that you *must* identify and separate those targets that can be reached directly from those that must be reached by the indirect route. And be very careful to use appropriate approaches for each.

GUILT OR SHOCK

For many years, pictures of starving, dirty children, and mutilated animals have been used to rattle our complacency. Others have appealed to our sense of guilt over our affluence or indifference to suffering. It would seem that the camps are still divided as to the more effective technique. I would suggest that qualitative research should be able to resolve the "shock versus guilt" issue for your cause. My own feeling is that since we live in the age of shock news we are sadly becoming increasingly inured and desensitized to even the most graphic portrayals of tragedy or cruelty. But this is a constantly changing situation, and yesterday's focus group may have delivered different results from today's.

My former colleague and friend, Barbara Fagan, who helped with so many aspects of this book, supplied me with an interesting example of this written in the mid-70s when she was at Lord Geller Federico. She was asked to create a fund-raising magazine insert designed to generate contributions for UNICEF, a major supplier of vitamins, food, and health services to children in developing countries. As Susan Moeller puts it in *Compassion Fatigue*, "the best of these ads promise that if we respond, we can throw off our fatigue and become once again a caring person." But how best to frame that promise?

As a mother, Barbara recalled her own "horror-gulp-turn-the-page" response to previous "damaged children" appeals, and was determined to show instead only positive "good fortune" visuals. She persuaded first-tier food photographer Henry Sandbank to donate some mouthwatering color shots of hamburgers, crisp salads, and juicy sirloins, and created a "spare a bite" appeal, which equated the cost of a hamburger and fries with the ability to positively impact a malnourished child for a month.

Even the clip-out coupon featured a picture of some delicious-looking french fries. Respondents were invited, in addition to sending their check, to request reprints to support fund-raising events in their own communities. The response was unprecedented. And yet, the next appeal from UNICEF went right back to the "visualized horror" approach.

Barbara's ad did another smart thing. Rather than just mounting a vague appeal to "send money," it equated the modest cost of some fast food with specific dollar amounts that delivered positive benefits: "$1 is a year's supply of multi-vitamins for a child in a crisis country, $15 can bring supplementary food and health services to five malnourished children for a month in some developing countries."

THE FUNDAMENTALS

Once you have selected your target and precisely and rigidly drawn your strategy, don't abandon these fundamentals of any sound advertising:

- Keep it simple. Be clear. Limit the number of ideas.
- Grab them early.
- Consider problem/solution.
- Be honest!
- Dramatize your benefit.

- Casting: the key.
- Ask for the order! Pick a memorable domain number or box number and keep it up there long enough to be remembered.
- Speak with one voice. Make sure all the elements (logo, typeface, theme line) are common.

And finally, let me repeat once again that odd-sounding admonition of Mark Twain: "Kill all your darlings." Or to paraphrase an old Y&R trade ad, don't let "that's a great ad" overwhelm "that's a great idea." About the only unfortunate aspect of Bill Bernbach's groundbreaking legacy, and that of the brilliant writers he discovered and nurtured, is that every so often, in their skilled pursuit of the essence of a product or service, they produced an outrageous but brilliant pun or a juxtaposition of words so unusual that it stuck forever in the consciousness of the readers. But those who would *emulate* them today so often pursue the mindsticker to the total exclusion of the central tenets of the product or cause.

A clear, moving, straightforward statement of your goals will always be better than the cleverest pun you can devise if the link between that "darling" phrase and the desired action of your ad is the slightest bit indirect or abstract.

TO BE PC OR NOT PC

Like many people I know, I often get annoyed when ultrasensitivity to issues or language that might be considered "politically incorrect" creates barriers to common-sense communication. There's a street sign at a sharp curve near my house that announces "limited sight distance." The first fifty or so times I passed it, I scratched my head. What the heck was that supposed to mean, especially to someone trying to be a safe driver? Then one day it hit me. That had to be the PC version of "*blind corner!*" It was designed not to offend our "visually challenged" friends. Actually, to not offend *their* friends because if they're truly visually challenged, they'd never see the sign in the first place. Give me a break!

However, if the cause organization you are creating ads for is dedicated to making the world a better place, and depends upon socially conscious people for funding, then perhaps you'd better put your work through the "PC Meter." Most breaching of political correctness is an unthinking use of stereotypes, but that does not excuse the harm it may ultimately do to a cause.

LOOK BOTH WAYS, THEN GO FOR IT!

In today's close, interconnected media age, it's a very common desire to have some input, to make an impact on the things we care about, on the people we love, on our country, on the world.

Advertising is a way to accomplish that. Its exposure is enormous, and its persuasive power is equally huge. An ad is, we hope, a media communication that affects people, rather than washing over them. It can provoke action. It can be a force for enormous change and economic impact. And it can be a tremendous force for good.

As a practitioner of advertising, you have great power in your hands. If you're a skilled practitioner, you possess a real gift. At the end of the day, if you've used it right, if you've carefully avoided all the unintended negatives, you can look back and say, "I made a positive difference!" That *is* true art, and it's a wonderful use of that gift.

Some wise guy once said that advertising is the most fun you can have with your clothes on. Well, I think cause marketing is the most fun you can have with your brain on.

Go on! Make a difference! And when the research is in and you realize how much of a difference you've made, it's one of the best feelings you'll ever have!

APPENDIX A

Advertising Council
Major Campaign Application

It Takes Time, but It's Worth the Effort

Thank you for taking the time necessary to complete the Advertising Council's Major Campaign Application. Your interest in obtaining Ad Council help is appreciated.

Your proposal is just that—a proposal. It need not be the last word on how your campaign should be conducted. Even so, it is important that you think clearly about your campaign idea and objectives from the very beginning of the application process.

We realize that answering all of the questions will take considerable effort. It is our hope that when you have worked through this application, you will not only have produced the best possible campaign proposal, but you will also have a better understanding of how effective public service advertising campaigns may be constructed.

Before You Complete the Application

- Carefully review the Ad Council's Campaign Selection Criteria and consider whether your proposal meets all standards or can do so in the future. Please also review Rules on Major Campaign Acceptance.

- Think through your campaign idea completely and reach a consensus about what the central goal of the campaign should be. Make sure that all of your senior decision-makers also understand the extent of the commitment you are proposing to undertake.

Before You Complete the Application, continued

- Give some preliminary thought to the following key questions about your proposed campaign:

  1. Who do I want to speak to? (Target audience)

  2. What do I want that person to understand? (Message)

  3. What do I want that person to DO? (Action Step)

  4. Why is it important? (Significance of Issue to Public)

  5. How is my organization equipped to help? (Qualifications)

- Please be prepared to commit the necessary budget and staff time to campaign development for a minimum of 3 years.

- The sample budget estimate of $350,000 per year is based on just one primary target audience, and includes production and distribution costs, research, campaign maintenance costs (such as monitoring placements of PSAs), and indirect Ad Council overhead reimbursement costs. You are strongly urged to make room in your proposed budget for pre- and post-launch research, new media opportunities, and high-use media such as out-of-home (bus shelter posters). The cost of direct-response fulfillment, such as a toll-free number and response piece, will also be your responsibility.

- Bear in mind that development of an Ad Council campaign is a team effort. The research, strategy, creative concepts and executions of your campaign will be developed by a team of leading communications industry professionals working as volunteers and Ad Council staff in cooperation with your own staff. All work must be approved by the Council's Campaigns Review Committee, as well as by you. Both the nonprofit partner and the Ad Council's signatures will appear on materials. The Ad Council is a communications and marketing *partner* throughout the entire public service effort.

- Please complete the attached application questionnaire and return it, along with all required attachments. Please answer questions briefly and in order, and use the same outline subheads on your reply. If you need help in answering any questions in this application, you may call the Advertising Council's Director, Local Campaigns and Proposals, Lynne Lee, at (212) 922-1500.

Good luck with your proposal!

Return applications to Ms. Lynne Lee, Director of Proposals, the Advertising Council, 261 Madison Avenue, New York, NY 10016-2303.

Major Campaign Proposal Questionnaire

I. Describe the Proposed Campaign

A. *What Is the Proposed Issue?*

What is the nature of the problem you believe can be alleviated with the help of public service communications?

- Please describe the problem briefly.
- Explain why the problem is important to the public.
- Explain any special impact on particular sub-groups.
- Document the problem using a few telling statistics.
- Append relevant research reports.

B. *How Can Public Service Advertising Help?*

Please explain briefly why you believe this issue could be successfully addressed through public service advertising.

- What is the single most important objective for your public service advertising campaign?
- Explain why advertising can help achieve this goal.
- Why do you need the Ad Council's help?

C. *Who Is the Intended Audience?*

Who do you want to reach with your public service message?

- Define target group(s) in terms of age, gender, any relevant demographics.
- Say why it is important to reach this group or groups.
- Would any part of your campaign be targeted to African Americans, Latinos, Asians, Native Americans, non-English speakers? Please explain how.
- If you have more than one target group, budget accordingly.

D. *What Is the Proposed Message?*

What do you want your target group(s) to understand about the issue you are addressing in your message?

- Describe what you think your target should know about your campaign issue.
- Describe any barriers or obstacles that might make understanding of the issue difficult for the public.

E. What Is the Proposed Call to Action?

Ideally, what action do you want your target audience to take in response to your public service message?

- Think of your target audience as an individual person. What can that person do in his or her home and/or community to help solve the problem in your campaign?

- Explain why this action is something an ordinary person can do.

- Explain why this action step will help solve the problem.

- Describe any impediments that might make it hard for your target audience to act.

F. Will Your Campaign Include Direct Response Fulfillment?

- Do you plan to use a local or national toll-free response number or response address in your advertising?

- Do you currently have or will you develop "collateral materials" such as brochures to use in reply to inquiries generated by your campaign?

- Have you or would you make arrangements to track and report the nature of inquiries generated by your campaign?

- Have you allocated sufficient funds to cover the costs of handling and tracking direct response fulfillment—budgeted separately from the main campaign budget?

- If you do not plan to use some kind of direct response mechanism in your campaign, please explain how you would plan to handle inquiries generated by your message, or say why a direct response mechanism would be unnecessary.

G. How Can Results Be Measured?

It is vital that you set goals for the results of your campaign from the outset, and plan ways to measure and assess the impact of your campaign.

Measurable results can include but are not limited to: direct replies to the advertising, such as calls to the toll-free number; positive changes in attitudes or behavior with respect to the campaign issue, measured through research studies; and indirectly, broad shifts in public attitudes and policies, reported through independent research studies, governmental surveys, or polls.

- In an ideal world, what in general would you like to see happen as a result of your public service campaign?

- Realistically, what specific goals would you like to achieve with your campaign in the first year? In three years? In five years? Set goals you believe you have a chance of meeting.

- How do you propose to measure progress towards specific goals?
- Have you conducted and/or do you plan to conduct research as a way of helping assess the impact of your campaign, and have you budgeted funds for this purpose?

H. Do You Meet Campaign Selection Criteria?

Without duplicating other answers in this questionnaire, briefly explain why your campaign proposal meets all of the Ad Council's criteria for campaign selection, which are included in this kit. If your proposal does not currently meet one or more of the criteria, explain how and when it could meet that standard in the future.

I. Timing and Support Considerations

- When do you propose to launch the campaign?
- Are there seasonal or event-related timing considerations?
- How long would you be prepared to support the campaign? (How many years?)
- How long would you continue the campaign and the program it supports if Ad Council assistance were withdrawn?
- Are you prepared to undertake a marketing program related to your campaign objective?
- What arrangements would you make to have the public service messages promoted among your associates, constituents and the media?

J. Budgetary Considerations

- Have funds been allocated and budgeted with which to conduct the public service advertising campaign? If so, what amount and for how many years?
- Please read "Rules for Campaign Acceptance," enclosed with this kit, and **see required attachments** section. Please supply all required attachments relating to your campaign budget and financing.

K. Background Considerations

- What other organization(s), private or governmental, presently offer public service messages addressed to the same problem or similar problems?
- How does your program differ?
- How does your program relate to Federal, State and Local City activities?

- Has an advertising agency already volunteered to create your campaign advertising? If so, please provide the name of the agency and identify your key contact there.

- Are you currently conducting or planning to conduct any other advertising campaign, whether public service in nature or paid? If so, please describe it in detail and explain why you need the Ad Council's help for a separate public service campaign.

II. Describe Proposed Campaign Nonprofit Partner

A. Nature of Proposed Campaign Partner

1. Please indicate the full name, address and telephone number of your organization, government agency, or coalition.

2. Please give the name and title of the person who would act as the liaison between your group and the Ad Council, and who would approve creative work if your campaign were accepted for development.

3. Please specify the nature of your organization, and **see required attachments** section.

   - Is yours a private, 501(c)3 nonprofit group? If not, what is your IRS tax-exempt designation?

   - Is proposed partner a government agency?

   - Is yours a coalition of private and/or governmental groups?

B. Questions for Private, Nonprofit Partners Only

1. When, where and for what purpose was your organization formed?

2. What service does your organization offer and who are the recipients?

3. How is your organization funded? **See required attachments.**

4. What expertise/resources does your organization possess with respect to the issue?

5. Please explain why your organization is sufficiently organized and staffed to manage a large public response as a result of your major national campaign effort.

6. What other organizations or individuals are familiar with your organization and can provide a reference or attest to your expertise on the proposed campaign issue? You are welcome to enclose a few selected testimonial letters with your application.

C. *Questions for Coalitions Only*

1. Please answer all questions requested for private, nonprofit sponsors.

2. In addition, please identify which group (either a 501(c)3 organization or government agency) will serve as the "convening" organization which will receive and disburse funds, and identify the name and title of the person who would approve campaign work, if other than the group and individual identified under "Nature of Proposed Campaign Sponsor."

3. Please list names, addresses, telephone numbers, name and title of key contact for each organization or government agency that is a member of the coalition.

4. Please describe briefly the background for each member of the coalition, and explain what expertise or resource each group brings to the coalition with respect to the campaign issue.

D. *Questions for Governmental Partners Only*

1. What programs and/or services does your branch of government offer to the public, and how do they relate to the campaign issue you are proposing?

2. What expertise/resources do you possess with respect to the proposed campaign issue?

3. Please explain how your branch of government is sufficiently organized and staffed to manage a large public response as a result of your major national campaign effort.

E. *Local Affiliations: Questions for All Proposed Campaign Partners*

1. Are there local groups, branches, chapters or related organizations affiliated with your national office, coalition, or government agency that can assist in marketing a major campaign at the community level? If so, please identify these affiliates and say where they are located. If necessary, you may append a list.

2. Have these local contacts committed themselves to assisting you with leveraging the effect of a public service campaign in their communities?

3. Do you have or can you obtain any other local assistance in marketing the campaign to media decision-makers and others?

4. Do you wish to adapt public service materials for particular key target markets as part of your campaign? This can increase the effectiveness of your messages. If so, have you allocated sufficient funds in your budget for this purpose?

III. Required Attachments

A. *Required documentation for private, nonprofit groups:*

The following must be submitted with proposal before Proposals Review Committee will consider application:

1. Documentation of IRS 501(c)3 status.

2. Audited financial statement from most recent fiscal year, no older than 12 months (or acceptable alternative, in judgment of Ad Council staff).

3. Most recent Annual Report.

4. Statement from National Charities Information Bureau or Philanthropic Advisory Service of Better Business Bureau showing that prospective sponsor organization meets their standards regarding compliance with fund-raising and organizational management (or acceptable alternative, in judgment of Ad Council staff).

5. Overall current year operating budget for sponsoring organization.

6. Written confirmation that funds for proposed campaign budget have been allocated and are immediately available for use. This confirmation shall be subject to review by the Ad Council to determine that satisfactory credit and funding is in place for this PSA campaign.

   or

   Written request for "Budgetary Conditional Acceptance," accompanied in writing by detailed, achievable fund-raising plan, specifying methods and time frames for obtaining whatever funds are lacking. See Rules on Major Campaign Acceptance.

B. *Required documentation for all campaign nonprofits:*

7. Please submit a realistic, rough separate budget for campaign, showing overall budget amount for each year, indicating number of years and showing in general what kinds of line items are planned. This does not represent final budget; if your campaign proposal is accepted, a final budget will be prepared in concert with campaign manager at Ad Council.

   There is no such thing as a "standard" budget. A rough rule of thumb—a "minimum" level for campaign funding per year, with only one target audience, is usually around $350,000 (including production and distribution costs, research, and indirect Ad Council overhead reimbursement costs, but excluding fulfillment).

   We understand that this is a significant funding requirement and have established policies that, on very rare occasions, enable the Ad Council to work with groups that do not have all necessary funds in hand at application time (see Rules on Major Campaign Acceptance). The Ad Council and its volunteer ad agencies do their best to ensure that campaign budgets are managed as cost-effectively as possible.

Give your best estimate of a budget amount. Factors that can affect actual costs include the kinds of media you imagine the campaign might use, costs of packaging and distribution, the amount of research you plan to conduct, the number of target audiences, the number of mailings each year, the number and kind of creative executions, etc. These specifics cannot be fixed until the campaign is actually prepared; so it is wise to allow a little "room to maneuver" in your budget.

The Director of Proposals will let you know if your initial proposed budget looks inadequate to sustain the kind of effort you are proposing.

APPENDIX B

Advertising Council
Endorsed Campaigns
Information and Application

What is an Endorsed Campaign?

Endorsement by the Ad Council is a way of recognizing the best of the many excellent public service messages produced by worthy organizations.

Endorsed Campaigns are public service advertising campaigns that are created outside of the Advertising Council. Campaign materials and information about their sponsors are submitted to the Ad Council, along with a complete application, for review and approval (see enclosed Application). Campaigns must meet specific criteria to win endorsement (see enclosed Criteria).

Only Endorsed Campaigns are entitled to be listed alongside the Advertising Council's own campaigns in the *Public Service Advertising Bulletin*. This publication is sent every two months to 17,000+ media decision-makers.

Why Request Ad Council Endorsement?

Ad Council endorsement of your campaign helps to heighten awareness and credibility of your effort, and enables media to contact you directly to request materials through a listing in the Council's *Public Service Advertising Bulletin*. Certain types of campaigns that generally would not be accepted as Major Campaigns with the Ad Council—such as fund-raising efforts, event-related campaigns, or campaigns dealing with international issues—can more readily be considered for acceptance as Endorsed Campaigns.

Many decision-makers in the media community report that they prefer to use PSAs that have been given Ad Council endorsement, which they look upon as a seal of quality. Ad Council endorsement has also been helpful on occasion to groups requesting PSA help from celebrity talent.

The Advertising Council
Endorsed Campaigns
Information and Application Questionnaire

The Advertising Council is pleased to announce a new designation for independently developed public service campaigns that meet its criteria:

Endorsed Campaigns

Formerly such campaigns were called Bulletin Campaigns. The new designation recognizes a change in the standards applied to such campaigns.

There are several key differences that benefit you:

- The Ad Council will now consider local public service campaigns for endorsement from the top ten media markets: New York, Los Angeles, Chicago, Philadelphia, San Francisco, Boston, Washington D.C., Dallas, Detroit and Atlanta. This was not the case in the past.

- Endorsed Campaigns must meet higher standards of excellence that are spelled out in a new set of campaign selection criteria.

The Endorsed Campaign information kit and application has been completely revised. We hope you will find it clearer and easier to use.

Nature of Endorsement

Endorsement of a public service campaign by the Ad Council is awarded after Ad Council staff and Board members have reviewed the complete campaign application, and approved.

Media are notified of the Ad Council's endorsement through a written description of the campaign, published in the *Bulletin*. Endorsed Campaign materials are to be provided free of charge and run in donated media time and space only. Endorsed Campaign sponsors are responsible for producing campaign materials and fulfilling media requests for ads.

Endorsed Campaigns do not bear the Ad Council logo, and are not distributed by the Council. However, Endorsed Campaign sponsors are entitled to rent selected Ad Council media mailing labels (but not the

Council's list itself) at a modest cost, on a one-time basis only, immediately following approval of the campaign.

The Ad Council's endorsement is valid for a year from the publication date of the *Bulletin* in which it is first announced, or upon expiration of talent permissions used in the advertising, whichever comes first. It applies only to the individual advertising executions submitted to and reviewed by the Ad Council; new materials created after approval is given must be submitted with a new application for endorsement.

Ad Council endorsement may not be applied to campaigns that directly or implicitly sell products of any kind, however worthy the beneficiary. For this reason, cause-related marketing efforts are not eligible for endorsement. Likewise, endorsement cannot be given to campaigns that advocate specific political or religious beliefs or activities, however meritorious.

By issuing an endorsement, the Advertising Council does not assume any legal responsibility for Endorsed Campaigns.

How to Apply

Please submit all requested materials in a complete application, all at once. *Applications must be complete to be considered.*

- Before submitting your application, please check to make sure you can meet criteria for selection. See enclosed criteria.
- Please submit your applications, *along with a one-time application fee of $250*, at least 4 months in advance of the Bulletin issue in which you wish your campaign to be listed. This application fee helps to cover the cost of administering endorsement campaigns. See attached schedule of submission deadlines.
- Complete attached questionnaire and submit it with ALL requested attachments. If you are submitting TV rough-cuts or final film, please include nine VHS tapes for circulation to the Endorsement Review Committe. Otherwise, you will be charged for duplication (approximately $45 for duplication and shipping charges).
- Return your completed application to the attention of Ms. Lynne Lee, Director of Proposals, The Advertising Council, 261 Madison Avenue, New York, NY 10016-2303.

Endorsement Listing Fee

If your application is approved, the Ad Council will issue a formal letter of endorsement, which you may use in your approaches to media. Public notice of endorsement is given in a written listing, published in the Ad Council's *Bulletin*, for which **there is a listing fee of $1,000 per insertion**, or 6 listings for $5,000.

Please designate the number of insertions desired and indicate the *Bulletin* issues in which you wish to be listed when your campaign is accepted. Payment for all requested insertions is due upon approval of your campaign.

CRITERIA FOR SELECTION AS AN ENDORSED CAMPAIGN

1. An Endorsed Campaign is a public service advertising campaign that is independently developed outside of the Advertising Council, reviewed by the Council, and approved for endorsement.

2. In general, campaigns must be *national in scope* in order to be accepted for endorsement, with the following **exceptions**:

   –Local campaigns from the top ten markets, including New York, Los Angeles, Chicago, Philadelphia, San Francisco, Boston, Washington D.C., Dallas, Detroit, and Atlanta are eligible for endorsement.

3. The campaign's Sponsor must be eligible for endorsement. Unless the campaign qualifies as an exception for local campaign endorsement, the Sponsor should be national in scope.

   Eligible:

   –Nonprofit organizations with 501(c)3 standing
   –Government agencies
   –Coalitions of eligible nonprofit or government organizations
   –Private, charitable, non-political foundations
   –Nondenominational groups
   –Recognized as expert in the issue featured in the campaign

   Not Eligible:

   –Nonprofit organizations without 501(c)3 standing
   –Trade associations or business advocacy nonprofits
   –"Cause-related marketing" efforts
   –Businesses
   –Political advocacy groups
   –Individuals

4. The primary purpose of the campaign should be public service; and the campaign issue should be of sufficient seriousness and public importance to warrant donations of space and time by media. **The campaign must be non-commercial, non-denominational, non-partisan politically, and not designed to influence legislation.**

5. The Advertising Council's endorsement applies only to creative materials submitted with the application, with the understanding that those materials are to be available free of charge, and run in donated time and space only.

APPLICATION QUESTIONNAIRE
FOR ENDORSED CAMPAIGN PROPOSAL

The Advertising Council will review your answers to the following questions and the advertisements submitted with your application. If your advertising is already in final form, you are welcome to submit it. It is the goal of this review process to help you achieve a successful public service advertising campaign; to that end, Ad Council staff may suggest revisions in your advertisements before an endorsement can be given. In order to avoid costly revisions, we prefer that you submit your advertising prior to completion in the following forms:

Radio:	Script.
Television:	Storyboard and Script or (9) VHS tapes if in rough-cut form or completed.
Newspaper and Magazine (or other) Print Ads:	Layout showing design and headline, with text and image attached.
Out of Home (Bus shelter, transit card, outdoor, etc.):	Layout showing design, with text and image attached.
Fulfillment Materials:	Layout showing design, with text and image attached, or completed piece.

Questions for all Applicants:

1. Please indicate the full name, address, and telephone number of your organization and the person who would act as the liaison between your organization and the Ad Council.

2. Is this your first time applying for an endorsement (formerly called a Bulletin Campaign listing)? Please state year and month of any previous endorsement.

3. What is your mission? What services does your organization offer, and who are the recipients?

4. What is the primary goal of your public service advertising campaign and who is your target audience?

5. When do you want the advertising to run? Is your campaign related to special timing for an event or season? Please indicate the Bulletin issue or issues for which you are applying: January/February, March/April, May/June, July/August, September/October, November/December.

6. Who has created or will create your advertising? Which media are you using? Television, radio, magazines, newspapers, transit, outdoor? Other? **Please append work in development or finished work for all executions for which endorsement is desired.**

7. Please explain whether you have obtained appropriate permissions or waivers from talent or other individuals featured in your ads, and indicate the expiration date of your campaign materials (if any).

Questions for Eligible Private Sector Groups Only:

8. Does your campaign have a direct response component, such as mail reply or a toll-free number? If so, is your organization sufficiently organized and staffed to handle a large public response as a result of your effort? Please explain how you plan to manage and fulfill this response. Please enclose samples of your fulfillment materials.

9. If yours is an eligible private sector group (ex, nonprofit organization or coalition), what is its tax-exempt status with the Internal Revenue Service? Please submit:

   –Copy of 501(c)3 nonprofit or 509(a) foundation IRS tax-exempt certification

   –Most recent annual report

   –Most recent audited financial statement

10. How is your organization funded?

11. Is your organization registered with the National Charities Information Bureau or the Council of Better Business Bureaus or the Philanthropic Advisory Service of the Better Business Bureau?

    a) If it is registered, do the Bureaus state in their current reports that your organization meets their standards?

    b) If your organization is not currently rated by one of these two groups, what other information can you provide to show that your nonprofit management practices meet similarly high standards? (You may cite references, append testimonials, or supply other appropriate credentials.)

12. If yours is a national fund-raising campaign, please list all copy points from your advertising that make claims regarding how donated funds will be used, and give a brief explanation substantiating these claims. We are sorry, but local fund-raising campaigns are not eligible for endorsement.

ENDORSED CAMPAIGN APPLICATION DEADLINES

Endorsed Campaigns are listed in the Ad Council's *Public Service Advertising Bulletin*, which is published every two months. To meet publication deadlines it is necessary to receive applications for Endorsement well in advance (allow at least four months) of issue dates.

Please submit your application for Endorsement according to the following schedule of deadlines:

Application Deadlines

January/February issue	October 1
March/April issue	December 1
May/June issue	February 1
July/August issue	April 1
September/October issue	June 1
November/December issue	August 1

APPENDIX C

Partnership for a Drug-Free America
Audits & Surveys
Student Survey, Grades Two and Three

On this page there are two pictures. One picture is of something bad which you should never take, and the other one is something that is OK to have sometimes.

Put a "BAD" sticker on the picture if you should never take it, and put an "OK" sticker on the picture if you can have it sometimes.

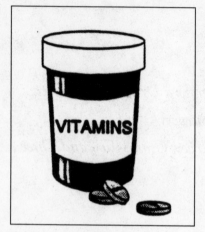

A. *Vitamins*

B. *Poison*

On this page are pictures of bad things you should never take and some things that are OK to have sometimes.

Put a "BAD" sticker on the picture if you should never take it, and put an "OK" sticker on the picture if you can have it sometimes. Start with soda . . .

A. Soda (Pop)

B. Wine Coolers

C. Things you sniff to get high

D. Beer

E. Pills you take to get high

F. Toothpaste

STOP

On this page are pictures of bad things you should never take and some things that are OK to have sometimes.

Put a "BAD" sticker on the picture if you should never take it, and put an "OK" sticker on the picture if you can have it sometimes.

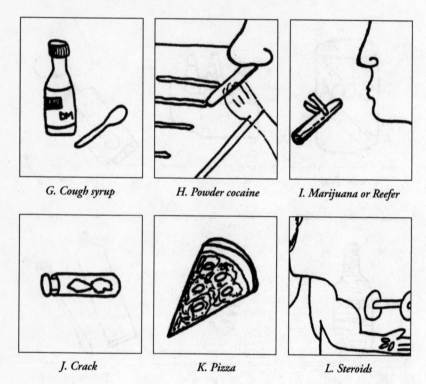

| *G. Cough syrup* | *H. Powder cocaine* | *I. Marijuana or Reefer* |

| *J. Crack* | *K. Pizza* | *L. Steroids* |

STOP

On this page are two pictures. One of these animals could be kept in an apartment as a pet, and the other one could not.

Put a "YES" sticker on the picture if you could keep it in an apartment, and a "NO" sticker if you could not keep it in an apartment.

A. Cat

B. Dinosaur

What are all the things that can happen to your <u>body</u> if you take drugs?

Put a "YES" sticker on the picture for the things that can happen, and a "NO" sticker if it can't happen.

If you take drugs, can you . . .

A. Get sick

B. Get crazy

C. Get smarter

D. Die

E. Get skinny

F. Get stronger

G. Play better

H. Think stupid

I. Get hooked and want to use drugs more and more

What can happen to your <u>life</u> if you use drugs?

Put a "YES" sticker on the picture for the things that can happen, and a "NO" sticker on the picture if it can't happen.

If you take drugs, can you . . .

A. Feel bad about yourself

B. Be cool

C. Be sad

D. Have fun

E. Have trouble making up your mind

F. Make your mom or dad sad

G. Quit school

H. Feel scared

I. Be more grown up

Do any of your friends your age use these?

Put a "YES" sticker on the picture if any of your friends your age use this, and a "NO" sticker if none of your friends your age use this.

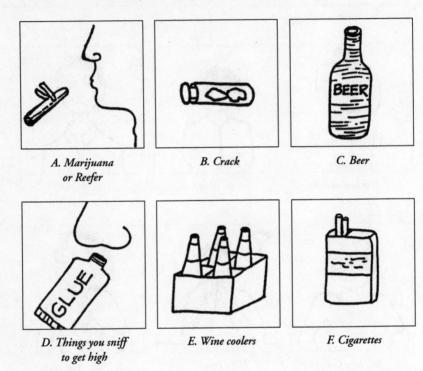

A. *Marijuana*   B. *Crack*   C. *Beer*
or Reefer

D. *Things you sniff*   E. *Wine coolers*   F. *Cigarettes*
to get high

Are these statements true? Circle the right answer below.

A. Ninja Turtles like to eat pizza.

   YES   NO   I DON'T KNOW

B. Ninja Turtles wear dresses.

   YES   NO   I DON'T KNOW

Are these statements true? Circle the right answer below.

A. Most people will try marijuana sometime
   YES   NO   I DON'T KNOW

B. I would like to try marijuana to see what it's like
   YES   NO   I DON'T KNOW

C. Drugs make people happy
   YES   NO   I DON'T KNOW

D. If you smoke marijuana, you'll want to use crack
   YES   NO   I DON'T KNOW

E. If you try marijuana, you'll mess up your life
   YES   NO   I DON'T KNOW

F. People who use drugs steal
   YES   NO   I DON'T KNOW

G. I am scared someone will make me take drugs
   YES   NO   I DON'T KNOW

Are these statements true? Circle the right answer below.

H. If someone tries to give me drugs I know a grown-up that I can tell

YES   NO   I DON'T KNOW

I. Kids who use drugs become drug dealers

YES   NO   I DON'T KNOW

J. I have someone to talk to when I'm scared

YES   NO   I DON'T KNOW

K. People who use drugs are scary

YES   NO   I DON'T KNOW

L. I worry I might want to try drugs someday

YES   NO   I DON'T KNOW

M. I know how to stay out of trouble on the street

YES   NO   I DON'T KNOW

Circle the right answer below.

A. Do you go to an after-school program for play, sports, music, reading or anything else?

YES   NO   I DON'T KNOW

B. If you go to an after-school program: Do you like to go? If you don't go: Would you like to go to an after-school program?

YES   NO   I DON'T KNOW

Circle the right answer.

A. How much do you learn about drugs from your school class?

A LOT   A LITTLE   I DON'T KNOW

B. How much do you learn about drugs from TV?

A LOT   A LITTLE   I DON'T KNOW

Circle the right answer.

C. How much do you learn about drugs on the street?

    A LOT   A LITTLE   I DON'T KNOW

D. How much do people at home tell you drugs are bad?

    A LOT   A LITTLE   I DON'T KNOW

Circle the right answer.

A. How good at games or sports are you?

    VERY   A LITTLE   NOT AT ALL

B. How special are you?

    VERY   A LITTLE   NOT AT ALL

C. How smart are you?

    VERY   A LITTLE   NOT AT ALL

D. How pretty or handsome are you?

    VERY   A LITTLE   NOT AT ALL

E. How hard is it for you to read?

    VERY   A LITTLE   NOT AT ALL

F. How much do you like school?

    A LOT   A LITTLE   NOT AT ALL

G. How often are you scared?

    A LOT   A LITTLE   NOT AT ALL

H. How often does someone tell you that you are good?

    A LOT   A LITTLE   NOT AT ALL

I. How often does someone tell you that you are being bad?

    A LOT   A LITTLE   NOT AT ALL

Circle the right answer.

A. Are you a boy or a girl?

    BOY   GIRL

B. What grade are you in?

    2ND   3RD

C. Are you: (You can circle more than one)

    BLACK   HISPANIC

    WHITE   ASIAN

    OTHER

D. Do your parents or grandparents speak Spanish?

    YES   NO

E. How old are you?

    6 OR YOUNGER   7   8   9 OR OLDER

F. Circle <u>all</u> the people you live with. (You can circle more than one)

    MOM   DAD   GRANDPARENTS

    BROTHER   SISTER   ANYONE ELSE

G. Does your mother have a job?

    YES   NO

H. Does your father have a job?

    YES   NO

APPENDIX D

Partnership for a Drug-Free America
Audits & Surveys
Student Survey, Grades Four
Through Six

Please take a few minutes to complete this survey about drugs. Your answers will help us understand the problems and needs of students all over New York City. This is not a test. There are no right or wrong answers. Just tell us what you know or think.

Your answers will be kept confidential. No one will know what answers you give. Do NOT write your name anywhere on the answer sheet.

When you are finished, a box will be passed around. Put your answer sheet in the box so no one will see your answers.

How dangerous are the things listed below?

A. Cigarettes

☐1 Very dangerous, never use

☐2 A little dangerous, but ok to try once or twice

☐3 Not at all dangerous, ok to use

☐4 I don't know what they are

B. Marijuana or Reefer

☐1 Very dangerous, never use

☐2 A little dangerous, but ok to try once or twice

☐3 Not at all dangerous, ok to use

☐4 I don't know what this is

C. Crack

☐1 Very dangerous, never use

☐2 A little dangerous, but ok to try once or twice

☐3 Not at all dangerous, ok to use

☐4 I don't know what this is

D. Liquor

☐1 Very dangerous, never use

☐2 A little dangerous, but ok to try once or twice

☐3 Not at all dangerous, ok to use

☐4 I don't know what this is

E. Heroin or Smack

☐1 Very dangerous, never use

☐2 A little dangerous, but ok to try once or twice

☐3 Not at all dangerous, ok to use

☐4 I don't know what this is

F. Wine Coolers

☐1 Very dangerous, never use

☐2 A little dangerous, but ok to try once or twice

☐3 Not at all dangerous, ok to use

☐4 I don't know what this is

How dangerous are the things listed below?

G. Powder Cocaine

☐1 Very dangerous, never use

☐2 A little dangerous, but ok to try once or twice

☐3 Not at all dangerous, ok to use

☐4 I don't know what this is

H. Steroids

☐1 Very dangerous, never use

☐2 A little dangerous, but ok to try once or twice

☐3 Not at all dangerous, ok to use

☐4 I don't know what they are

I. Things like glue that you sniff to get high

☐1 Very dangerous, never use

☐2 A little dangerous, but ok to try once or twice

☐3 Not at all dangerous, ok to use

☐4 I don't know what they are

J. Beer or malt liquor

☐1 Very dangerous, never use

☐2 A little dangerous, but ok to try once or twice

☐3 Not at all dangerous, ok to use

☐4 I don't know what this is

K. PCP or Angel dust

☐1 Very dangerous, never use

☐2 A little dangerous, but ok to try once or twice

☐3 Not at all dangerous, ok to use

☐4 I don't know what this is

L. Pills you take to get high

☐1 Very dangerous, never use

☐2 A little dangerous, but ok to try once or twice

☐3 Not at all dangerous, ok to use

☐4 I don't know what they are

Can this happen to your <u>body</u> if you take drugs? Could you . . .

		YES	NO
a.	Get sick	☐1	☐2
b.	Be sexier	☐1	☐2
c.	Get AIDS	☐1	☐2
d.	Get taller	☐1	☐2
e.	Get too thin	☐1	☐2
f.	Mess up your brain	☐1	☐2
g.	Get bigger	☐1	☐2
h.	Think stupid	☐1	☐2
i.	Live longer	☐1	☐2
j.	Get stronger	☐1	☐2
k.	Die	☐1	☐2
l.	Get smarter	☐1	☐2
m.	Go crazy	☐1	☐2
n.	Do better at sports	☐1	☐2

Can this happen to your <u>life</u> if you use drugs? Could you . . .

		YES	NO
a.	Make your parents sad	□₁	□₂
b.	Get your sister or brother to use	□₁	□₂
c.	Be more popular	□₁	□₂
d.	Get a boyfriend or girlfriend	□₁	□₂
e.	Go to jail	□₁	□₂
f.	Feel bad about yourself	□₁	□₂
g.	Get pregnant too soon	□₁	□₂
h.	Do better in sports	□₁	□₂
i.	Become a drug dealer	□₁	□₂
j.	Drop out of school	□₁	□₂
k.	Lose your money	□₁	□₂
l.	Have fun	□₁	□₂
m.	Hang out with older kids	□₁	□₂
n.	Get a bad report card	□₁	□₂
o.	Make a lot of money	□₁	□₂
p.	Join a gang	□₁	□₂
q.	Lose control	□₁	□₂
r.	Have trouble making decisions	□₁	□₂
s.	Go to parties more	□₁	□₂
t.	Feel happier	□₁	□₂
u.	Get hooked and want to use drugs more and more	□₁	□₂
v.	Make your dad or mom angry	□₁	□₂
w.	Be cool	□₁	□₂
x.	Be sad	□₁	□₂
y.	Be in danger	□₁	□₂

How many of your friends ever use the following?

A. Crack

☐₁ Some

☐₂ None

☐₃ I don't know what this is

B. Marijuana or Reefer

☐₁ Some

☐₂ None

☐₃ I don't know what this is

C. Powder cocaine

☐₁ Some

☐₂ None

☐₃ I don't know what this is

D. Beer or malt liquor

☐₁ Some

☐₂ None

☐₃ I don't know what this is

E. Things like glue that you sniff to get high

☐₁ Some

☐₂ None

☐₃ I don't know what they are

F. Liquor

☐₁ Some

☐₂ None

☐₃ I don't know what this is

G. Wine coolers

☐₁ Some

☐₂ None

☐₃ I don't know what they are

A. How much do you learn that drugs are bad from your <u>school class</u>?

   ☐$_1$ A lot

   ☐$_2$ A little

   ☐$_3$ Nothing

B. How much do you learn that drugs are bad from your <u>parents or grandparents</u>?

   ☐$_1$ A lot

   ☐$_2$ A little

   ☐$_3$ Nothing

C. How much do you learn that drugs are bad from your <u>brother or sister</u>?

   ☐$_1$ A lot

   ☐$_2$ A little

   ☐$_3$ Nothing

D. How much do you learn that drugs are bad from your <u>friends</u>?

   ☐$_1$ A lot

   ☐$_2$ A little

   ☐$_3$ Nothing

E. How much do you learn that drugs are bad from <u>TV commercials</u>?

   ☐$_1$ A lot

   ☐$_2$ A little

   ☐$_3$ Nothing

F. How much do you learn that drugs are bad from <u>TV shows, news or movies</u>?

   ☐$_1$ A lot

   ☐$_2$ A little

   ☐$_3$ Nothing

G. How much do you learn that drugs are bad from <u>after school activities</u>?

   ☐$_1$ A lot

   ☐$_2$ A little

   ☐$_3$ Nothing

H. How much do you learn that drugs are bad <u>on the street</u>?

   ☐$_1$ A lot

   ☐$_2$ A little

   ☐$_3$ Nothing

Do you ever see or hear messages that say drugs are bad:

	YES	NO
On TV	□₁	□₂
On radio	□₁	□₂
On large billboards	□₁	□₂
On posters, on buses, bus stops, or subways	□₁	□₂
In movie theaters	□₁	□₂

How much do you agree with these statements?

A. Most people will try marijuana sometime.

□₁ I agree a lot

□₂ I agree a little

□₃ I don't agree at all

B. I would like to try marijuana to see what it's like.

□₁ I agree a lot

□₂ I agree a little

□₃ I don't agree at all

C. If you smoke marijuana, you'll want to use crack.

□₁ I agree a lot

□₂ I agree a little

□₃ I don't agree at all

D. Everyone tries drugs sometimes

□₁ I agree a lot

□₂ I agree a little

□₃ I don't agree at all

E. It's hard for a kid to say no to drugs around cool kids who are using drugs.

□₁ I agree a lot

□₂ I agree a little

□₃ I don't agree at all

How much do you agree with these statements?

F. People who use drugs steal.

☐₁ I agree a lot

☐₂ I agree a little

☐₃ I don't agree at all

G. If a kid uses marijuana, friends will stop hanging out with him or her.

☐₁ I agree a lot

☐₂ I agree a little

☐₃ I don't agree at all

H. I am different than other kids because of how I feel about drugs.

☐₁ I agree a lot

☐₂ I agree a little

☐₃ I don't agree at all

I. I worry I might want to try drugs someday.

☐₁ I agree a lot

☐₂ I agree a little

☐₃ I don't agree at all

J. It's ok to help someone sell drugs.

☐₁ I agree a lot

☐₂ I agree a little

☐₃ I don't agree at all

K. If a girl is pregnant, smoking marijuana can hurt the baby.

☐₁ I agree a lot

☐₂ I agree a little

☐₃ I don't agree at all

L. I am scared someone will make me take drugs.

☐₁ I agree a lot

☐₂ I agree a little

☐₃ I don't agree at all

How much do you agree with these statements?

M. Trying cocaine is part of growing up.

☐₁ I agree a lot

☐₂ I agree a little

☐₃ I don't agree at all

N. I know what to do if someone offers me drugs.

☐₁ I agree a lot

☐₂ I agree a little

☐₃ I don't agree at all

O. Most kids my age are scared to take drugs.

☐₁ I agree a lot

☐₂ I agree a little

☐₃ I don't agree at all

Does this describe someone who sells drugs?

	YES	NO
a. Has many friends	☐₁	☐₂
b. Is scared all the time	☐₁	☐₂
c. Uses drugs	☐₁	☐₂
d. Dies young	☐₁	☐₂
e. Goes to jail	☐₁	☐₂
f. Is a good friend	☐₁	☐₂
g. Is scary	☐₁	☐₂
h. Gets respect	☐₁	☐₂
i. Is lonely	☐₁	☐₂
j. Has lots of girlfriends or boyfriends	☐₁	☐₂

Does this describe a girl who hangs around with someone who sells drugs?

	YES	NO
a. Has many friends	☐1	☐2
b. Is scared all the time	☐1	☐2
c. Uses drugs	☐1	☐2
d. Goes to jail	☐1	☐2
e. Is a good friend	☐1	☐2
f. Gets used	☐1	☐2
g. Gets respect	☐1	☐2
h. Has nice jewelry and clothes	☐1	☐2
i. Has babies young	☐1	☐2
j. Makes her own decisions	☐1	☐2

What would you do if someone you know gives you drugs? (Circle up to 3 answers you think are true.)

a. (1) Walk away
b. (2) Try them
c. (3) Tell a teacher
d. (4) Tell mom
e. (5) Tell the police
f. (6) Tell a school counselor
g. (7) Say no
h. (8) Fight the person
i. (9) Tell them not to use
j. (1) Change the subject
k. (2) Keep it a secret

What is most important to you? (Circle up to two answers.)

a. (1) Live in a different neighborhood
b. (2) Have a happy family
c. (3) Have a lot of money
d. (4) Make mom or dad proud of me
e. (5) Be popular
f. (6) Graduate high school
g. (7) Have a good job
h. (8) Go to college
i. (9) Feel safer
j. (0) Have a car

Do you go to an after-school or weekend program for play, sports, music, reading or anything else?

☐₁ Yes

☐₂ No

☐₃ I don't know

If you go to an after-school program: Do you like to go?
If you don't go: Would you like to go to an after-school program?

☐₁ Yes

☐₂ No

☐₃ I don't know

I have an adult to talk to about my problems.

☐₁ Yes

☐₂ No

☐₃ I don't know

I wish I had an adult to talk to about my problems.

☐₁ Yes

☐₂ No

☐₃ I don't know

☐₄ Already have an adult to talk to about my problems

A. How good at games or sports are you?

   ☐₁ Very   ☐₂ A little   ☐₃ Not at all

B. How pretty or handsome are you?

   ☐₁ Very   ☐₂ A little   ☐₃ Not at all

C. How sexy are you?

   ☐₁ Very   ☐₂ A little   ☐₃ Not at all

D. How special are you?

   ☐₁ Very   ☐₂ A little   ☐₃ Not at all

E. How cool are you?

   ☐₁ Very   ☐₂ A little   ☐₃ Not at all

F. How smart are you?

☐₁ Very ☐₂ A little ☐₃ Not at all

G. How good are you at helping out at home?

☐₁ Very ☐₂ A little ☐₃ Not at all

H. How often are you scared?

☐₁ A lot ☐₂ A little ☐₃ Not at all

I. How often do you get into trouble?

☐₁ A lot ☐₂ A little ☐₃ Not at all

J. How much do you like school?

☐₁ A lot ☐₂ A little ☐₃ Not at all

K. How often does someone let you know that you are good?

☐₁ A lot ☐₂ A little ☐₃ Not at all

L. How often does someone tell you that you are being bad?

☐₁ A lot ☐₂ A little ☐₃ Not at all

Mark the answers below:

A. Are you a boy or a girl?

☐₁ Boy
☐₂ Girl

B. What grade are you in?

☐₁ 4th
☐₂ 5th
☐₃ 6th

C. Are you: (You can X more than one)

☐₁ Black
☐₂ White
☐₃ Hispanic
☐₄ Asian
☐₅ Other

D. Are you: (You can X more than one)

☐₅ Other

☐₁ African American

☐₂ West Indian (Haitian, Jamaican, Trinidadian, Barbadian, etc.)

☐₃ Hispanic (Puerto Rican, Cuban, Colombian, Mexican, Dominican, etc.)

☐₄ Other

E. How old are you?

☐₁ 8 or younger

☐₂ 9

☐₃ 10

☐₄ 11

☐₅ 12 or older

18. Who do you live with? (Put an X by all the people you live with)

☐₁ Mother

☐₂ Father

☐₃ Brother(s)

☐₄ Sister(s)

☐₅ Grandmother

☐₆ Grandfather

☐₇ Other(s)

Thank you for your answers. This is the end of the survey.

APPENDIX E

*Partnership for a Drug-Free America
1993 New York City Grade School Study
(Summary)*

Increased Awareness of Risks, Decreased Perceptions of Benefits among Children*

Perceived Risks of Using Drugs	1992	1993	Prop. Change
	%	%	
Make Your Mom or Dad Sad	90	93	+3%
Feel Bad About Yourself	85	90	+6%
Feel Scared	79	87	+10%
Be Sad	80	86	+8%
Die	89	92	+3%
Get Sick	86	91	+5%
Think Stupid	84	87	+3%
Get Crazy	85	89	+5%
Get Skinny	83	86	+4%
Perceived Benefits of Using Drugs			
Be More Grown Up	19	16	−18%
Be Cool	17	14	−17%
N =	(2378)	(2477)	

*below poverty 2nd and 3rd graders
Proportional change given only where statistically significant.
Margin of error at the 95% confidence level is approximately +/−3%.

Deglamorized Images of Drug Dealers and Their Girlfriends: Preteens*

Image of Drug Dealer	1992 %	1993 %	Prop. Change
Goes to Jail	85	90	+5%
Dies Young	87	89	
Uses Drugs	77	81	+6%
Is Scary	73	79	+9%
Is Lonely	68	72	+6%
Is Scared All the Time	54	54	
Is a Good Friend	10	8	–22%
Has Many Friends	24	22	
Has Lots of Girlfriends/Boyfriends	17	17	
Image of Dealer's Girlfriend			
Uses Drugs	75	79	+6%
Gets Used	77	82	+7%
Goes to Jail	77	84	+10%
Is Scared All the Time	62	64	
Has Many Friends	22	20	
N =	(2594)	(3157)	

*below poverty 4th–6th graders
Proportional change given only where statistically significant.
Margin of error at the 95% confidence level is approximately +/–3%.

Greater Ability to Resist Drugs

Children*	1992	1993	Prop. Change
	%	%	
I Worry I Might Want to Try Drugs Someday	21	15	−29%
N =	(2378)	(2477)	

Preteens**	1992	1993	Prop. Change
	%	%	
If Someone Offered Me Drugs, I Would Walk Away	79	85	+7%
If Someone Offered Me Drugs, I Would Tell Them Not to Use	10	12	+30%
I Have an Adult to Talk to About My Problems	85	88	+3%
I Wish I Had an Adult to Talk to	16	15	
N =	(2594)	(3157)	

*below poverty 2nd and 3rd graders
**below poverty 4th–6th graders
Proportional change given only where statistically significant.
Margin of error at the 95% confidence level is approximately +/−3%.

Sources of Information

Preteens* Learned "A Lot" About Drugs From . . .

	1992	1993	Prop. Change
	%	%	
School Class	84	83	
Parents/Grandparents	82	84	
TV Shows	71	71	
TV Commercials	66	70	+ 6%
On the Street	67	66	
Brother/Sister	58	60	
Friends	55	56	
After-School Activities	52	53	
N =	(2594)	(3157)	

*below poverty 4th–6th graders
Proportional change given only where statistically significant.
Margin of error at 95% confidence level is approximately +/–3%.

Differences and Gains by Ethnicity
Children's* Perceived Risks/Benefits of Using Drugs

	Total			Black			Hispanic		
	1992 %	1993 %	Prop. Change	1992 %	1993 %	Prop. Change	1992 %	1993 %	Prop. Change
Die	89	92	+3%	85	92	+8%	93	92	
Get Sick	86	91	+5%	84	91	+8%	87	91	+4%
Get Crazy	85	89	+5%	81	89	+11%	89	90	
Think Stupid	84	87	+3%	80	88	+9%	88	88	
Get Skinny	83	86	+4%	78	87	+12%	87	86	
Make Your Mom or Dad Sad	90	93	+3%	86	93	+9%	93	93	
Feel Bad About Yourself	85	90	+6%	81	91	+12%	88	91	
Feel Scared	79	87	+10%	74	87	+17%	83	88	+6%
Be Sad	80	86	+8%	75	87	+16%	83	86	
Be Cool	17	14	–17%	24	14	–40%	12	13	
Be More Grown Up	19	16	–18%	24	17	–29%	17	14	
Have Fun	13	11		18	13	–27%	9	10	
N =	(2378)	(2477)		(795)	(854)		(1348)	(1397)	

*below poverty 2nd and 3rd graders
Proportional change given only where statistically significant.
Margin of error at the 95% confidence level is approximately +/–3%.

Differences & Gains by Ethnicity
Preteens'* Perceived Benefits of Using Drugs

	Total			Black			Hispanic		
	1992 %	1993 %	Prop. Change	1992 %	1993 %	Prop. Change	1992 %	1993 %	Prop. Change
Hang Out with Older Kids	57	51	–11%	59	55		56	46	–17%
Get a Boyfriend or Girlfriend	10	8		12	8	–28%	7	8	
Do Better in Sports	7	5		8	5	–38%	4	5	
Go to Parties More	44	41		46	48		41	35	–15%
N =	(2594)	(3157)		(1043)	(1280)		(1307)	(1534)	

*below poverty 4th and 6th graders
Proportional change given only where statistically significant.
Margin of error at the 95% confidence level is approximately +/–3%.

Differences & Gains by Ethnicity
Preteens'* Images of Drug Dealers and Their Girlfriends

	Total			Black			Hispanic		
	1992	1993	Prop. Change	1992	1993	Prop. Change	1992	1993	Prop. Change
	%	%		%	%		%	%	
Dealer Goes to Jail	85	90	+5%	83	89	+8%	89	91	
Dealer Uses Drugs	77	81	+6%	73	80	+11%	81	81	
Dealer Is Scary	73	79	+9%	70	76	+8%	76	82	+8%
Dealer Is Lonely	68	72	+6%	66	68		70	76	+8%
Dealer Is a Good Friend	10	8	–22%	11	10		9	7	
Dealer Has Many Friends	24	22		25	24		25	20	–18%
Girlfriend Goes to Jail	77	84	+10%	73	83	+14%	81	85	+6%
Girlfriend Gets Used	77	82	+7%	74	81	+9%	80	83	
Girlfriend Uses Drugs	75	79	+6%	71	80	+12%	78	78	
Girlfriend Makes Her Own Decisions	56	53		50	52		61	55	–10%
N =	(2594)	(3157)		(1043)	(1280)		(1307)	(1534)	

*below poverty 4th and 6th graders
Proportional change given only where statistically significant.
Margin of error at the 95% confidence level is approximately +/–3%.

BIBLIOGRAPHY

British Design and Art Direction (D&AD). *The Copy Book*. D&AD in association with Rotovision SA. ISBN 2-88046-258-4. A D&AD Mastercraft series publication, pages 46, 84, 102, 114, 120, 126, 151.

Buckley, Christopher. *Thank You for Smoking*. New York: Random House, 1994, pages 124–25.

Kotler, Philip, and Alan R. Andreason. *Strategic Marketing for Nonprofit Organizations*. Upper Saddle River, NJ: Prentice Hall, 1996, pages 304–5.

Massing, Michael. *The Fix*. New York: Simon and Schuster, 1998, pages 174, 273.

McLuhan, Marshall. *Understanding Media*. Cambridge: MIT Press, 1994, pages 7, 22, 299.

Moeller, Susan D. *Compassion Fatigue*. New York: Routledge, 1999, pages 9, 39.

Ogilvy, David. *Ogilvy on Advertising*. New York: Random House, 1983, pages 67, 166.

Peppers, Don, and Martha Rogers, Ph.D. *The One to One Future*. New York: Doubleday, 1993, pages XXV–XXVII, 14–15.

Roman, Kenneth, and Jane Maas. *How to Advertise*. New York: St. Martin's Press, 1992, pages 78–83.

Schrag, Peter. *Paradise Lost*. New York: The New Press, 1998, pages 18, 244–45.

Steel, Jon. *Truth, Lies, and Advertising*. New York: John Wiley and Sons, Inc., 1998, pages 36–38, 143, 149, 160.

Sullivan, Luke. *"Hey, Whipple, Squeeze This!"* New York: John Wiley and Sons, Inc., 1998, page 91.

INDEX

ABOUT THE
AUTHOR

Richard Earle majored in English and American Studies at Amherst College. His advertising career spanned more than thirty years at six U.S. agencies, the most recent being Saatchi & Saatchi, New York, where he held the position of executive vice president, group creative director.

During this time, Dick wrote and supervised major national campaigns for clients such as Procter & Gamble, Johnson & Johnson, Revlon, MGM, Canada Dry, and New York Life. He also created or supervised a number of award-winning public service campaigns, including the Keep America Beautiful "Crying Indian" series, and the first national anti-drug–abuse campaign for the National Institute of Mental Health. His work has won the Gold Lion at Cannes, two "Effies," five "Clios," and more than fifty other major industry awards.

He has served as president of the Washington-based National Coordinating Council on Drug Education. His *Reader's Digest* article, "How to Talk to your Child About Drug Abuse," was the magazine's most-requested reprint. As creative director on Johnson & Johnson's Tylenol brand, Earle was responsible for all strategy and advertising leading to that brand's survival after two separate tampering incidents. The story of that remarkable recovery is widely studied by business schools throughout the world.

Recently, Earle has served as an advertising and media consultant to a number of public interest and political initiative organizations such as U.S. Term Limits, the Massachusetts Department of Public Health Tobacco Control Program, and the Massachusetts Council on Compulsive Gambling.

An occasional playwright and lyricist, Richard Earle is a member of the Dramatist's Guild, and lives with his wife Pat in Gloucester, Massachusetts.